Implementation of a Data
Reliability Program

By Orlando López

E Book: 978-1-968165-11-6

Paperback: 978-1-968165-12-3

Hardcover: 978-1-968165-13-0

Published by **Author Publications**: 2025

https://www.authorpublications.com

+1 (771) 203-5560

Dedication

For Lizette, Mikhail, István, Christian, and Mikhail Jr

Disclaimer

The regulatory requirements and guidelines detailed in this book primarily focus on the lifecycle data of medicinal products for human use. However, it is important to recognize that the topics discussed are equally pertinent across various industries that handle critical data.

The recommendations for implementing a data reliability program presented in this book are based on the author's extensive experience in data management, spanning thirty-seven years.

While these suggestions aim to provide valuable insights, they should not be interpreted as formal processes mandated by relevant global regulatory authorities, standards, or guidelines. Furthermore, this book is not intended to establish a definitive paradigm or model.

Table of Contents

Preface

Understanding and prioritizing data integrity, reliability, and quality are not just crucial for effective data management, but they also form the backbone of our profession. As data managers, data governance officers, and data quality assurance analysts, we bear the responsibility of ensuring that the data we work with is accurate, consistent, and trustworthy.

Data integrity [1]

Data integrity is not just a technical term; it is the bedrock of data management. It is the key to the accuracy and consistency of data throughout its lifecycle, ensuring that data is not corrupted, altered, or tampered with in unauthorized or unintended ways. For instance, a data integrity violation could occur if a hacker gains unauthorized access to a database and alters the data, leading to inaccurate results and potentially damaging decisions. Understanding and prioritizing data integrity is crucial for effective data management.

Data integrity is a technical aspect of data management and a fundamental principle that ensures the trustworthiness of data. It protects data from unauthorized modifications or errors, ensuring reliability and security.

Data integrity mechanisms, such as validation rules that check data accuracy and consistency, access controls that limit who can view or modify data, and encryption that protects data from unauthorized access, help safeguard data against integrity violations.

Data reliability [2]

Data reliability is not just about trust; it is about practicality. It is the assurance that data can be counted on to be accurate and consistent over time, making it a valuable asset in any data-driven organization. This practicality is what makes data reliability so important in our daily activities. It is not just a concept but a tool we can rely on in our work.

Data integrity is a prerequisite for data reliability. Data with high integrity, meaning it is accurate and consistent, can be relied upon to remain accurate and consistent over time, which is a key aspect of data reliability. In simpler terms, data integrity ensures that the data is accurate and consistent at all times. In contrast, data reliability ensures that it can be trusted to remain accurate and consistent over time, even as it is used in various transactions and activities.

Data reliability encompasses factors such as accuracy, consistency, completeness, and timeliness, collectively contributing to the overall quality of the data.

Data quality [3]

Data quality encompasses not only accuracy and completeness, but also other aspects. It is a comprehensive concept that encompasses data integrity and reliability. It focuses on the overall excellence of data, encompassing its accuracy, completeness, consistency, relevance, and timeliness, ensuring no aspect of data is left untouched. This all-encompassing nature is what makes data quality so valuable. It is not just about one aspect but the overall condition of data and its ability to meet users' needs and expectations.

Data quality efforts aim to ensure data fits its intended purpose, making it valuable and actionable.

Data integrity and data reliability are critical components of data quality. Without data integrity, data cannot be trusted, and without reliable data, the quality of data is compromised.

In summary, data integrity is a foundational element that ensures data is protected from unauthorized changes. In contrast, data reliability is built upon this integrity, ensuring that data is trustworthy and dependable. On the other hand, data quality is a comprehensive goal encompassing integrity and reliability, focusing on producing secure, consistent data that is valuable and fit for use in decision-making and analysis.

Organizations typically implement a combination of data governance, data management practices, data validation processes, and security measures to achieve high data quality, maintain data integrity, and ensure data reliability. Ultimately, the synergy of these three concepts is essential for organizations to make informed decisions, conduct meaningful analyses, and maintain the credibility and usefulness of their data assets.

This book intends to guide readers in effectively managing data and e-records reliability vulnerabilities and raise essential compliance.

Enjoy the reading. If you have suggestions for improvement or questions, send them to olopez6102@gmail.com.

Orlando López
SME - E-Records Quality

References.

[1] Data integrity is the property of data that has not been retrieved or altered without authorization since creation and until disposal (NIST SP 800- 57P1, IEEE, ISO-17025, INFOSEC, 44 USC 3542, 36 CFR Part 1236, and other standards).

[2] Data reliability is not just about trust; it is about practicality. It is about being able to depend on data for subsequent transactions and activities.

[3] Data quality encompasses not only accuracy and completeness, but also other aspects. It is about the overall condition of data and its ability to meet users' needs and expectations. It is about being reliable, trustworthy, and suitable for analysis, decision-making, and other purposes.

Additional Readings.

- HMA, *"Reliability"* in Data Quality Framework for EU Medicines Regulation, October 2023.

Chapter 1
Introduction

Data [1] is considered reliable if it provides a complete and accurate representation of subsequent transactions or activities and if it can be relied upon during these transactions or activities [2]. In the context of medicine manufacturing, where the quality and safety of the products are of utmost importance, data reliability plays a crucial role in ensuring the efficacy and compliance of the manufactured medicines.

Data reliability is not just about consistency and repeatability; it is about trust. It denotes the consistency and repeatability of data over time, regardless of the methods or tools used to collect it. A dataset is considered reliable if it consistently produces the same results, regardless of whether it is measured multiple times or obtained by different researchers or methods. For instance, if an experiment yields the same results every time it is performed, it is considered reliable.

"Data reliability is fundamentally compromised when there is a failure to record or maintain complete and accurate records of test results or conditions associated with all tests. Furthermore, the lack of reliable data compromises the quality unit's (QU) ability to ensure compliance with applicable standards."

Amman Pharmaceutical Industries US FDA Warning Letter, MARCS-CMS 668867, February 2024.

5

Reliable data is one of the fundamental principles of data quality. Data quality measures how well data meets users' requirements and expectations for its intended purpose. Data reliability refers to the accuracy and truthfulness of the data.

In addition to reliability, several attributes govern data quality, including accuracy [3], completeness [4], conformity [5], consistency [6], objectivity [7], suitability [8], integrity, validity [9], source authentication [10], and timeliness [11] with the intended use. These attributes ensure that the data is not only reliable but also trustworthy [12], instilling a sense of security and confidence in the work being done.

Manufacturers operate under a quality system as critical players in the data reliability ecosystem. Their responsibility is not just to develop and document control procedures but to complete, secure, protect, and archive records, including data that provides evidence of their operational and quality system activities [13]. This empowerment to contribute significantly to data reliability in their operations is a testament to their integral role in ensuring data accuracy and integrity. Manufacturers play a key role in ensuring data reliability by implementing robust data collection and management processes, contributing to the quality and safety of the medicines they produce. Their actions directly influence the reliability of the data used in subsequent transactions and activities, making them key stakeholders in the data reliability process.

The reliability program ensures that a product or system functions consistently without failure over a specified period under normal operating conditions. The data obtained from the products or systems is reliable and trustworthy, providing evidence of the operational and quality system activities. This data can be used confidently in subsequent transactions and activities.

Reliable data is accurate, authentic [14], and has integrity; it is also highly usable [15]. This usability enables it to be used confidently for decision-making, analysis, and other critical purposes. For instance, in manufacturing medicine, reliable data can help predict equipment failures, optimize production schedules, and ensure compliance with regulatory standards. Data reliability in these processes cannot be overstated, as it forms the bedrock of trustworthy and effective decision-making, providing confidence and security in your actions. For example, reliable data can be used to predict the failure of critical manufacturing equipment, enabling timely maintenance and preventing production delays. Similarly, it can be used to optimize production schedules, ensuring efficient use of resources and meeting market demands. Lastly, it can ensure compliance with regulatory standards, avoid penalties, and maintain the manufacturer's reputation.

For features that ensure reliable data maintenance on your computer systems, refer to "Trustworthy Computer Systems" [16].

Book Chapters and Appendices.

This book is divided into twenty-two chapters and three appendices. It discusses the key elements to be addressed in a Data Reliability Implementation Program (DRIP), with a specific focus on production and quality control systems in medical manufacturing environments. Each chapter and appendix is designed to provide comprehensive guidance on different aspects of data reliability, from setting objectives to managing external data sources.

A reliability program ensures that a product or system functions consistently without failure over a specified period under normal operating conditions. Chapter 2 provides a detailed account of the DRIP.

Chapter 3, "Define Objectives and Goals," emphasizes the significance of setting clear objectives and goals for a DRIP. These objectives and goals are pivotal in guiding the efforts and providing a framework for implementing and sustaining data reliability initiatives within an organization. This chapter is crucial to achieving data reliability.

Chapter 4 outlines the identification of individuals or teams responsible for overseeing the data reliability program and guiding efforts and initiatives to ensure data reliability within an organization.

Data inventory and classification processes enable organizations to understand better and manage their data assets. They ensure that data is adequately treated based on its significance, sensitivity, and importance to business operations. Chapter 5 discusses data inventory and classification.

Data Quality Assessments are an essential component of a Data Reliability Program. They are crucial in improving decision-making, building trust, ensuring compliance, enhancing operational efficiency, reducing costs, promoting data integration, increasing customer satisfaction, and driving continuous improvement. Chapter 6 provides the framework for the Data Quality Assessments.

Chapter 7, Data Quality Standards, defines the data quality standards and metrics that align with the organization's goals. These standards include accuracy, completeness, consistency, timeliness, and integrity.

Chapter 8 outlines the activities related to data cleansing and transformation. These activities focus on enhancing the quality and usability of the data, which is crucial for ensuring that the data is accurate, consistent, and meets the required standards for reliable analysis and informed decision-making.

Documentation is a critical aspect of data engineering. It refers to creating, maintaining, and organizing records for various aspects of the workflow and ensuring that these processes are well-understood, scalable, and maintainable. Documentation provides detailed information about an organization's structure, content, and data usage. Chapter 9 discusses the purpose of documentation and the benefits of the data reliability program.

Chapter 10 outlines the Data Governance Framework, a structured methodology designed to manage an organization's data quality, reliability, and security throughout its entire data lifecycle.

A robust data access control system is crucial for maintaining the confidentiality, integrity, and availability of sensitive information. It is an essential component of overall information security strategies. Chapter 11 deals with data access control.

Chapter 12 discusses Data Monitoring and Auditing, which are crucial aspects of a reliability program. This is especially true in industries such as pharmaceutical manufacturing, where the dependability and performance of systems, processes, or products are crucial.

Chapter 13 discusses Data Lifecycle Management (DLM), a comprehensive approach to managing data from its creation or acquisition to its archival and disposal. DLM involves defining policies and procedures for data retention that comply with legal requirements and the typical stages in the data lifecycle.

Chapter 14 focuses on Continuous Improvements within the context of a data reliability program. Continuous improvements involve an ongoing commitment to refining processes, addressing issues, and optimizing the overall data ecosystem to ensure that data remains reliable, accurate, and valuable for decision-making. This emphasis on continuous improvement should reassure you of the forward-thinking nature of the data reliability program.

In the Data Reliability Program, External Data Sources refer to any data obtained from outside the organization or system where the data reliability program is practiced. While the benefits of External Data Sources are significant, organizations must implement robust processes within their data reliability programs to ensure the accuracy, reliability, and ethical use of external data. Proper data validation, documentation (Chapter 9), and ongoing monitoring (Chapter 12) are crucial for effectively managing external data within a data reliability framework. Chapter 15 explains robust processes applicable to external data sources within the context of a data reliability program.

In data management and business operations, compliance entails ensuring that an organization adheres to the applicable laws, regulations, and ethical frameworks relevant to its activities. Ensuring compliance is necessary for maintaining data reliability, security, and privacy. Chapter 16, Reporting and Communication, discusses this topic.

Chapter 17 covers Compliance and Regulations during the implementation of a data reliability program. Integrating compliance and regulation into the Data Reliability Program enables organizations to meet legal requirements, enhances data reliability and security, and fosters a trustworthy and responsible data environment.

Chapter 18 discusses data recovery and disaster planning, critical components of a comprehensive data reliability program. These elements ensure that an organization can effectively recover its data in the event of unexpected incidents or disasters.

Chapter 19 outlines the KPIs. In the context of a Data Reliability Program, defining key performance indicators (KPIs) and measurable metrics is a quantifiable indicator used to assess the effectiveness, performance, and quality of data-related processes and outcomes. The metrics discussed in this chapter provide a basis for measuring progress, identifying areas for improvement, and ensuring that the objectives of the data reliability initiative are met.

Chapter 20 discusses feedback and iteration, which achieve continuous improvement and adaptability in a Data Reliability Program.

Scalability and future readiness, as discussed in Chapter 21, are key features of a Data Reliability Program, particularly in the rapidly evolving landscape of data management and analytics.

A DRIP applicable to outsourced activities, as outlined in Chapter 22, is essential for organizations that rely on outsourced manufacturing, testing, or data processing, where data quality can have a direct impact on decision-making, regulatory compliance, and overall business performance.

This book applies to any data-driven industry. The author selected the medicinal products manufacturing industry as an example. In this environment, properly recorded information serves as the basis for manufacturers to ensure the identity, strength, purity, and safety of their products. This book highlights the implementation of data suitability, associated risk-assessed controls, and data handling.

The author refers the reader to relevant medicinal manufacturing product regulations and guidance for additional information. Some descriptions are based on listed regulations and guidance, and judicious editing is necessary to fit the context of this book.

This book aims to ensure that accurate, complete, and legible copies of data are available for review, guide readers in effectively managing data and e-record reliability vulnerabilities, and promote essential compliance in this area.

This book aligns with the definitions of data reliability in data engineering standards.

The recommendations to implement data-record controls, as described in this book, are based solely on the authors' standpoint and opinion and should be considered a suggestion only. They are not supposed to serve as the regulators' official implementation process.

References.

[1] The principles outlined in this book apply to data generated by both electronic and paper-based systems.

[2] NARA, *"Universal Electronic Records Management (ERM) Requirements,"* Version 3.0, June 2023.

[3] This is a dimension of data quality. Data accuracy refers to the extent to which data accurately represents real-life entities.

[4] It is one dimension of data quality. Data completeness refers to the extent to which all required data elements or values are present in a dataset without missing or null values.

[5] Data conformity refers to data adhering to specific definitions, such as its type, size, and format.

[6] Data consistency is one dimension of data quality. Data consistency refers to the accuracy, reliability, and coherence of data within a system or database.

[7] Objectivity is based on factual information, with minimal influence from personal opinions or feelings.

[8] Data suitability refers to the appropriateness and fitness of a dataset for a particular purpose or analysis.

[9] Data validity refers to the accuracy, correctness, and suitability of the data.

[10] Source authentication refers to data that has a verifiable source, accompanied by well-documented evidence or reliable witnesses.

[11] Data timeliness refers to the degree to which data is current and up-to-date at the point in time when it is needed for analysis, decision-making, or other business processes.

[12] Trustworthy data - Reliability, authenticity, integrity, and usability are the main characteristics of trustworthy data from a record management perspective. (NARA)

[13]US FDA, *"Guidance for Industry Quality Systems Approach to Pharmaceutical CGMP Regulations,"* September 2006.

[14] Data authenticity refers to the quality or state of being genuine, trustworthy, and unaltered.

[15] Usable data refers to information that is accessible, understandable, and applicable for its intended purpose.

[16] López, O., *"Trustworthy Computer Systems,"* Journal of GxP Compliance, Vol 19 Issue 2, July 2015.

Additional References.

- Data Reliability Standards and frameworks - https://www.linkedin.com/posts/orlandolopezrodriguez_the-term-data-reliability-can-be-defined-activity-7181016993808969728-Dgq2?utm_source=share&utm_medium=member_desktop

- Data reliability relationship with complete, consistent, accurate, and trustworthy data - https://www.linkedin.com/pulse/data-reliability-relationship-complete-consistent-accurate-lopez-rgqec/?trackingId=DLm8ZQAfRwybAnT1jrJ0GA%3D%3D

Chapter 2
Implementation of a Data Reliability Program

Introduction

Data reliability, crucial in the pharmaceutical industry, is a responsibility shared by all pharmaceutical professionals. Their dedication and expertise are instrumental in ensuring the medicinal products are high quality, safe to use, and

> *Data is considered reliable if it ensures a complete and accurate representation of the subsequent transactions or activities and if it can be depended upon during subsequent transactions or activities.*
>
> **NARA, "Universal Electronic Records Management (ERM) Requirements," Version 3.0, June 2023**

effective. By adhering to strict regulatory guidelines, pharmaceutical companies, with the guidance of these professionals, must maintain data integrity throughout the entire product lifecycle, from research and development to manufacturing and distribution. Data reliability refers to the accuracy, consistency, and completeness of data recorded and reported in various documents, such as laboratory records, production logs, and quality control reports. The pharmaceutical guidelines emphasize the importance of implementing robust data management systems, secure electronic records, and thorough documentation practices to prevent data manipulation, unauthorized changes, or inaccuracies. A commitment to data reliability, led by these professionals, ensures that pharmaceutical companies produce reliable and traceable data, contributing to product quality assurance, patient safety, and regulatory compliance in the highly regulated pharmaceutical landscape.

A reliability program is not just a technical necessity; it is a tool that empowers pharmaceutical professionals to enhance their capabilities and improve patient outcomes. Reliable data is not only accurate but also trustworthy, providing a complete and accurate representation of transactions, activities, or facts. It remains dependable during subsequent transactions and activities. For instance, reliable data can be used to identify trends in patient responses to a particular drug or to make informed decisions about the safety and efficacy of a new product. These characteristics underscore the practical benefits of a reliability program, as it enables informed decisions and valuable insights and instills confidence in the professionals, knowing that their analyses and decisions are based on trustworthy data.

Data reliability is about the consistency and repeatability of data over time, regardless of the methods or tools used to collect it. A dataset is considered reliable if it consistently produces the same results, even when measured multiple times or obtained by different researchers or methods. To illustrate, consider an experiment that consistently yields the same results every time it is performed. This experiment is a prime example of data reliability [2].

Data reliability is not just a technical aspect; it is the foundation of making informed decisions [3], obtaining valuable insights, and maintaining the integrity of an organization's operations. The term "trusted" is relevant to data reliability since it requires a combination of data quality, integrity, and security to ensure that the data is reliable, accurate, and trustworthy. Decisions based on reliable and accurate data can yield positive outcomes or negative consequences. Ensuring data reliability is a significant responsibility, as it directly impacts the success and safety of pharmaceutical operations.

Various factors must be weighed to ensure that data is trusted, including data quality, integrity, and security. Implementing a data reliability program is a systematic process that involves a series of activities to guarantee the accuracy, authenticity, integrity, and usability of data utilized within an organization.

Data Reliability Key Components.

As an element of Data Governance (Chapter 10), the Data Reliability Program is a structured approach and set of activities to ensure that data used within an organization is accurate [4], authentic [5], with integrity [6], usable [7], and can be confidently used for decision-making, analysis, and other purposes. Data reliability is crucial for making informed decisions [8], generating meaningful insights, and maintaining the integrity of an organization's operations.

This book provides a detailed step-by-step guide for implementing a data reliability program.

- *Define Objectives and Goals.*

Clearly articulate the objectives and goals of the Data Reliability Program. These include improving data accuracy, reducing errors, enhancing data consistency, and ensuring data complies with relevant regulations.

- *Establish Governance and Ownership.*

Identify individuals or teams responsible for overseeing the program. This is where the role of data stewards becomes crucial. Data stewards are not only responsible for ensuring data quality; they are also the guardians of data reliability, ensuring that every piece of data is accurate, authentic, and usable. They are responsible for maintaining data quality and integrity, ensuring that it meets the organization's standards and regulatory requirements, and promoting a culture of data reliability throughout the organization. Data stewards play a key role in data governance, ensuring data is managed effectively and appropriately.

- *Data Inventory and Classification.*

Catalog all the data sources within the organization. Categorize data based on its importance, sensitivity, and relevance to business operations. For example, customer data might be classified as highly important and sensitive, while operational data might be less sensitive but still crucial for daily business operations. Understand how data flows through the organization, from collection to use in various processes.

- *Data Quality Assessment.*

Conduct an initial data quality assessment by identifying common issues such as duplicates, inconsistencies, missing values, and outliers. Develop key performance indicators (KPIs) to measure data quality.

- *Data Quality Standards.*

Define data quality standards and metrics that align with the organization's goals. These standards include accuracy, completeness, consistency, timeliness, and integrity.

Adhering to these standards ensures that the data used for decision-making and analysis is reliable and trustworthy, providing professionals with reassurance and security.

- *Data Cleansing and Transformation.*

Implement data cleansing and transformation processes to rectify data quality issues. These processes may involve using tools and technologies for data cleaning, normalization, and enrichment.

- *Data Documentation.*

Create metadata repositories and data dictionaries to document data sources, definitions, and lineage. Data lineage records the origins, changes, and movements of data throughout its lifecycle. This documentation helps data users understand the meaning and origins of the data, and it is crucial for ensuring the accuracy and authenticity of the data, as it provides a clear trail of how the data was collated, processed, and used. For example, data lineage can reveal when and how a particular piece of data was collected, who modified it, and how it was utilized in various analyses, providing a comprehensive history of the data's journey.

- *Data Governance Framework.*

Develop and implement a data governance framework that includes policies, procedures, and workflows for data management, access control, and data stewardship [9].

- *Data Access Control.*

Ensure that access to data is controlled and that only authorized personnel can view, modify, or delete data [10]. Implement role-based access controls (RBAC) and data encryption where necessary.

- *Data Monitoring and Auditing.*

Set up continuous monitoring and auditing mechanisms to track data quality and compliance over time. Automated alerts can notify stakeholders of data issues in real time.

- *Data Training and Awareness.*

Provide training and awareness programs for employees to understand the importance of data reliability and how to adhere to data quality standards.

- *Data Lifecycle Management.*

Define data lifecycle stages: capture, processing, storage, usage and access, archiving, and disposal. Implement data retention policies and procedures in accordance with applicable regulatory and legal requirements.

Refer to Chapter 13.

- *Continuous Improvement.*

Review and refine data reliability processes regularly based on feedback, monitoring results, and changing business needs. Continuously update data quality standards. This commitment to continuous improvement ensures that the data reliability program remains practical and relevant, engaging all pharmaceutical professionals.

- *External Data Sources.*

Extend data reliability efforts to include data from external sources or third-party vendors, ensuring that external data meets the same quality standards.

- *Reporting and Communication.*

Share data quality reports and findings with key stakeholders, including senior management, to maintain transparency and accountability.

- *Compliance and Regulation.*

Ensure data reliability practices align with industry regulations (e.g., General Data Protection Regulation (GDPR), Health Insurance Portability and Accountability Act (HIPAA)) and internal compliance requirements.

- *Data Recovery and Disaster Planning.*

Develop data recovery and disaster recovery planning strategies to ensure data can be restored in the event of unexpected events or data loss.

- *Performance Metrics and Key Performance Indicators.*

Continuously measure and report on data reliability metrics, KPIs, and the progress of the Data Reliability Program.

- *Feedback and Iteration.*

Collect feedback from data users and stewards to identify areas for improvement and iterate on the program's processes and procedures [11].

- *Scalability and Future Readiness.*

Ensure the Data Reliability Program can scale with the organization's growth and adapt to emerging technologies and data sources.

Final Comment.

Implementing a Data Reliability Program is an ongoing effort that requires commitment, resources, and a culture of data quality within the organization. It helps ensure that data remains a reliable asset that can be leveraged for decision-making and strategic planning.

Establishing and maintaining data reliability often involves data quality assurance processes, cleaning, documentation, and robust data management practices. High data reliability contributes to better decision-making, improved research outcomes, and increased trust in the data's usefulness and accuracy.

The following chapters in this book describe each critical component of the data reliability program.

References.

[1]López, O., *"Are Data Quality and ALCOA attributes equivalent?"* GMP Journal, Issue #38, November 2023.

[2]United States National Archives and Records Administration (https://www.archives.gov/)

[3]What Does Attribute Data Mean? https://www.bizmanualz.com/library/what-does-attribute-data-mean

[4]Data is accurate when it reflects the activity or measurement performed (EMA, *"EMA Questions and Answers: Good Manufacturing Practice Data Integrity,"* August 2016).

[5]Authentic is the property of being genuine and being able to be verified and trusted, with confidence in the

validity of a transmission, a message, or a message originator. See authentication (NIST Special Publication 800-18).

[6]Data/e-records integrity is the property that data has not been unauthorizedly altered since created and until disposal (NIST SP 800-57P1).

[7]Usable data refers to information that is accessible, understandable, and applicable for its intended purpose.

[8]Data is reliable if its content can be trusted as a complete and accurate representation of the transaction, activities, or facts to which it attests, and it can be dependent upon during subsequent transactions and activities (NARA)

[9]McGuire, M., *"Defining Your Data Strategy: Balancing Offense and Defense"*, December 2023. https://www.dataedification.com/p/defining-your-data-strategy-balancing

[10] Enhance Regulatory Adherence with LIMS in Chemical Processing - Rhodes Caribbean. http://rhodes-caribbean.com/technology/enhance-regulatory-adherence-with-lims-in-chemical-processing.htm

[11] How to Implement a Data Governance Framework | Secoda. https://www.secoda.co/learn/how-to-implement-a-data-governance-framework

Additional References.

- HMA-EMA, *"Reliability,"* in Data quality framework for EU medicinal regulation, HMA-EMA Joint Big Data Steering Group, October 2023, pp. 15-18 (https://www.ema.europa.eu/en/documents/regulatory-procedural-guideline/data-quality-framework-eu-medicines-regulation_en.pdf).

- What is Data Reliability? Definition, Examples, and Best Practices | Metaplane. https://www.metaplane.dev/blog/data-reliability-definition-examples

- WHO (TRS 996 Annex 5), *"Designing and validating systems to assure data quality and reliability,"* Guidance on sound data and record management practices, 2016, pp. 183-186. Note: This guidance document was replaced by the WHO Guideline on Data Integrity (TRS No.1033, Annex 4) in March 2021.

Chapter 3
Define Objectives and Goals

Introduction

Defining objectives and goals in a DRIP is not just a task; it is a strategic move. This process empowers you to guide your efforts and initiatives, ensuring data reliability within your organization. The strategic nature of this task instills a sense of engagement and purpose in your role.

Objectives and goals are not just markers; they serve as a compass that sets the direction for your program, providing a clear roadmap for enhancing data quality, accuracy, and consistency. This guidance keeps you focused on the path toward reliable data, ensuring that your efforts are always directed toward the desired outcomes.

Concepts

The following outlines the definition of the DRIP's objectives and goals.

- *Define Objectives.*

Objectives are specific, measurable, achievable, relevant, and time-bound (SMART) statements that outline the desired outcomes of the DRIP.

Example Objectives.

- – Improve data accuracy by reducing data entry errors by 20% within the next six months.

- Enhance data consistency across all databases and systems to achieve a 95% consistency rate by the end of the year.

- Establish a robust data governance framework to ensure ongoing monitoring and maintenance of data quality.

- Implement data validation processes to detect and correct errors at the point of entry.

- *Define Goals.*

Goals are broad, high-level statements that express the DRIP's overarching aims. They provide a sense of purpose and direction, guiding the organization toward the desired state of reliable data.

Example Goals.

- Achieve high data reliability to support accurate decision-making and business operations.

- Foster a data-driven culture within the organization by promoting awareness of the importance of reliable data.

- Establish a comprehensive data quality management framework for collecting, storing, processing, and reporting data.

- Enhance overall organizational efficiency by minimizing the impact of unreliable data on business processes.

- *Alignment with Organizational Objectives.*

Aligning your DRIP's objectives and goals with your organization's broader objectives is not just a formality; it is a strategic move that can significantly contribute to your organization's mission, vision, and goals. This alignment can make your DRIP an integral part of your organization's strategy, enhancing its value and impact.

- *Measurable Metrics.*

Refer to Chapter 19.

- *Timeframe.*

Set clear timeframes for achieving objectives and goals. Establishing deadlines provides a sense of urgency and helps monitor progress over time.

- *Stakeholder Involvement.*

Stakeholder involvement in your DRIP is not just a checkbox; it is a critical aspect of its success. You are not just part of the process but integral to its success.

The following explains the stakeholder involvement.

- – Identification of Stakeholders.

Begin by identifying all relevant stakeholders who have a vested interest in ensuring the reliability of the data. The relevant stakeholders may include quality assurance personnel, data stewards, information technology professionals, data analysts, business leaders, and end-users.

- – Assessment of Stakeholder Needs and Expectations.

Gathering stakeholder input and insights through interviews, surveys, or workshops is essential to tailor the DRIP to meet the organization's requirements and address any concerns.

– Clear Communication.

Establishing clear and open lines of communication with stakeholders, including outlining the objectives, goals, and benefits of data reliability initiatives, is crucial. Transparent communication is crucial for building trust and ensuring that stakeholders are well-informed about the program's purpose and progress [1].

– Involvement in Goal Setting.

Ensure key stakeholders are involved in defining DRIP's goals and objectives to align with organizational priorities and meet expectations.

– Collaborative Planning.

During the program's planning phase, involve stakeholders in a collaborative effort to identify potential challenges, understand resource requirements, and establish realistic timelines for implementation.

– Feedback Gathering.

Gathering feedback from stakeholders throughout the program, including during planning, implementation, and post-implementation reviews, is essential. This enables adjustments and improvements based on the evolving needs of stakeholders.

- Training and Support.

It is essential to provide training and support to stakeholders, especially those directly involved in data management processes. The training and support help ensure stakeholders have the necessary skills and knowledge to implement data reliability measures successfully.

- Addressing Concerns and Resistance.

Acknowledge and address stakeholders' concerns or resistance to change to improve data reliability. Open discussions, clarifications, and highlighting the initiative's benefits can help gain support.

- Involvement in Decision-Making.

It is important to involve stakeholders in decision-making processes related to the DRIP. Collaborative decision-making fosters a sense of ownership and commitment among stakeholders.

- Celebrating Successes.

Acknowledging achievements and milestones with stakeholders is crucial for ensuring the reliability of data initiatives.

- Adaptability and Flexibility.

Flexibility and adaptability are essential, especially in response to unexpected challenges. Regularly evaluate the program and adjust based on feedback and changing organizational priorities.

Stakeholder involvement is a dynamic and ongoing process that requires active engagement and collaboration. By incorporating stakeholders' perspectives, needs, and contributions, organizations can enhance the likelihood of success in implementing a Data Reliability Program [2]. It promotes a shared understanding of goals, facilitates smoother implementation, and fosters a culture of data reliability within the organization.

- *Continuous Improvement.*

Consider incorporating a culture of continuous improvement within your DRIP. Regularly reassess objectives and goals based on changing business needs, technological advancements, and stakeholder feedback to ensure their effectiveness and relevance.

Refer to Chapter 14.

- *Risk Mitigation.*

Identify potential risks and challenges associated with achieving objectives and goals.

Identifying potential risks enables the implementation of data reliability requirements in modern industry practices and globalized supply chains [3].

Develop mitigation strategies to address these risks and ensure the success of the DRIP [4].

For reference, the CEFIC guide [5] can be consulted.

Benefits

Defining objectives and goals in a DRIP context is critical to ensuring the initiative's success and effectiveness. It is not just a bureaucratic step but a strategic move that can significantly enhance the value and impact of the data reliability program. Here are several benefits:

Here are several benefits:

- *Clarity of Purpose.*

The objectives and goals of a DRIP help define its purpose, expected outcomes, and measures of success. This clarity ensures that all stakeholders are aligned and focused on achieving specific targets.

- *Measurable Outcomes.*

When you set clear objectives and goals, you establish measurable outcomes that serve as benchmarks to track and evaluate progress. These measurable outcomes help identify necessary adjustments or improvements.

- *Resource Allocation.*

Clear objectives and goals are essential to determining the resources required to implement a data reliability program. By understanding what needs to be achieved, organizations can allocate the necessary financial, human, and technological resources effectively. Resource allocation ensures that resources are used efficiently and effectively to support the program's objectives [6].

- *Motivation and Accountability.*

Clear objectives and goals motivate teams involved in an implementation program. When individuals understand what they are working towards and how their efforts contribute to the overall success (Zuniga, C., & Boosten, G. (2020). A Practical Approach to Monitor Capacity under the CDM Approach. Aerospace, 7(7), 101.), it fosters a sense of purpose and accountability. The motivation and accountability, in turn, lead to increased engagement and productivity throughout the implementation process.

- *Risk Management.*

Setting objectives and goals is crucial in identifying potential risks and challenges while implementing a data reliability program. By clearly defining the desired outcomes, organizations can anticipate obstacles and develop effective strategies to mitigate risks. This proactive approach to risk management helps ensure the smooth progress of the program and minimizes disruptions to its progress.

- *Stakeholder Alignment.*

Having clear and well-defined objectives and goals is crucial for achieving alignment among stakeholders in the data reliability implementation program. When everyone comprehensively understands the overarching objectives and what success should look like, it promotes collaboration and cooperation across various departments or teams. This alignment is crucial for breaking down silos and ensuring that all efforts are coordinated toward achieving common goals [7].

- *Continuous Improvement.*

Objectives and goals provide a framework for continuous improvement throughout the DRIP. By regularly reviewing progress against established targets, organizations can identify areas for enhancement and implement necessary adjustments [8]. This iterative approach enables organizations to adapt effectively to changing circumstances and emerging needs.

Defining objectives and goals in a DRIP context is essential for providing clarity, driving progress, ensuring accountability, and achieving success in improving data reliability within an organization.

Summary

Adequately defined objectives and goals are critical to guide the efforts and provide a framework for implementing and sustaining data reliability initiatives within an organization.

Objectives and goals provided to the DRIP:

- Objectives are SMART statements that outline the program's desired outcomes. Goals are broader, high-level aims that express the overarching purpose.

- Objectives and goals should align with the organization's mission, vision, and strategic priorities. They provide direction and help prioritize efforts to improve data quality and reliability.

- Involving stakeholders in setting objectives and goals fosters ownership, ensures alignment with needs and expectations, and facilitates implementation.

- Measurable metrics are essential to track progress over time. Clear timeframes create urgency and accountability.

- Risk mitigation strategies should be developed to address challenges to achieving objectives and goals [9].

- A culture of continuous improvement enables regular reassessment and refinement of objectives and goals based on the changing business landscape.

- Well-defined objectives and goals communicate the purpose and benefits, guide planning and decisions, and provide the basis for policies and procedures to support reliable data.

In summary, adequately defined objectives and goals are crucial for guiding efforts and providing a framework for implementing and sustaining data reliability initiatives within an organization.

References

[1]Branding and Design Agency Sydney - Bettermade. https://www.bettermade.com.au/).

[2]Breslow, L. (1973). Research in a Strategy for Health Improvement. International Journal of Health Services. https://doi.org/10.2190/422y-u3tg-ma4k-b82a

[3]Russian Federal State Institute of Drugs and Good Practices, "*Data integrity & computer system validation,*" (draft) August 2018.

[4]Securing funding for the RPA revolution. https://cxotechmagazine.com/dont-miss-out-on-the-rpa-revolution-heres-how-to-secure-funding/).

[5]CEFIC, *"Practical risk-based guide for managing data integrity,"* April 2022 (Version 2).

[6]AI Resource Allocation Generator | Taskade. https://www.taskade.com/generate/project-management/resource-allocation

[7]Productroadmap.ai. https://www.productroadmap.ai/okrs/what-are-okrs-google-a-comprehensive-guide

[8]Best Practices for Efficient Document Review Processes. https://generisonline.com/best-practices-for-efficient-document-review-processes/

[9]Risk Assessment Vs. Deadline Estimation (Confusion Resolved). https://organisationalproductivity.com/risk-assessment-vs-deadline-estimation-confusion-resolved/

Chapter 4
Establish Governance and Ownership

Introduction

Data Governance and Ownership are not just components but the backbone of a Data Reliability Program. They play a pivotal role in ensuring that an organization's data is managed effectively, maintained securely, and used responsibly. These concepts are not just about establishing accountability, defining processes, and providing a framework for maintaining data reliability. They also highlight each professional's crucial and active role in this process, making them feel more involved and responsible.

The Data Governance Framework is explained in Chapter 10.

Data Governance

Data Governance refers to the management of an organization's data availability, usability, reliability, and security. It involves defining policies, standards, and procedures to ensure that data is handled consistently and complies with applicable regulations and business requirements.

It also involves an organizational structure that includes written policies and procedures, as well as documenting processes to prevent and detect situations that may impact data reliability. It includes defining roles and responsibilities, measuring, reporting, and taking action to resolve any issues identified [2].

The United Kingdom (UK) Medicines and Healthcare Regulatory Agency (MHRA) stresses data governance in its GMP Data Integrity Definitions and Guidance for Industry (Chapter 6.5). A robust data governance approach ensures that data are "complete, consistent, and accurate" [3].

According to the MHRA, the scope of the data reliability governance should include:

- relevant policies.

- training in the importance of data reliability.

- procedures; and

- computer system access controls.

Note that implementing technology alone will not resolve the data reliability issues. In a Notice of Concern by the World Health Organization (WHO) on September 2015, associated with data deleted on laboratory equipment, it was stated on this Statement of Concern that "new equipment and usage of a server, on its own, is not deemed sufficient to ensure the absence of data reliability issues and to prevent the manipulation of analytical data." [4] Implementing practical behavioral, procedural, and technical steps based on a clear understanding of risk will ensure that the system promotes the correct behavior, enhances compliance, and provides improved product quality assurance [5].

This chapter discusses data governance based on the MHRA guidance, highlighting the key elements of data reliability in governance.

The governance system to be implemented must adopt a 'quality risk management' approach across all areas impacted by data reliability. This approach is not only important but crucial in identifying and mitigating potential risks, thereby ensuring the reliability and integrity of the data.

Data governance should address data ownership throughout the lifecycle and consider the design, operation, and monitoring of processes/systems to comply with the principles of data reliability, including control over intentional and unintentional changes to the information.

Following a systematic process that includes implementing policies, strategies, plans, procedures, and guidelines is critical to defining, documenting, and implementing data governance. Implementing these documents will involve staff planning, training, and enforcing the governance-related policies and procedures.

Data governance and related measures should be integrated into a quality system and are essential to ensure the reliability of data and records in Good Manufacturing Practice (GxP) activities [7].

For more details on data governance, refer to Chapter 10 - Data Governance Framework.

Data Ownership

Data Ownership is not just about assigning responsibility for specific datasets or domains. It is about entrusting individuals or groups within the organization with the overall well-being of the data they oversee. This includes the availability, maintenance, and security of that system's datasets or data domains, instilling a sense of responsibility and commitment in data owners.

Data governance should establish clear ownership and accountability throughout the lifecycle (Chapter 10).

The critical components of data ownership are:

Accountability.

Designate specific individuals or teams as data owners responsible for the data's accuracy, completeness, and reliability under their purview.

Decision-Making Authority.

It empowers owners to decide on data definitions, access permissions, and usage policies. This empowerment includes determining who can access, modify, or use specific datasets. As a data owner, you have the authority to make decisions that directly impact the reliability and security of our data, which demonstrates the trust and responsibility placed in your hands.

Communication and Collaboration.

Facilitate communication and collaboration between data owners, stewards, and other stakeholders to ensure a shared understanding of data requirements and priorities.

Alignment with Business Goals.

Ensuring data ownership aligns with broader business objectives. Data owners should understand the strategic importance of their data in supporting organizational goals.

Data Access and Permissions.

Defining and managing access controls ensures that only authorized individuals can access and modify specific datasets. These types of permissions also consider data privacy and security requirements.

Benefits

Governance and Ownership in a data reliability program ensure data integrity, security, and effective management.

Governance.

- *Data Quality Assurance.*

Effective governance practices are essential for maintaining data quality standards and ensuring data accuracy, consistency, and reliability. These practices are especially essential in a data reliability program, where the main objective is maintaining high-quality data.

- *Regulatory Compliance.*

A well-implemented data governance framework ensures compliance with industry guidelines, regulations, and data protection laws, which is crucial for protecting sensitive information and maintaining stakeholder trust.

- *Risk Mitigation.*

Data governance helps mitigate data risks, such as unauthorized access or data breaches, by implementing controls and monitoring mechanisms, thereby improving data reliability.

Ownership.

- *Accountability.*

Clearly defined data ownership ensures accountability for the reliability of specific datasets. Data owners are responsible for maintaining the accuracy and integrity of the data, fostering a sense of ownership and commitment to data quality.

- *Effective Decision-Making.*

Data owners deeply understand the context and business requirements associated with their datasets. This knowledge is essential for making informed decisions about data management, quality improvement, and strategic initiatives within the data reliability program.

- *Collaboration and Communication.*

Ownership encourages collaboration between different stakeholders involved in the data reliability program. Clear lines of ownership facilitate communication, coordination, and knowledge sharing, improving overall data reliability. Your collaboration with other stakeholders is crucial in ensuring the reliability and integrity of our data, and your communication and coordination skills are key in this process.

Summary

Data governance and ownership are essential to a Data Reliability Program as they establish data management standards, controls, and accountability. Data governance ensures that data is treated as a valuable organizational asset, and ownership provides a mechanism for assigning responsibility and fostering collaboration to enhance data reliability. Together, these elements create a robust foundation for maintaining the integrity and trustworthiness of an organization's data.

In simpler terms, data governance and ownership provide the structure and accountability necessary to maintain data reliability. They help address issues promptly and support an organization's data-driven decision-making processes. When properly defined and consistently implemented, data governance and ownership enhance the trustworthiness and value of an organization's data assets.

References

[1] This book defines "establish" as meaning to define, document, and implement.

[2] ITIL Service Design, 2011 Edition.

[3] Churchward, D., *"Good Manufacturing Practice (GMP) data Integrity: a new look at an old topic," Part 1 of 3*, MHRA Inspectorate Blog, June 2015.

[4] WHO, Notice of Concern to Svizera Labs, September 2010.

[5] Churchward, D., *"Good Manufacturing Practice (GMP) data integrity: a new look at an old topic,"* Part 3 of 3, MHRA Inspectorate Blog, August 2015.

[6] MHRA, *"MHRA GMP Data Integrity Definitions and Guidance for Industry,"* March 2018.

[7] *TRS 1033 - Annex 4: WHO guideline on data integrity*. (n.d.). World Health Organization (WHO). https://www.who.int/publications/m/item/annex-4-trs-1033.

Additional Readings.

- Nagula, V. a. P. B. A. (n.d.). *Data Governance: policies, procedures, and benefits*. TDAN.com. https://tdan.com/data-governance-policies-procedures-and-benefits/32589

Chapter 5
Data Inventory and Classification

Introduction

Data inventory and classification processes are fundamental in organizations, empowering data engineers to comprehend and actively manage their data assets. By ensuring that data is treated based on its significance, sensitivity, and importance to business operations, you not only contribute but also lead your organization's data management strategy. This empowerment gives you a sense of control and confidence in your role.

Without a data inventory and classification system, organizations risk data loss, misuse, or non-compliance with regulations. Therefore, these processes ensure data availability, integrity, and accuracy, providing security and compliance within the organization.

Data Inventory

A data inventory is a detailed list or database that documents and describes an organization's data assets. It provides a comprehensive view of the collected data, including storage location, ownership, processing methods, and the individuals with access to it.

The inventory should include details such as the data identity, the individual responsible for the data type, the location, the archiving organization (e.g., cabinet, shelf, folder, binder, box, database), the retention time, and other relevant information.

The primary objective of data inventory is to provide a comprehensive view of the data being collected, stored, and processed. Maintaining a comprehensive data inventory provides a deeper understanding of your organization's data landscape, empowering you to make more informed decisions and support various data management initiatives. This empowerment makes you feel more capable in your role.

A data inventory helps organizations identify where their data resides, whether in databases, file systems, cloud storage, or other repositories.

It provides visibility into the organization's data types, facilitating informed decision-making regarding data management and security measures.

A well-maintained data inventory is crucial for meeting regulatory compliance requirements, particularly in relation to data protection and privacy laws.

The following are critical aspects of data inventory.

- *Identification of Data Assets.*

A data inventory identifies and lists all the different types of data an organization collects and manages. The data types include structured data (e.g., databases), unstructured data (e.g., documents, images), and semi-structured data (e.g., Extensible Markup Language (XML) files).

- *Location and Storage.*

The data inventory indicates where each type of data is stored. Storage types could include on-premises servers, cloud storage, databases, file systems, or other data repositories.

- *Data Sources.*

The data inventory specifies the data sources from which data is collected. These may include customer interactions, website forms, sensor data, internal applications, and other relevant data sources.

- *Data Formats and Structures.*

The data inventory details the formats and structures of the data. For example, it might specify whether data is stored in a relational database, a non-SQL (NoSQL) database, a spreadsheet, or another format.

- *Data Usage and Processing.*

The data inventory describes how the organization processes, uses, and transforms data. These processes encompass information about data processing pipelines, transformations, and the systems or applications that interact with the data.

- *Access and Permissions.*

The data inventory outlines who has access to each data type and what permissions or restrictions are in place. This outline is crucial for data security and access control.

- *Data Lifecycle.*

The data inventory provides insights into the data lifecycle, including when it is created, modified, and archived. Understanding the data lifecycle is essential for effective data management and governance. Refer to Chapter 13.

- *Data Ownership.*

The data inventory may include information about the individuals or departments responsible for different data sets throughout the lifecycle [1].

Establishing clear data ownership is crucial for ensuring accountability and effective management.

- *Regulatory Compliance.*

A data inventory helps organizations understand which data is subject to specific regulations or compliance requirements. This inventory ensures adherence to data protection laws and industry standards.

- *Updates and Maintenance.*

A data inventory is a living document that requires regular updates and maintenance to reflect changes in the data landscape. New data sources, modifications to existing data sources, or retirements of old data sources should be accurately documented.

Creating and maintaining a data inventory is a foundational step in effective data governance, security, and overall data management within an organization. It provides a clear picture of the data environment, enabling more informed decision-making, effective risk management, and enhanced compliance efforts.

Data Classification

Proper data classification is critical for regulatory compliance and the integrity and reliability of your organization's data. By categorizing data based on its sensitivity, value, and the level of protection it requires, you are playing a crucial role in maintaining the integrity of your organization's data.

Regulators emphasize the need for documented policies and controls in the Data Governance around different data classifications. Data classification involves categorizing data based on its sensitivity, value, and level of protection it requires. Typical classifications include public, internal use, confidential, regulatory [2], and restricted.

Such compliance classifications include legal or ethical standards such as Data Privacy, the General Data Protection Regulation (GDPR), GxP [3], the Sarbanes-Oxley Act (SOX), and so on.

In the medicinal manufacturing environments, data classification is based on product quality, safety and efficacy, and data reliability. Some standard data classifications in pharma include regulatory data, stability data, reference standards data, and so on. These categories align controls to data criticality.

The data management procedure should, at least where applicable, include data classification, confidentiality, and privacy [4].

Data classification is a crucial aspect of a Data Access Control System (Chapter 11) that helps organizations manage and secure their data effectively. It plays a key role in data governance by ensuring that data is appropriately handled and protected, and in data security, it enables the implementation of granular access controls.

Data classification policies aid information technology teams in determining appropriate electronic controls for different servers, databases, and backup systems. It allows for the implementation of appropriate security controls based on the sensitivity of the data.

Classifying data enables organizations to implement granular access controls, ensuring that only authorized individuals or systems can access and manipulate sensitive information.

The primary goal is implementing appropriate access controls to protect sensitive information and prevent unauthorized access.

In a security incident, data classification aids in prioritizing response efforts based on the criticality of the affected data

Data classification helps organizations assess and manage the risks associated with different data types.

As machine learning and artificial intelligence (AI) continue expanding in the industry, high-quality, well-classified data sets will be essential for developing robust models. Data classification ensures that the correct data is used for training these models, improving their accuracy and reliability.

Integration with Data Reliability Program

- *Reliability Assessment.*

A data reliability program ensures data reliability, accuracy, and availability. Understanding the data inventory and classifying data based on its importance and impact allows organizations to prioritize efforts in maintaining the reliability of critical data [5].

- *Data Quality Assurance.*

Knowing the types of data and their significance enables organizations to implement data quality assurance measures tailored to the specific needs of each data category.

- *Backup and Recovery Planning.*

Critical data identified through classification can be subject to robust backup and recovery planning to ensure its availability in case of data loss or system failures.

Automation and Tools

- *Data Discovery Tools.*

Automated tools can assist in discovering and cataloging data across the organization, helping maintain an up-to-date data inventory.

- *Classification Tools.*

Automated classification tools use predefined rules or machine learning algorithms to classify data based on content and context, streamlining the classification process.

Employee Training and Awareness

Organizations can establish clear guidelines on handling different types of data based on their sensitivity, ensuring that employees know the appropriate measures to take.

Benefits

Data Inventory Benefits.

- *Visibility.*

A data inventory gives organizations visibility into their entire data asset landscape, enabling them to determine where their data is stored.

- *Governance.*

It provides a framework for implementing policies and standards for data governance to ensure consistent handling and compliance with regulations.

- *Risk Management.*

Assists in identifying and mitigating risks associated with data, including unauthorized access, data breaches, and issues with data quality.

Data Classification Benefits.

- *Security.*

Ensures the highest level of protection for sensitive/high-risk regulatory data, reducing the risk of data breaches.

- *Efficient Resource Allocation.*

Organizations can optimize security investments by allocating resources based on data importance.

- *Compliance.*

This feature helps ensure compliance with different data protection regulations / regulatory data by identifying and safeguarding sensitive information.

Summary

Data inventory and classification are essential elements of a data reliability program, providing the foundational knowledge to implement effective data management, security, and reliability measures. By understanding where data is stored, its nature, and its criticality, organizations can establish a more robust and tailored approach to ensure the reliability and integrity of their data assets.

Data Inventory.

- Detailed list of an organization's data assets.

- Provides visibility into data types, locations, formats, usage, access permissions, lifecycle, and ownership.

- Critical for data governance, security, and compliance.

Data Classification.

- Category data is based on sensitivity and required protection levels.

- Typical classifications: public, internal, confidential, restricted.

- Enables granular access controls according to sensitivity.

- Help assess and manage data risks.

- Prioritize security efforts in case of incidents.

- Tailor reliability assurance to data criticality.

References

[1]ICH, *"Good Clinical Practice (GCP) Guideline, E6(R3),"* Draft, May 2023.

[2]In the context of this book, regulatory data is the bioanalytical data, animal health data, preclinical data (cell-based and animal-based laboratory data), spontaneous adverse drug reporting data, and chemical and manufacturing control data.

[3]GxP - The underlying international life science requirements, such as those outlined in the US FD&C Act, US PHS Act, FDA regulations, EU Directives, Japanese MHL.W regulations, Australia TGA, or other applicable national legislation under which a company operates (GAMP Good Practice Guide, IT Infrastructure Control and Compliance, ISPE 2005).

[4]WHO, *"Guideline on Data Integrity,"* (TRS No.1033, Annex 4) March 2021.

[5]Critical data poses a high risk to product quality, efficacy, or patient safety (ISPE GAMP COP Annex 11— Interpretation, July/August 2011).

Chapter 6
Data Quality Assessment

Introduction.

In drug manufacturing, quality is viewed as a required objective achieved through production process management. Data are the results of the production process, and the way this process is performed affects the data accuracy [2].

Data quality is the extent to which all data (electronic, paper-based, or hybrid) are accurate, auditable, in conformance, complete, consistent, with integrity, provenance, and valid throughout the data lifecycle. Data defines product quality and ensures public safety.

Understanding that data reliability and accuracy are local and global concerns is crucial. The United States Food and Drug Administration (US FDA) and numerous other international medicinal regulatory agencies prioritize this issue. This global recognition not only underscores the critical role of data quality assessment in the pharmaceutical industry but also validates the importance of your work as an industry professional. It highlights your responsibility and commitment to data reliability and accuracy [3].

Current Good Manufacturing Practices (CGMP) require companies to use up-to-date technologies to meet worldwide medicinal regulatory expectations. When operating under a quality system, manufacturers must develop and document control procedures to capture, create, protect, access, use, migrate, transform, archive, and destroy e-records. The e-records provide evidence of operational and quality system activities. This will provide a quality system approach to fulfilling oversight and review of CGMP records.

A quality management system (QMS) is not merely a collection of policies, processes, and procedures. It is a comprehensive framework essential for planning and execution in an organization's core business area. The control procedures that ensure data reliability must be equally comprehensive, providing a solid foundation of evidence for operational and quality system activities. This underscores the thoroughness required in data management [4].

Data reliability is not just about trustworthiness but also about usefulness. More is needed for data to be trustworthy; it must also be helpful. This is achieved by integrating data quality into data handling practices, a crucial aspect of data reliability [5].

Data quality assessments are a central and critical component of a data reliability/quality program. Periodic verifications of data accuracy, completeness, consistency, and reliability are crucial for making informed decisions, gaining meaningful insights, and maintaining trust in an organization's data-driven processes. A data reliability program encompasses various strategies and practices to enhance data dependability, and data quality assessments play a central role in achieving this objective.

This chapter discusses the significance of data quality and the criteria for assessing and maintaining the quality of data sets. The attributes used to assess data to establish quality are accuracy, suitability, conformity, completeness, consistency, integrity, provenance, and validity. Quality data must meet all these criteria. Without just one attribute, it could compromise any data-driven initiative [5].

Principle

Data integrity ensures that information has not been improperly tampered with. Data reliability confirms that the content is a trustworthy representation of the recorded transactions or events and can be relied upon in future dealings. Meanwhile, quality data is characterized by its accuracy, completeness, reliability, consistency, and relevance.

Ensuring strong data integrity and reliability indicates that you work with high-quality data.

As an industry professional, your role in maintaining data reliability is crucial. You are not just a part of the process but an integral component. Your efforts to ensure the data you work with is dependable are a key factor in the success of your organization. Your commitment to data reliability makes the pharmaceutical industry a trusted source of life-saving products.

Refer to Table I for this chapter's data integrity, reliability, and quality definitions.

Data Degradation.

Data degradation is the deterioration in stored data's accuracy [6], completeness [7], consistency [8], and reliability [9]. This issue can occur over time due to various factors and poses a significant challenge to data reliability. For businesses that rely on accurate and consistent data for decision-making, analysis, and other crucial functions, it is essential to understand and address data degradation.

Data degradation can occur for various reasons, such as human errors in data entry, system failure due to hardware or software malfunctions, inadequate data management processes, and data duplication due to system errors or human oversight.

The following are some common types of data degradation:

- Data inconsistency occurs when data is recorded differently in different places or times, leading to confusion and inaccuracies.

- Data duplication arises when data is duplicated, leading to inconsistencies and inaccuracies.

- Data outdatedness occurs when data is not updated promptly, leading to inaccurate and outdated information.

- Data incompleteness occurs when data needs to be included or completed, leading to inaccuracies and gaps in information.

- Data Corruption occurs when data is altered or damaged due to hardware or software malfunctions, leading to inaccuracies and inconsistencies.

Establishing proper data management processes, including regular data quality checks, cleaning, and validation, is essential to preventing data degradation. Organizations should also invest in high-quality data management systems and training programs to ensure employees have the skills to manage data effectively.

By proactively addressing data degradation through regular data quality checks, cleaning, and validation, organizations can enhance their data's reliability and ensure that information remains accurate and usable over the long term. This approach underscores the importance of preventive measures in maintaining data reliability.

Data Quality.

According to the Federal Information Processing Standards (FIPS), [10] data quality is considered accurate, auditable, in conformance to requirements, complete, consistent, with integrity, provenance, and valid, making data both correct and valuable (Figure 6-1).

The Medicines and Healthcare Products Regulatory Agency (MHRA) data integrity guidance highlights, "This guidance primarily addresses data integrity and not data quality since the controls required for integrity do not necessarily guarantee the quality of the data generated." [11].

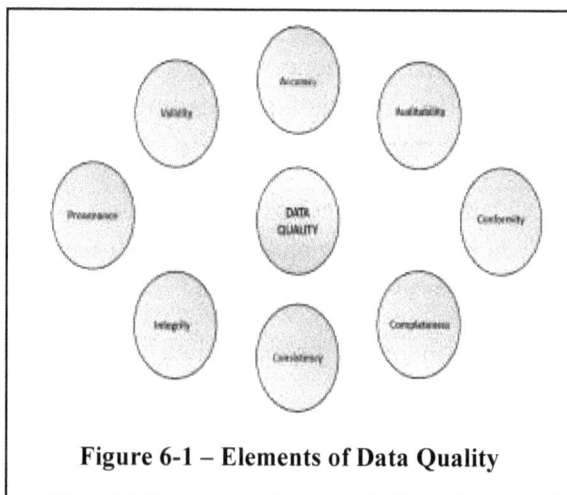

Figure 6-1 – Elements of Data Quality

The above is evident. Only four out of six attributes defined by FIPS are contained in the data integrity guidance documents. Conformity and validity should be included in the industry definitions. Only two out of six attributes defined by FIPS are contained in FDA expectations. Conformity, validity, consistency, and completeness are missing from the FDA's expectations.

As we conclude, it is important to remember that data quality cannot exist without data reliability, and data reliability cannot exist without data integrity. This interconnectedness underscores the importance of your work in maintaining these aspects of data in the pharmaceutical industry. It makes you feel integral to the process, emphasizing the significance of your role.

Table I: Definitions: Data Integrity, Data Reliability, and Data Quality

Data Integrity (NIST SP 800-57P1, ISO 17025, INFOSEC, 44 USC 3542, 36 CFR Part 1236.10, and ANSI/IEEE)	Data Reliability (US National Archives and Records Administration [12])	Data Quality (ISO 9000:2015)
Data integrity is the property that data has not been altered unauthorizedly. It covers data entry or collection, storage, transmission, and processing.	A reliable record is one whose content can be trusted as a complete and accurate representation of the transactions, activities, or facts to which it attests and can be dependent upon in subsequent transactions or activities.	The degree to which a set of data characteristics fulfills requirements. Characteristics include accuracy, conformity, validity, consistency, reliability, and completeness.

The precise collection and management of CGMP data is the total quality. ALCOA (Attributable, Legible, Contemporaneous, Original, Accurate) and ALCOA+ (Attributable, Legible, Contemporaneous, Original, Accurate, Complete Consistent, Enduring, Available) are features related to data reliability, but ALCOA and ALCOA+ fell short of the expectation in the data quality arena 13].

The following is a brief description of each attribute of data quality. Some attributes incorporate simple examples.

Data Accuracy.

Data accuracy is how data correctly represents "real-life" entities. It refers to whether the data values stored for an object are correct and describes the real-world context it refers to. To be correct, data values must be the right values and must be represented in a consistent and unambiguous form. One dimension of data accuracy is data reliability.

Example:

	The email address of Paul
Database	paul@gmail.com
Reality	Paul1@gmail.com

Data accuracy is designed to decrease the risks of preserving the content and meaning of the data. It includes built-in checks for the correct and secure data entry and processing [14]. European Union (EU) Annex 11 (Rev 1.0) paragraphs associated with data accuracy are 4.8, 6, 7.2, 10, and 11 [15].

Data accuracy is an element of a workflow that verifies the correctness of the collected data. During the Project Stage in the system lifecycle (SLC), these accuracy-related workflows are tested and periodically verified during the Operational Stage in SLC as part of the inputs and outputs (I/Os) verifications [16].

Data Auditability.

Changes to a set of data need to be traceable. A history of updates is essential to track what, when, and by whom data edits were made.

The EU Annex 11 (Rev 1.0) paragraph associated with data audibility is 9 [17].

Data Conformity.

Conformity means the data follow a set of standard data definitions like data type, size, and format.

Example:

Name	Unsubscribed
Paul	True
John	True
Sam	False

This workflow is designed as part of the Project Stage in the SLC and executed during the transformation; subsequently, the sensor(s) signals are captured, and the data are in transient mode. These workflows are tested during the Project Stage in the SLC. During the Operational Stage in the SLC, these workflows are periodically verified as part of the I/O verifications.

Data Completeness.

Completeness is the property that all necessary parts of the entity in question are included. A product's completeness is often used to express that it has met all the requirements.

The EU Annex 11 (Rev. 1) paragraphs associated with data completeness are 4.8, 7.1, and 9 [14].

Data Consistency.

Data consistency refers to data accuracy, reliability, and coherence within a system or database. Adherence to a set of rules among data is designed during the project stage in the SLC. The consistency is tested and periodically verified as part of the I/O verifications.

The EU Annex 11 (Rev. 1) paragraphs associated with data accuracy are 4.8 and 5 [15].

Data Integrity.

Data/e-records integrity is the property that data has not been unauthorizedly altered since created and until disposal. It covers data entry or collection, transmission, storage, and processing.

The controls associated with security start early in the lifecycle of the system. The security requirements can be expressed as technical features (e.g., access controls), assurances (e.g., background checks for system developers), or operational practices (e.g., awareness and training).

System security requirements, like other system requirements, are derived from several sources, including law, policy, applicable standards and guidelines, functional needs of the system, and cost-benefit trade-offs.

A record risk assessment considers the sensitivity of the information to be processed. It should also consider legal implications, organization policy, and the system's functional needs. Risk assessment supports decision-making.

System security testing includes testing the parts of the system that have been developed or acquired and testing the entire system. Security management, physical facilities, personnel, procedures, commercial or in-house services (such as networking services), and contingency planning affect the entire system's security but may be specified outside the development or acquisition cycle. Because only items in the development or acquisition cycle will have been tested during system acceptance testing, separate tests or reviews may need to be performed for these additional security elements.

Many security activities take place during the system's operational phase. These fall into three areas: security operations and administration, operational assurance, and periodic re-analysis of security.

Data Provenance.

Data provenance is the confidence of the data source systems. Instituting data quality rules at the source enhances this confidence.

This data reliability issue is relevant in the data warehouse environment, where data is extracted from source systems.

With standards and business processes, the data across all source systems will line up. When the data is inconsistent, we have created nonconformance to the data fields holding the source systems' data.

Data quality in source systems involves:

- Data entered or generated directly in computer systems is the raw data and official record for CGMP purposes. It must comply with data requirements. The usage of source data must comply with the regulated entity procedural control(s) covering the electronic data utilization.

- All entries in data fields, both text and from selection lists, must be:

    - contemporaneous – entered at the time the work is done or soon afterward,

    - reliable – a complete and accurate representation of the transactions, activities, or facts to which they attest and

    - usable – can be located, retrieved, presented, and interpreted separately and combined with other data.

- Audit trails record all changes to electronic data, as applicable.

Data profiling is the technical analysis of data to describe its content, consistency, and structure to uncover the degree of data quality in a source system. As soon as a candid data source is identified, a quick data profiling assessment should be made to provide a go/no-go decision about proceeding with the project. Once the fundamental strategic decision is made to include a data source in the project, a lengthy tactical data profiling effort should be made to identify as many data problems as possible.

The profile must be used for data standard enforcement across platforms.

Data Validity.

Data validity refers to data accuracy, correctness, and fitness. It is about the correctness and reasonableness of data conforming to the syntax and structure defined by the business requirements.

Example:

	email
Paul	paul@g@gmail.com

Regarding data accuracy, this workflow is designed as part of the Project Stage in the SLC and executed during the transformation; subsequently, the sensor(s) signals are captured, and the data is in transient mode. During the Project St e in the SLC, these workflows are tested and periodically verified as part of the I/O verifications.

Data Quality Design.

The e-records lifecycle incorporates two stages: defining the planning, requirements, and design of the e-records model and the functionality of managing the e-records model.

During the Project Stage in the SLC, it should be designed to detect and prevent data defects before they corrupt databases or end-user applications.

The controls to be instituted as part of the design may include the following:

- Data design review.

- Accuracy checks for data entered manually [18].

- Built-in checks for the correct and secure data entry and processing [12].

- Until the transient data are recorded to durable media, the transient data must ensure that the transient data may be subject to transformation, not manipulation [11].

- During the operational stage in the SLC, controls must be implemented to collect and store error/defect data for future or real-time evaluation.

- During the Operational Stage in the SLC, periodically cleansing data ensures data quality. The following section reviews "data cleansing."

- During the Operational Stage in the SLC, the correctness of data loaded to the data storage area must be periodically reconciled. The technique and method to be used in the data reconciliation process, the frequency of data reconciliation, the rationale for the choice of subsets of data to reconcile, and documentation of the results of data reconciliation must be defined during the design and implemented according to the specifications.

The software may be designed to reject or adjust specific I/Os data that does not conform to some predetermined criterion or otherwise falls within certain pre-established limits. This type of edit can help reduce manual data entry errors and lead to accuracy checks [14]. Edits can also falsify information and give the erroneous impression that a function is under control [19]. Edits are a vulnerability to e-records because software applications alter them.

Quality Control to Data.

There must be a recovery mechanism to detect and correct corrupt or inaccurate e-records from an e-record set, table, or database; this process should identify incomplete, incorrect, inaccurate, or irrelevant parts of the data and then replace, modify, or delete dirty or coarse data [20]. Correcting damaged e-records provides a mechanism for accurately reproducing an original e-record discovered to be stained, marred, or otherwise damaged.

Data cleansing or scrubbing ensures data quality. Any error should be investigated to prevent it from happening again.

When an e-record is discovered unreadable, it can be restored from a true copy. If a valid copy is unavailing, look for a trustworthy backup copy of the record and restore it from the backup set.

If the data set being cleansed consists of CGMP-relevant e-records, any changes and deletions must generate an audit trail. The reason for the migration must be documented in the e-record. Audit trails must be available, converted to an intelligible form, and regularly reviewed [17].

Damaged e-records may be considered an incident and investigated.

Benefits.

Data Quality Assessments are critical in a Data Reliability Program to ensure an organization's data accuracy, consistency, and reliability.

The benefits of including Data Quality Assessments in Data Reliability are as follows.

Improved Decision-Making.

Accurate and reliable data are crucial for making informed decisions. Data quality assessments are essential to identify and rectify any discrepancies, errors, or inconsistencies in the data. This ensures that decision-makers have trustworthy information on which to base their decisions.

Enhanced Trust and Credibility.

Reliable data is essential to building trust among internal and external stakeholders. A Data Reliability Program with regular Data Quality Assessments demonstrates a commitment to maintaining high data standards, which enhances the organization's credibility.

Compliance and Risk Mitigation.

Industries and regulatory bodies require strict data accuracy. Data Quality assessments ensure compliance, reducing legal risk.

Operational Efficiency.

High-quality, accurate, and consistent data results in increased operational efficiency. The operational efficiencies reduce the time and resources spent on error correction and discrepancy resolution, allowing organizations to focus on productive activities.

Cost Savings.

Ensuring high-quality data is crucial to preventing costly mistakes and disruptions in operations. By performing Data Quality Assessments early on, organizations can detect and rectify errors before they cause downstream issues. This preemptive approach can save businesses significant money in the long run, avoiding the negative consequences of poor data quality.

Improved Data Integration.

In organizations, data from different sources must undergo Data Quality Assessments before integration to ensure consistency.

Enhanced Customer Satisfaction.

Data accuracy is vital for customer satisfaction if an organization provides products or services based on customer data. Conducting Data quality assessments helps maintain high accuracy in customer records, improving customer trust and satisfaction.

Continuous Improvement.

Implementing Data Quality Assessments as part of a Data Reliability Program creates a framework for continuous improvement. Organizations can adapt to changing data landscapes and technologies by regularly evaluating and enhancing data quality processes to ensure sustained reliability.

Summary.

Data Quality Assessments are an essential component of a Data Reliability Program. They are crucial in improving decision-making, building trust, ensuring compliance, enhancing operational efficiency, reducing costs, promoting data integration, increasing customer satisfaction, and driving continuous improvement. Organizations can effectively identify and address data quality issues by conducting regular assessments and fostering a culture of data reliability and accountability.

A data quality assurance and security program must ensure that operations and decision-making are supported with data that meets the needs of accuracy, conformity, validity, consistency, reliability, and completeness.

Instead of emphasizing data reliability, regulated companies should concentrate on data quality to meet quality requirements in the respective medicines' manufacturing practices regulations.

References.

[1]López, O., *"Introduction to Data Quality,"* Journal of Validation Technology, April 2020.

[2]Veregin, H., *"Data Quality Parameters,"* Geographical information systems, 1999.

[3]US FDA, *"Data Integrity and Compliance with Drug CGMP - Questions and Answers, Guidance for Industry,"* December 2018.

[4]ISO 9001:2015 Quality Management Systems – Requirements.

[5]Syncsort Editors, *"Data Integrity Vs Data Quality: How Are They Different?"* https://blog.syncsort.com/2019/01/data-quality/data-integrity-vs-data-quality-different/, January 2019.

[6]   Accuracy is a dimension of data quality. Data accuracy is how data correctly represents "real-life" entities.

[7]   Completeness - It is one dimension of data quality. Data completeness refers to the extent to which all required data elements or values are present in a dataset without missing or null values.

[8]   Consistency—Data consistency is one dimension of data quality. It refers to data accuracy, reliability, and coherence within a system or database.

[9]   A reliable record is one whose content can be trusted as a complete and accurate representation of the transactions, activities, or facts to which they attest and can be depended upon in subsequent transactions or activities (NARA).

[10] Federal Information Processing Standards (FIPS), Publication 11-3, *"American National Dictionary for Information Systems,"* Windrowed, July 1979.

[11] MHRA, *Guidance on GxP data integrity.* (2018, March 9). GOV K. https://www. v.uk/go rnment/publications/guidance-on-gxp-data-integrity.

[12]US NARA, *"Records Management Guidance for Agencies Implementing Electronic Signature Technologies,"* October 2000.

[13] López, O., *"Are Data Quality and ALCOA attributes equivalent?"* GMP Journal, Issue 38, October/November 2023, pages 7-11.

[14]EU GMP Annex 11 p5, *"Computerised Systems,"* June 2011.

[15]PIC/S PI 041-1, *"Good Practice for Data Management and Integrity in Regulated GMP/GDP Environments,"* Jul 2021, (https://picscheme.org/docview/4234).

[16]US FDA, 21 Code of Federal Regulations Part 211.68(b), December 2008.

[17]EU GMP Annex 11 p9, *"Computerised Systems,"* June 2011.

[18]EU GMP Annex 11 p6, *"Computerised Systems,"* June 2011.

[19]US FDA, *"Guide to Inspection of Computerized Systems in the Food Processing Industry,"* April 2003.

[20] CEFIC, *"Practical risk-based guide for managing data integrity,"* April 2022 (Version 2)

Additional Reading.

- McDowall, R.D., *"Data Quality and Data Integrity Are the Same. Wrong!"* Spectroscopy Vol 34 Issue 11, November 2019, pages 22-29.

Chapter 7
Data Quality Standards

Introduction.

Data Quality Standards establish guidelines for data accuracy, completeness, consistency, timeliness, and integrity that align with the organization's goals.

Some of these standards are key performance indicators (KPI) elements.

Critical Components.

Data Quality Standards are guidelines and criteria to ensure that data meets specific requirements for accuracy, completeness, consistency, reliability, and timeliness. For instance, a data quality standard for accuracy could be that all numerical data should be within a specific range of the actual value. In a data reliability program, these standards play a crucial role in maintaining the integrity and trustworthiness of the data used for various purposes, such as decision-making, analysis, and reporting. For example, data quality standards could ensure that all sales figures are accurately recorded and consistent across different sources in a sales analysis.

Some critical components of Data Quality Standards within a data reliability program are:

- *Accuracy.*

Data accuracy is how data correctly represents "real-life" entities. It should be free from errors, inconsistencies, or biases that could lead to incorrect interpretations or decisions.

Inaccuracies can lead to incorrect conclusions and flawed decision-making. For example, if a data quality standard for accuracy is not met, a company might make a business decision based on incorrect sales figures, leading to financial losses. This underscores the importance of adhering to data quality standards to avoid such consequences. Measures must be taken to minimize errors and ensure data accuracy to enhance reliability.

https://www.linkedin.com/posts/orlandolopezrodriguez
_according-to-worldwide-medicinal-regulatory-activity-
7147240521470492672-q-
nm?utm_source=share&utm_medium=member_desktop

- *Completeness.*

Data should be comprehensive and include all necessary information without significant gaps or missing values. Incomplete data can lead to skewed analyses and unreliable insights.

Ensuring data is complete is essential to enhancing data reliability.

https://www.linkedin.com/posts/orlandolopezrodriguez
_httpslnkdinggu82j6b-activity-7146162759808761856-
rV9A?utm_source=share&utm_medium=member_desktop

- *Consistency.*

Data consistency refers to data accuracy, reliability, and coherence within a system or database. Consistency ensures that the information maintains significance and relevance across different contexts. Inconsistencies can arise due to discrepancies in data collection methods, formats, or definitions, undermining the reliability of analyses and comparisons.

- *Reliability.*

Data is reliable if its content can be trusted as a complete and accurate representation of the transaction, activities, or facts to which it attests and can be depended upon during subsequent transactions and activities (NARA). If the data is reliable, the collection processes are robust, well-documented, and subject to validation and verification procedures.

- *Timeliness.*

Data timeliness refers to the degree to which data is current and up-to-date about the point in time when it is needed for analysis, decision-making, or other business processes.

- *Relevance.*

Data should be relevant to the organization's objectives, requirements, or use case. Irrelevant or extraneous data can clutter datasets and distract from meaningful analysis.

- *Security and Privacy.*

Data should be protected against unauthorized access, alteration, or disclosure to maintain confidentiality, integrity, and privacy. Compliance with relevant regulations and standards, such as Good Clinical Practices (GCP), GDPR, or HIPAA, is essential to ensure data security and privacy. Data Quality Standards also play a role in data privacy and security, as they ensure that data is accurate, complete, and consistent, reducing the risk of data breaches or unauthorized access.

Benefits.

Implementing Data Quality Standards within a data reliability program offers several benefits, including contributing to the data's integrity, trustworthiness, and usability. This enhances the quality of our work and inspires us to strive for excellence in data management.

The following are some of the key advantages.

- *Enhanced Decision-Making.*

High-quality data ensures that decisions are based on accurate, reliable, and relevant information. By adhering to Data Quality Standards, organizations can minimize the risk of making decisions based on erroneous or incomplete data, leading to better outcomes and reduced uncertainty. This empowerment in decision-making instills a sense of confidence in the data's reliability.

- *Increased Operational Efficiency.*

Reliable data reduces the time and resources spent correcting errors, reconciling inconsistencies, and dealing with data-related issues. By establishing consistent data quality practices, organizations can streamline data processes, improve workflow efficiency, and focus resources on value-added activities.

- *Improved Customer Satisfaction.*

Data Quality Standards help ensure customer data is accurate, up-to-date, and secure. This leads to improved customer experience, as organizations can provide personalized services, make informed recommendations, and maintain trust by safeguarding sensitive information. Adhering to these standards has a key benefit: the positive impact on customer relationships.

- *Better Strategic Planning.*

Reliable data is a foundation for strategic planning, forecasting, and performance measurement. With access to trustworthy data that adheres to established standards, organizations can confidently analyze trends, identify opportunities, and mitigate risks.

- *Compliance and Risk Mitigation.*

Adhering to Data Quality Standards helps organizations comply with regulatory requirements and industry data integrity, security, and privacy standards. This proactive approach to data management mitigates non-compliance risk by avoiding penalties, legal issues, and reputational damage associated with data breaches or violations. It instills a sense of security and confidence in the organization's data management practices.

- *Increased Stakeholder Trust.*

Reliable data introduces confidence among stakeholders, including customers, investors, partners, and regulators. When stakeholders trust an organization's data accuracy and reliability, they are more likely to engage in collaborative efforts, invest in initiatives, and support strategic goals.

- *Facilitated Data Integration and Interoperability.*

Consistent data quality standards make integrating data from diverse sources and systems easier. Data Integration and Interoperability enable organizations to break down data silos, improve data sharing and collaboration, and enhance interoperability across departments, functions, and external partners.

- *Continuous Improvement.*

Implementing Data Quality Standards fosters a culture of continuous improvement within an organization. This underscores the importance of our ongoing commitment and dedication to maintaining and enhancing data quality. By monitoring data quality metrics, identifying areas for enhancement, and implementing corrective actions, we can ensure that our data remains accurate, reliable, and valuable.

Summary.

Implementing and following data quality standards is essential to ensuring that data is accurate, reliable, and valuable in a data reliability program. Data quality involves technical solutions like data validation tools and organizational practices like data governance frameworks and training programs. Data analysts, data scientists, and data managers play a crucial role in implementing these standards, ensuring data accuracy, and maintaining data reliability. Their expertise and dedication are instrumental in the continuous monitoring and improvement efforts required to maintain and improve data quality.

These standards can reap numerous benefits for organizations, including better decision-making, increased operational efficiency, enhanced customer satisfaction, and more vital stakeholder trust.

Combining these data quality components contributes to the overall reliability of data.

Additional Reference.

- Data reliability through various standards and frameworks – Appendix IV.

- López, O., *"Are Data Quality and ALCOA attributes equivalent*?" GMP Journal, Issue #38, November 2023.

Chapter 8
Data Cleansing and Transformation

Introduction.

Data cleansing and transformation, which focus on enhancing the quality and usability of the data, are critical processes in which data analysts play a pivotal role. Their expertise is crucial to ensuring the data is accurate and consistent and meets the required reliable analysis and decision-making standards.

Data Cleansing.

Data degradation (Chapter 6) is a phenomenon in which data accuracy, completeness, consistency, and reliability deteriorate over time for various reasons, such as human error, system failure, hardware or software malfunctions, inadequate data management processes, and data entry mistakes. This is considered a decline in data quality and, consequently, a lack of data reliability.

Adequate data management controls, including frequent data accuracy checks (Annex 11 to the EU GMP guideline, p. 6 (Rev, 1)), cleansing, and data validation [1], are crucial to maintaining and maximizing data quality.

Data Cleansing, also known as data scrubbing or data cleaning, is a meticulous process. It involves identifying and correcting dataset errors, inconsistencies, and inaccuracies. The primary objective is to enhance the accuracy and reliability of the data by addressing issues such as missing values, duplicates, formatting errors, and outliers. This process ensures the data is free from errors that could negatively impact the analysis or decision-making processes.

Key data cleansing activities.

- *Handling Missing Data.*

Identify and address missing values by blaming them based on statistical methods or removing them if appropriate.

- *Duplicate Removal.*

Detect and eliminate duplicate records or entries to prevent redundancy and maintain data integrity.

- *Outlier Detection and Treatment.*

Identify and handle outliers or extreme values that may skew the overall dataset by correcting or investigating their validity.

- *Standardizing Formats.*

Ensure consistent data formatting, such as date formats, unit conventions, and naming conventions, to improve consistency.

- *Addressing Inconsistencies.*

Resolve inconsistencies in data values, particularly in fields where there should be uniformity, to avoid confusion and ensure accurate analysis.

- *Correcting Data Types.*

Ensure data types are appropriate for each variable, correcting any discrepancies that may impact analysis.

- *Conforming to Business Rules.*

Align data with predefined business rules to meet organizational standards and requirements.

- *Data Validation.*

Implement validation checks to verify the accuracy and reliability of data values against predefined criteria [1].

If CGMP data [2] are present in the dataset, the US FDA requires that processes be designed to prevent data modification without a record [3].

Any change in the raw data [4] during the data cleansing should clarify the previous entry. The change should indicate its reason and be dated, signed, or initiated by the individual making it [5].

Data Transformation.

Data Transformation involves converting, mapping, and restructuring data from its original format into a more suitable form for analysis, reporting, or integration with other datasets. This process is crucial for ensuring that data is in a format that supports meaningful insights and decision-making.

Key data transformation activities.

- *Normalization.*

Standardize data to a standard scale, facilitating comparisons and analysis across different variables.

- *Aggregation and Summarization.*

Aggregate and summarize data to create more meaningful and manageable datasets, especially when dealing with large volumes of information.

- *Encoding and Decoding.*

Convert categorical data into numerical codes to make it compatible with analysis tools and algorithms.

- *Data Integration.*

Combine data from multiple sources or formats to create a unified dataset for comprehensive analysis.

- *Derivation of New Variables.*

Create new variables or features from existing data to provide additional insights or enhance the dataset's utility.

- *Temporal Adjustments.*

Adjust timestamps or date-related fields to align data with specific periods or time zones for accurate temporal analysis.

- *Handling Units and Conversions.*

Ensure that units of measurement are consistent and convert them if necessary to facilitate meaningful comparisons.

- *Data Masking or Anonymization.*

Implement techniques to protect sensitive information while allowing for meaningful analysis, especially in cases where privacy concerns are paramount.

Benefits.

Data cleansing and transformation are essential components of a data reliability program to guarantee that an organization's data is accurate, consistent, and reliable.

The following are key benefits of data cleansing and transformation.

- *Accuracy Improvement.*

Data cleansing involves identifying and correcting errors and inconsistencies in the data. This process helps eliminate typos, missing values, or outdated information, improving data accuracy.

- *Consistency Enhancement.*

Consistent formatting and data structure across sources enables easier integration and analysis, reducing errors.

- *Quality Assurance.*

Organizations can improve decision-making by maintaining high data quality standards through data cleaning and transformation.

- *Compliance and Regulatory Requirements.*

Data cleansing and transformation are crucial for organizations to comply with industry regulations and standards. Regulatory bodies require businesses to maintain accurate and up-to-date records, and an effective data reliability program ensures adherence to these requirements.

- *Operational Efficiency.*

Clean and well-organized data simplifies business processes, reduces manual data correction, and frees up employee time for value-added tasks.

- *Enhanced Data Integration.*

Converting data into a standardized format makes integrating other systems easier, resulting in seamless data flow across departments and systems.

- *Improved Decision-Making.*

Organizations must clean and transform data to provide accurate information for informed decision-making.

- *Cost Savings.*

Data errors can result in expensive mistakes, primarily if decisions are based on inaccurate information. Investing in data cleansing and transformation can help organizations avoid these errors, leading to cost savings overall.

- *Customer Satisfaction.*

Reliable and accurate data improves customer service, ensuring interactions are based on up-to-date information and enhancing satisfaction and loyalty.

- *Risk Mitigation.*

Inaccurate or inconsistent data can cost an organization and damage its reputation. A robust data reliability program that includes data cleansing and transformation can mitigate these risks by ensuring reliable and trustworthy data.

Summary.

In a Data Reliability Program, data cleansing and transformation are ongoing processes that should be performed systematically and consistently. These activities contribute significantly to maintaining the overall quality and reliability of the data, ensuring that it remains a valuable and trusted asset for organizational decision-making and analysis. The benefits of these processes include improved accuracy, consistency, and overall data quality, leading to better decision-making, operational efficiency, and compliance with regulatory requirements.

Data cleansing and transformation are vital in a data reliability program; they are transformative. These two processes offer improved accuracy, consistency, and overall data quality, contributing to better decision-making, operational efficiency, and compliance with regulatory requirements. Implementing these processes can inspire a positive change in your data management practices.

References.

[1]López, O., *"Data and E-records Validation"*, in Data Lifecycle and its Integrity, (Book Publishing Pros, Los Angeles, CA, 1st ed, 2024) pp. 246-252. (https://www.amazon.com/Data-Lifecycle-Integrity-Orlando-Lopez/dp/191743880X?ref_=ast_author_dp&th=1&psc=1)

[2]CGMP data - Transient data becomes a data point saved to a repository during recording. When the data point is generated to satisfy a CGMP requirement, it becomes CGMP data.

[3]US FDA, *"Data integrity and compliance with drug CGMP - questions and answers*, December 2018.

[4]Raw data - Original records and documentation retained in the format in which they were initially generated (e.g., paper, or electronic) or as a "true copy."

[5]OECD (2021), GLP Data Integrity, OECD Series on Principles of Good Laboratory Practice and Compliance Monitoring, No. 22, OECD Publishing, Paris, https://doi.org/10.1787/45779212-en.

Chapter 9
Data Documentation

Introduction.

Data engineering involves creating, developing, and managing data infrastructure, pipelines [1], and systems to facilitate data collection, processing, and storage.

The data engineer practitioner's role in data documentation is crucial as a data engineer, scientist, or analyst. The practitioner creates and manages the data infrastructure, pipelines, and systems. As a data scientist, the practitioner analyzes and interprets the data; as an analyst, the practitioner provides insights and recommendations based on the data. It is not just about creating, maintaining, and organizing records for various aspects of the workflow. It is about ensuring these processes are well-understood, scalable, and maintainable. The information provided about an organization's structure, content, and data usage makes the data management process effective and reliable.

Data documentation is crucial in a data reliability program, a systematic approach to ensuring data accuracy, consistency, and reliability. It provides a systematic way to capture and communicate information about data within an organization. By implementing data documentation as part of a data reliability program, you can significantly enhance the quality and reliability of your data, thereby supporting effective data management and instilling confidence in your data processes.

The data documentation generally includes information related to its specifications, such as descriptions of applicable functions, requirements, and procedures.

Rest assured, the design and implementation of data documentation must adhere to CGMP. The controls to the data documentation, including any changes, are meticulously drafted, reviewed, and approved by the relevant organizational units. The quality control unit also plays a crucial role in reviewing and approving these controls, ensuring the highest data management standards delineated in US FDA 21 CFR 211.100 [2].

Type of data-related documentation.

There are various types of data-related documentation, each serving a specific purpose.

The following are some common types of data-related documentation.

- *Data Dictionary.*

The data dictionary provides a detailed description of each data element used in a database or system. It includes data types, field lengths, allowable values, table relationships, and constraints.

The data dictionary promotes a common understanding of data elements across teams, reducing ambiguity and promoting data consistency.

- *Data Flow Diagrams (DFD).*

A DFD is a graphical representation that shows how data flows through a system, including processes, stores, and flows. It illustrates the data flow from its source to the destination, highlighting the processes that transform the data.

A DFD is a valuable tool for visualizing and understanding the flow of data within a system. It can help identify potential bottlenecks, data reliability risks, or areas for improvement.

- *Entity-Relationship Diagrams (ERD).*

An ERD represents the relationships between different entities in a database. It includes entities, attributes, and the relationships between entities.

An ERD provides a graphical representation of the database schema, helping stakeholders understand the structure and relationships between different data entities.

- *Metadata Documentation.*

The metadata [3] documentation describes the metadata associated with datasets, including information about data sources, transformations, and quality. It details data lineage [4], transformations (Chapter 8), quality measures, and source information.

The documentation facilitates understanding of the context and quality of data, aiding in data governance and decision-making.

- *Data Quality Documentation.*

The data quality documentation describes the procedures and standards for maintaining data quality. It provides data quality metrics, validation rules, and data quality improvement processes.

The data quality documentation ensures that data is accurate, consistent, and reliable, supporting informed decision-making.

- *Data Security Documentation.*

The data security documentation outlines the security measures to protect sensitive data. It provides access controls, encryption methods, and data classification standards.

The data security documentation helps ensure compliance with regulations, protects against unauthorized access, and maintains the confidentiality of sensitive information.

- *Data Governance Policies.*

The data governance policies define the rules and procedures for managing data within an organization. It contains data ownership, stewardship responsibilities, and lifecycle management policies.

The data governance policies establish accountability, consistency, and control over data assets, supporting effective data management.

Refer to Chapter 10.

Data Documentation.

The design and implementation of data recording and review formats must assure data reliability.

In a data reliability program, data documentation serves several essential purposes.

- *Understanding Data Sources.*

Documenting the sources of data helps in understanding where the data comes from. Data sources include information about data providers, collection methods, and any transformations applied to the raw data.

Refer to Chapter 15.

- *Data Definitions and Metadata.*

Clearly defining the data elements and providing metadata, such as data types, units, and allowable values, ensures a common understanding of the data across the organization. It is critical for maintaining consistency and accuracy in data interpretation.

- *Data Quality Metrics.*

Data quality metrics are numerical measures used to evaluate and measure the accuracy, completeness, reliability, and overall quality of data. These metrics are essential in helping organizations assess the state of their data and pinpoint areas that require improvement. Good data quality is crucial for making informed decisions, conducting reliable analyses, and ensuring the efficiency of business processes.

Recording data quality metrics and standards is critical in establishing benchmarks for data reliability. It specifies the criteria for data accuracy, completeness, consistency, and other quality dimensions. This documentation serves as a guide for evaluating data quality and supporting initiatives to enhance it.

- *Data Lineage.*

Data lineage is the process of monitoring and visualizing data movement and changes throughout its lifecycle in a data system or pipeline. It involves identifying the data source, documenting any transformations applied, and tracking its movement across different systems.

This process provides a comprehensive record of the data's origin, the processes it undergoes, and the destinations it reaches. It helps to ensure transparency and traceability in data management. By establishing data lineage, organizations can gain better visibility into their data and more easily identify the root cause of any issues that arise during their data analytics processes.

It is crucial to track data's lineage from its source to its different transformations and uses. Data documentation should include details about how data moves through different systems, processes, and organizational changes. Tracking data's lineage enhances transparency and traceability, which are essential for data management.

- *Data Governance.*

Data documentation supports data governance by providing a foundation for defining and enforcing data policies and standards. It helps establish data management, access, and usage rules, ensuring compliance with regulatory requirements and internal policies.

Refer to Chapter 10.

- *Facilitating Collaboration.*

Imagine the possibilities of a data-driven culture within your organization. Well-documented data can encourage collaboration among different teams, sparking innovative ideas and solutions. As stakeholders, you can work more efficiently and effectively with access to transparent, comprehensive documentation, paving the way for a genuinely data-driven future.

- *Change Management.*

As data evolves, documentation becomes essential for managing changes. Change Management, in the context of data documentation, includes tracking modifications to data structures, definitions, and processes. Understanding how changes impact data reliability is critical for maintaining trust in the data. By documenting these changes, you can ensure that all stakeholders are aware of the modifications and their implications, thereby maintaining the reliability and quality of your data.

- *Troubleshooting and Debugging.*

Documenting data flows and process maps to simplify troubleshooting and debugging is recommended to ensure data reliability.

This documentation assists in identifying and rectifying issues and providing insights into the data context.

Moreover, the primary purpose of the documentation is to aid data engineering in maintenance and quality assurance activities.

Benefits.

The following are the key benefits of data documentation.

- *Understanding Data Structure.*

Clear documentation, including data types, field names, and relationships between elements, is vital for interpreting and analyzing data accurately.

- *Facilitating Data Discovery.*

Clear documentation with metadata and context helps users find relevant datasets, making analysis and decision-making easier.

- *Improved Collaboration.*

Documentation facilitates effective collaboration among teams in an organization. It fosters a shared understanding of data structures and definitions, enhancing communication and facilitating the more efficient use of data resources.

- *Reducing Ambiguity.*

Clear documentation ensures consistency and reduces ambiguity among teams analyzing the same dataset.

- *Enhancing Data Quality.*

Documentation provides information on data sources, transformation processes, and data lineage. This transparency helps identify potential data quality issues and enables organizations to implement measures to enhance data quality.

- *Compliance and Auditing.*

Data documentation is crucial for compliance with regulatory requirements and auditing purposes. It provides a transparent record of data sources, transformations, and usage, which is essential for demonstrating compliance with data governance and privacy regulations.

- *Simplifying Onboarding.*

New personnel can easily go onboard and work with data when comprehensive documentation is available, minimizing the learning curve.

- *Effective Change Management.*

Effective data management requires proper documentation to track changes to data structures or definitions. Change Management ensures that stakeholders remain informed and minimizes disruptions and errors associated with modifications.

- *Supporting Data Governance.*

Documentation is crucial to data governance. It establishes and enforces data standards, naming conventions, and usage policies, ensuring consistent data management in accordance with organizational guidelines.

- *Facilitating System Integration.*

Clear documentation aids system integration by providing information on data formats, APIs, and integration points. System integration is crucial in complex IT environments with multiple systems and data sources.

- *Risk Mitigation.*

Accurate and comprehensive documentation minimizes the risk of misinterpreting or misusing data. It serves as an explicit reference for users, reducing the likelihood of errors and potential negative impacts on decision-making and operations.

Summary.

Data documentation is a fundamental component of a data reliability program. It helps ensure that data is accurate, consistent, and trustworthy. It also supports transparency, collaboration, and effective data management practices, contributing to the overall reliability and usefulness of an organization's data assets.

Adequate data-related documentation is essential for fostering a data-driven culture, ensuring data quality, and promoting the overall success of data management initiatives within an organization.

References.

[1]A data pipeline is a set of processes and tools that ingest, process, transform, and move data from one or more sources to a destination for storage, analysis, or other purposes.

[2]21 CFR Part 211 -- Current Good Manufacturing Practice for Finished Pharmaceuticals. (n.d.). https://www.ecfr.gov/current/title-21/chapter-I/subchapter-C/part-211.

[3]López, O., *"Metadata"* in E-records Integrity Requirements, Lopez, O., Eds. (Nova Science Publisher, New York, NY, 1st ed., 2022) pp. 129-137.

[4]Read elsewhere in this chapter.

Chapter 10
Data Governance Framework

Introduction.

A data governance framework is a structured methodology designed to oversee an organization's data quality, reliability, and security throughout its entire data lifecycle. Refer to Chapter 13.

Your involvement in cross-functional teams, including Business Intelligence (BI) and Information Technology (IT) teams, is crucial and integral to ensuring that Master Data Management practices are governed and standardized across transactional and analytical systems.

Data governance encompasses the creation of policies, procedures, workflows, and standards for managing data, controlling access, and ensuring data quality, security, and privacy.

The primary goals of data governance include compliance with regulations, alignment with organizational objectives, and ensuring data reliability. Given the data-centric nature of today's world, data governance plays a crucial role in enabling organizations to make well-informed decisions, manage risks effectively, and establish trust with stakeholders.

The framework outlines the processes, procedures, and governance structure responsible for managing data within an organization, encompassing Business Intelligence and IT teams, to ensure that Master Data Management practices are consistently governed and standardized across the organization's transactional and analytical systems. It encompasses strategy, policies, plans, procedures, working instructions, and workflows for data management, access control, and data stewardship.

A robust data governance approach ensures that electronic records are "complete, consistent, and accurate"— qualities that are fundamental to reliable data. Developing and enforcing policies, procedures, and standards is integral to data governance, ensuring high quality, security, privacy, and effective use of data assets.

Leadership is crucial in establishing an effective data governance system. Senior management leads the way in integrating data governance into the quality system, emphasizing the implementation of necessary policies, procedures, training, monitoring, and other systems.

Effective data asset management is crucial for organizations, so they adopt data governance as a fundamental practice. The framework serves as a guiding structure to navigate the complexities of data management, ensuring that data is treated as a valuable organizational asset and used to align with the organization's goals and regulatory requirements.

Components and Principles.

The following are key components and principles of data governance.

- *Data Stewardship.*

Data governance assigns responsibility for data to individuals or teams, known as data stewards, who are accountable for ensuring data quality, security, compliance, accuracy, consistency, and adherence to standards within an organization.

- *Data Policies and Standards.*

Data governance involves creating and enforcing data policies and standards to ensure the integrity and consistency of data. These policies outline the rules governing data access, storage, retention, and usage. They also address data privacy and compliance with relevant regulations, such as the 21 CFR Parts 210/211 (US Drug GMPs), the EU General Data Protection Regulation (GDPR), or the US Health Insurance Portability and Accountability Act of 1996 (HIPAA).

- *Data Quality Management.*

Data governance encompasses profiling, cleansing, validation, and monitoring to ensure the accuracy and reliability of data.

Refer to Chapter 6.

- *Data Security.*

Protecting sensitive data from unauthorized access and breaches is crucial for data governance. Data security involves implementing access controls, encryption, and other security measures to protect sensitive information.

- *Data Catalog and Metadata Management.*

Maintaining a comprehensive data catalog [1] and metadata repository is crucial for tracking and comprehending an organization's data assets. Metadata provides information about data lineage, sources, and definitions.

- *Data Lifecycle Management.*

Data governance involves managing data from creation to disposal. It includes defining retention policies and ensuring proper disposal of sensitive information.

- *Data Compliance and Risk Management.*

Compliance with data-related regulations varies by regulatory authority and applicable predicate regulation. Data governance manages risks and ensures adherence to established standards and regulations.

- *Data Ownership and Accountability.*

Clear data accountability and ownership must be established to establish effective data governance. Data ownership and accountability help individuals or teams understand their responsibilities and roles for specific data assets. For instance, the computer system owner is responsible for ensuring the security of the data stored on that system.

- *Data Culture.*

Encouraging a data-driven culture is a significant aspect of data governance. It involves promoting data literacy, training on best practices, and fostering trust and collaboration to enhance data-driven decision-making.

Benefits.

A robust data governance framework offers several benefits in the context of a data reliability program, providing you with assurance and confidence in your data-driven processes:

- *Data Quality Assurance.*

Establishing standards and procedures for data quality is fundamental for maintaining the reliability, accuracy, and consistency of the data used within the organization.

- *Data Standardization.*

Standardization ensures consistent data formats, naming conventions, and definitions for reliable integration and analysis across various sources.

- *Data Lifecycle Management.*

These guidelines cover the entire data lifecycle, from acquisition to disposal, ensuring that data remains accurate and reliable.

Refer to Chapter 13.

- *Risk Management.*

Establishing a data governance framework (Chapter 10) can mitigate risks associated with data, including data breaches, unauthorized access, and data quality issues, by safeguarding data integrity and security through controls and policies.

- *Compliance with Regulations.*

Adhere to regulatory requirements and industry standards when managing data to ensure compliance and accuracy. Compliance with regulations is crucial for adhering to data protection laws, privacy regulations, global medicinal manufacturing standards, and other legal requirements.

- *Data Ownership and Accountability.*

A clear definition of data ownership and the assignment of data management tasks foster accountability, ensuring the accuracy and reliability of specific datasets.

- *Improved Decision-Making.*

Accurate and reliable data, ensured by a well-governed data environment, are essential for informed decision-making. This emphasis on the benefits of data governance in improving decision-making processes instills confidence and security in the audience's data-driven processes.

- *Data Stewardship.*

Data Stewardship's role is to ensure that organizational data and metadata meet quality, accuracy, format, and value criteria and that data is properly defined and understood (standardized) across the enterprise. Data stewards are responsible for implementing data governance policies and procedures, ensuring data quality, and promoting data standardization and consistency across the organization. They play a crucial role in the data governance process, making them feel integral to the organization's data management efforts.

Organizations should assign data stewards to ensure that data and metadata meet quality, accuracy, format, and value criteria. This crucial role of data stewards in implementing data governance policies and procedures not only empowers them to standardize data across the enterprise but also makes them feel integral to the data governance process.

- *Enhanced Data Collaboration.*

Establishing common data standards and definitions, a crucial function of data governance, fosters collaboration and communication among diverse teams and business units. This shared understanding fosters a sense of unity and collaboration in the audience.

- *Data Auditing and Monitoring.*

Organizations can conduct regular audits to monitor data quality and usage, enabling them to identify and rectify issues promptly and maintain the reliability of their data. Data auditing and monitoring are crucial components of data governance, as they provide valuable insights into the health of an organization's data and help ensure that data quality standards are consistently met.

- *Facilitates Change Management.*

Provides a framework for managing changes to data structures, definitions, and processes. Facility change management ensures that changes are documented, communicated, and implemented in a controlled manner to maintain data reliability.

- *Efficient Data Integration.*

It provides data mapping, transformation, and compatibility guidelines for seamless data integration from diverse sources. Efficient data integration is essential for maintaining the reliability of integrated datasets.

- *Continuous Improvement.*

Establishing a culture of continuous improvement in data management processes by regularly reviewing and updating the data governance framework helps organizations adapt to evolving data needs and technologies.

The data governance framework should be reviewed to ensure compliance with new and existing laws. This may involve updating policies, retraining staff, or implementing new data protection measures.

Summary.

Effective data governance is crucial for managing data assets efficiently.

A well-designed data governance framework is integral to a data reliability program. It provides the structure and guidelines to ensure data quality, integrity, and security, ultimately contributing to reliable and trustworthy data for decision-making and business operations.

The data governance program should encompass policies, procedures, and standards that ensure high-quality, secure, private, and effective data management, ownership, and accountability throughout the data lifecycle. It should also consider the design, operation, and monitoring of processes and systems to ensure compliance with the principles of data reliability, including control over intentional and unintentional changes to data [2].

Data governance should, at the very least, include data classification, confidentiality, and privacy.

Effective data governance can lead to several benefits for an organization, including improved decision-making, reduced operational risks, enhanced data security, better compliance with regulations, and increased stakeholder trust. It helps organizations leverage their data as a strategic asset and ensures that data is managed to align with business goals and objectives.

It aims to comply with regulations, support organizational goals, and ensure the reliability of data, which is critical in today's data-driven world.

Outlines processes, procedures, and governance structure to manage data. Includes strategy, policies, plans, and workflows for data management, access control, and stewardship.

References.

[1]   A data catalog is a centralized repository and management system for storing and organizing metadata and information about an organization's data assets. It is a critical component of data management and governance initiatives, enabling users to discover, understand, and effectively utilize the organization's data resources.

[2] MHRA, *"GxP Data Integrity Guidance and Definitions,"* March 2018.

Additional Readings.

- López, O., *"Electronic Records Governance"* in Data Integrity in Pharmaceutical and Medical Devices Regulation Operations. (Routledge, Boca Ratón, FL, 1st ed., 2021), pp 133-141.

- Lawrence, V. a. P. B. A. (n.d.). *"Rethinking Data Policies in the Age of AI Governance."* TDAN.com. https://tdan.com/rethinking-data-policies-in-the-age-of-ai-governance/32613

Chapter 11
Data Access Control Systems

Introduction.

The data integrity service, a crucial element in data reliability, is a security function that preserves information in its original form and can be audited to confirm its reliability through audit trails. Data access control, a vital part of this service, is designed to manage and regulate access to sensitive data, ensuring that only authorized individuals or systems can view or manipulate it. By preventing unauthorized modifications, access to data is restricted to authorized individuals or systems. These access control mechanisms, such as user authentication and permissions, are not just features but necessities for maintaining data authenticity and security.

As a regulated user, you play a crucial role in our efforts to maintain data integrity. It is your responsibility to exercise appropriate controls, ensuring that changes to CGMP e-records can be made only by authorized personnel.

(US FDA 21 CFR 211.68(b)).

Robust data access control systems are your shield, ensuring the security and compliance of your data. They prevent data leaks, giving you a sense of security and confidence that provides peace of mind in the face of potential threats.

Data access control systems are not just a feature but a critical necessity in our computer systems and networks. They are designed to regulate and manage access to data, ensuring that only authorized individuals or systems can view, modify, or interact with specific data. These systems play a vital role in protecting sensitive information, maintaining data integrity, preventing unauthorized access or data breaches, and providing a sense of security. Their implementation is urgent and of the utmost importance.

For manufacturers of medicinal products, it is essential to establish and implement a method to document the access privileges of authorized personnel for each electronic system and data repository.

Access Controls Models.

Access control models play a crucial role in managing access to resources. They establish the regulations and techniques that oversee the authorization of users or systems to resources and the actions they can execute once authorization is granted.

Access controls should ensure strict segregation of duties. This means that the regulated user access rights and permissions should align with personnel responsibilities, ensuring users can access only the resources necessary for their role [1].

Different access control models exist, each with its principles and methods. The following are three common access control models.

- *Discretionary Access Control (DAC).*

In DAC, the data owner controls who can access the data and what actions they can perform. Access permissions are typically based on user identities and roles. Users or administrators are assigned access rights based on their identity or role.

Key features:

- − The resource owner makes access decisions.

- − Users can grant or revoke permissions to others.

- − It is commonly used in file systems where users control their files and directories.

- *Mandatory Access Control (MAC).*

In MAC, access is determined by a set of rules and policies established by system administrators. Users have limited control over access permissions, often based on security labels or classifications.

Key features:

- − System-wide security policies determine access.

- − Security labels are assigned to resources and users.

- − It is commonly used in environments with strict security requirements, such as government or military systems.

- *Role-Based Access Control (RBAC).*

Data access rights and permission rules should be based on the function, activity, or business process related to the e-records. This approach enables organizations to make changes without affecting the access and permission rules [2].

RBAC is a significant change in access control. It assigns access permissions to roles, and users are associated with one or more roles. Access decisions are based on a user's role within an organization, simplifying administration and ensuring the principle of least privilege. This role-based approach streamlines access to rights management, making administration more efficient and reducing the likelihood of errors.

Typically, users with elevated access rights (e.g., admin) should refrain from conducting regular work tasks on the system.

Key features:

- Access is based on job function or role.

- Users inherit permissions associated with their roles.

- Reduces administrative overhead by managing access at the role level.

Computer system users shall have access to only the functionality required by their job role within the system. User roles and responsibilities shall be pre-determined and documented in controlled documentation.

It is important to note that the access control models mentioned above are not mutually exclusive. Some systems may use elements from multiple models to create a hybrid or layered approach. The choice of access control models should be based on the security requirements and specific characteristics of the system or organization implementing it.

Access Control Lists (ACLs).

ACL is a set of rules or entries that specify the permissions or access rights granted to users or system processes regarding objects, such as files, directories, or network resources. Access Control Lists (ACLs) are commonly used in computer systems and networks to control and manage access to various resources. The primary purpose of an ACL is to define who (or what) can perform specific actions on a particular object and under what conditions.

ACLs are widely used in operating systems, such as Windows and Unix/Linux, to control access to files and directories.

They are also used in network devices, such as routers and switches, to control traffic flow.

ACLs offer a flexible and granular approach to managing resource access, allowing administrators to define specific permissions for various users or groups. They are an essential component of security in various computing environments.

Authentication and Authorization.

Authentication, a fundamental aspect of information security, verifies a user's, system's, or entity's identity to ensure they are who they claim to be. Its primary goal is to ensure that only authorized individuals can access sensitive information or perform specific actions. In data security, authentication is crucial as it protects access to sensitive resources, such as computer systems, networks, applications, and data, thereby maintaining data integrity and ensuring the confidentiality, integrity, and availability of data.

Authentication typically involves using credentials, information known only to the individual or system being authenticated.

The following are common types of credentials.

- *Usernames and Passwords.*

Usernames and passwords are the most common form of authentication. Users provide a unique username (often their email address or a chosen identifier) and a secret password. The system then compares this information against stored credentials to determine whether to grant or deny access.

- *Biometric Authentication.*

This type of authentication involves using individuals' unique biological traits, such as fingerprints, iris patterns, voice recognition, or facial features, to identify them.

- *Two-Factor Authentication (2FA) or Multi-Factor Authentication (MFA).*

In addition to a password, users must provide a second form of identification, such as a temporary code sent to their mobile device or generated by a hardware token.

- *Smart Cards and Tokens.*

Users carry a physical card or token that contains authentication information. These devices can be used with a personal identification number (PIN) or password.

- *Certificates.*

Digital certificates issued by a trusted authority are used to authenticate the identity of individuals or systems in electronic communication.

Authentication is crucial to ensuring the security of information and systems. Without proper authentication mechanisms, unauthorized individuals or systems could gain access to sensitive data, leading to potential security breaches, data loss, or unauthorized activities. Organizations implement various authentication methods based on their security requirements, the sensitivity of the information involved, and the usability considerations for their users.

Authorization determines whether an authenticated user, system, or entity has the necessary permissions to access a particular resource, perform a specific action, or use certain functionalities within a system. While authentication verifies a user's identity, authorization ensures that the authenticated user has the appropriate access rights to perform desired operations.

Key concepts related to authorization include:

- Access Control refers to the mechanisms and policies governing users' or systems' actions. Access control can be based on user roles, groups, or specific attributes.

- Permissions are rules or settings associated with a user that determine what actions they can take or what resources they can access. For example, a user may have read-only access to specific files or be granted administrative privileges for a particular system.

- Roles are predefined permissions assigned to users based on their job functions or responsibilities. Roles simplify access management by grouping related permissions, rather than assigning individual permissions to each user.

- Authorization policies define the rules and criteria that dictate who has access to resources and under what conditions. Administrators often configure and manage these policies to ensure compliance with security requirements.

Principle of Least Privilege (PoLP).

This security principle states that a user or system should be granted the minimum access or permissions necessary to perform its job functions. This principle helps reduce the potential impact of security breaches or misuse.

Authorization is a crucial component of overall system or network security. Even if a user is successfully authenticated, they must still be authorized to perform specific actions or access certain data. This layered approach enables organizations to control and mitigate potential security risks, ensuring that users have only the necessary access to perform their tasks without exposing the system to unnecessary vulnerabilities. Implementing strong authentication and authorization mechanisms collectively contributes to a robust security posture.

Encryption.

Encryption plays a critical role in ensuring the security of sensitive data by providing a powerful mechanism to control data access. Encryption converts data into a secure format that can only be deciphered with the appropriate decryption key. It is especially vital for safeguarding sensitive information. Encrypted data can only be decrypted and read by individuals with the appropriate decryption key.

It helps to protect data confidentiality, particularly during transmission or storage. It is applied to data at rest (stored data) and in transit (transmitted over networks) to prevent unauthorized access.

Encryption can be used to control access to specific pieces of information on a selective basis. For instance, different encryption keys can encrypt different data sets, and only authorized personnel with the corresponding keys can access that data.

It can also be integrated with role-based access control mechanisms. Only users with the appropriate roles and corresponding decryption keys can access specific encrypted data.

In summary, encryption is a fundamental tool in data access control. It provides a robust layer of protection, securing data at rest and in transit, and is crucial in ensuring that only authorized individuals can access and comprehend sensitive information. Implementing encryption as part of a comprehensive data security strategy is crucial for organizations seeking to safeguard their valuable assets and ensure regulatory compliance.

Audit Trails and Logging.

Audit trails and logging are critical to data access control and information security. They are necessary for monitoring and ensuring the integrity, confidentiality, and availability of sensitive data within an organization's systems.

Let us examine these ideas within the framework of controlling access to data.

- *Audit Trails.*

An audit trail records system activity, such as logins, file accesses, and configuration changes, and provides a detailed account of who did what, when, and from where within a system.

An audit trail aims to track and document data access and system operations activities. This documentation is vital for investigating security incidents, ensuring compliance with regulations, and identifying potential security breaches or unauthorized access.

Audit trails typically include user identification, timestamps, IP addresses, actions performed, and success or failure indicators.

The audit trail requirements in the United States (US) are outlined in 21 CFR Part 11, Section 11.10(e). The computer system must create an audit trail independently of the operators, including who performed what actions, wrote what, and when.

- *Logging.*

Logging involves generating and storing detailed records, known as log records, of events and transactions within a system.

Logging is crucial for capturing significant events and actions within a system. In the context of data access control, logging helps track user activities, detect anomalies, and generate alerts for suspicious behavior.

Log entries may contain information about authentication events, file accesses, system configuration changes, and other relevant activities.

Integration of data access control systems with Audit Trails and Logging.

Audit trails and logging monitor who accesses what data, when, and under what circumstances. This information is critical for identifying and addressing potential security issues.

Many regulatory standards and compliance frameworks require organizations to maintain detailed audit trails and logs to demonstrate accountability and adherence to security policies.

Audit trails and logs play a crucial role in forensic analysis following a security incident or data breach, enabling security teams to understand the scope and impact of the incident.

Access Control Mechanisms.

Access control mechanisms are security features or processes that regulate and restrict access to resources, systems, or information within a computer network or a computing environment. These mechanisms ensure that only authorized entities (users, processes, or systems) can access specific resources and perform certain actions. Access control mechanisms are implemented through various technologies and techniques, and they are a fundamental aspect of overall information security.

The following are fundamental access control mechanisms.

- Authentication and Authorization. Read elsewhere in this chapter.

- Access Control Lists. Read elsewhere in this chapter.

- Role-Based Access Controls. Read elsewhere in this chapter.

- Biometric Access Control. For authentication, biometric access control uses individuals' unique physical or behavioral characteristics, such as fingerprints, iris scans, or facial recognition. The biometric data is captured and compared against stored templates to verify the user's identity.

- Encryption. Read elsewhere in this chapter.

- Physical Access Controls. Securing physical access to servers, data centers, and storage facilities is a foundational aspect of data protection.

- Network Access Controls. Implementing firewalls, intrusion detection systems, and virtual private networks (VPNs) to control access to data over a network.

- Endpoint Security: Securing individual devices (computers, smartphones) to prevent unauthorized access or data leakage.

Dynamic Access Controls.

Some systems implement dynamic access controls that adjust access permissions based on changing conditions, such as the user's location, time of day, or the system's security status.

Access Revocation.

It is important to revoke access rights promptly for individuals who no longer require access to specific data. Access revocation helps minimize the risk of unauthorized access.

Benefits.

Data access control systems play a vital role in a data reliability program by managing and regulating access to organizational data.

There are numerous benefits to implementing robust data access control systems in a data reliability program.

- *Security and Confidentiality.*

Access control systems ensure only authorized users can access regulatory, sensitive, and/or confidential data. It enhances critical security and helps maintain the confidentiality of proprietary or private data.

- *Data Integrity Protection.*

Access control systems restrict unauthorized personnel from altering data, ensuring their integrity.

Data integrity service maintains information as entered/captured and is auditable (e.g., audit trails) to affirm its traceability [3].

- *Compliance with Regulations.*

Access control systems help organizations comply with data protection and worldwide medicinal manufacturing regulations. They enable the implementation of access policies that align with regulatory requirements, reducing the risk of legal and compliance issues.

- *Prevention of Data Leaks.*

Unauthorized access is a common cause of data leaks. Access control systems prevent unauthorized users from accessing sensitive information, reducing the risk of data breaches, and protecting the organization's reputation.

- *Granular Control Over Data Access.*

Organizations can define specific access permissions based on roles, ensuring data security by minimizing unnecessary access to data for job responsibilities.

- *Auditability and Accountability.*

Organizations can limit data access based on job roles to ensure data security.

- *Reduced Insider Threats.*

Limiting access to only those who require it through access control systems mitigates the risk of insider threats to data reliability.

- *Data Governance Alignment.*

Access control systems align with data governance initiatives by enforcing data access, sharing, and protection policies. It ensures that organizational governance standards manage data.

- *Prevention of Data Overwrites or Conflicts.*

Controlled access prevents data inconsistencies and unintentional errors that can compromise reliability.

- *Enhanced Trust in Data.*

When access is limited and controlled, users can have greater confidence in data reliability, fostering a data-driven culture within the organization.

- *Efficient Collaboration.*

Access control systems allow authorized users to collaborate and share data securely within defined parameters, ensuring reliable and accurate information exchange.

Summary.

A robust data access control system is crucial for maintaining the confidentiality, integrity, and availability of sensitive information. It is an essential component of overall information security strategies.

The following are the key points about data access control systems.

- Data access control involves managing and regulating access to sensitive information to ensure that only authorized individuals or systems can view or manipulate the data. This helps maintain data integrity and prevent unauthorized alterations or access.

- Access control models, such as discretionary (DAC), mandatory (MAC), and role-based (RBAC), establish regulations and techniques to authorize users and systems, as well as the actions they can execute.

- ACLs specify permissions to users/systems regarding resources like files, directories, and networks.

- Authentication verifies user identities, while authorization determines if authenticated users have appropriate access rights.

- Encryption converts data into a secure format that can only be decrypted with appropriate keys, protecting confidentiality.

- Audit trails record system activity to track data access and operations. Logging records essential events and actions.

- Access control mechanisms, including authentication, authorization, access control lists (ACLs), role-based controls, encryption, physical controls, and network controls, regulate and restrict access to resources and information.

- Dynamic, context-aware access controls, along with the prompt revocation of unnecessary access, minimize security risks.

Data access control systems are essential components of a data reliability program. They provide a layer of security and governance that safeguards data integrity, ensures compliance, and enhances overall trust in the organization's data assets.

References.

[1]CEFIC, "*Practical risk-based guide for managing data integrity*," April 2022 (Version 2).

[2]López, O., "*E-records Integrity Requirements*," Nova Science Publisher, Inc., NY, 1st ed., 2022.

[3]López, O., "*Security*," in Data Integrity in Pharmaceutical and Medical Devices Regulation Operations (CRC Press, Boca Raton, FL, 1st ed., 2017), pp. 162-166.

Additional Readings.

- 21 CFR Part 211.68(b) – Current Good Manufacturing Practice for Finished Pharmaceuticals, Subpart D—Equipment, Automatic, mechanical, and electronic equipment, April 2009.

- EU Commission Directive 2003/94/EC, Article 9 – Documentation, Paragraph 2, October 2003.

- OECD 17, *"Physical, logical security and data integrity"* in The Application of the OECD principles of GLP to computerised systems, pages 22-23, November 2022.

- OECD 22, *"Access to* Data" in Advisory Document of the Working Party on GLP-on-GLP Data Integrity, pages 29-30, September 2021.

- PIC-S PI 041-1, *"System Security for Computerized Systems,"* in Good Practice for Data Management and Integrity in Regulated GMP/GDP Environments, pages 40-44, July 2021.

- Russian Federal State Institute of Drugs and Good Practices (FSI SID&GP), *"Security,"* in Data Integrity and Validation of Computerized Systems (Rev 1), page 25, July 2022.

Chapter 12
Data Monitoring and Auditing

Introduction.

Data monitoring and auditing are essential components of a reliability program, relying heavily on the expertise and diligence of industry professionals, such as data engineers. These professionals play a crucial role in designing and implementing data monitoring systems, analyzing the collected data, and ensuring the reliability of the auditing process.

In the medicinal manufacturing industry, where the performance and dependability of systems, processes, and products are critical, a data engineer's role in data monitoring and auditing is invaluable in tracking data quality and compliance over time.

Data Monitoring.

Data monitoring is continually observing and analyzing relevant data to assess a system's performance, health, and reliability.

The primary goal of data monitoring is to detect any deviations or anomalies in real-time or near real-time, allowing for prompt corrective actions. Data governance, a crucial aspect of this process, should include monitoring applicable processes and systems to ensure compliance with the principles of data integrity, including control over intentional and unintentional changes to data. These processes in data governance ensure that data is accurate, reliable, and secure, thereby enhancing the effectiveness of data monitoring and auditing.

Monitoring involves using sensors, instruments, or software tools to collect data on parameters such as temperature, pressure, vibration, or other relevant indicators. For instance, in medicinal manufacturing, data on the temperature and pressure in a reactor during a chemical reaction can be monitored to ensure the reaction is proceeding as expected and to detect any potential issues early on.

Automated alert systems can be integrated to notify stakeholders when data falls outside predefined thresholds, indicating potential issues with reliability.

As noted previously, quality and performance monitoring may incentivize data falsification [1].

Therefore, quality metrics should include monitoring to track the number of actual reliability failures and their relevant follow-up.

Data governance should consider monitoring processes and systems to ensure compliance with the principles of data reliability, including control over intentional and unintentional changes to data [1].

Regulated entities should ensure that they have sufficient resources to monitor their data governance systems, data, and associated risks. This monitoring should be proportional to the complexity of their systems, operations, and the importance of the data, as well as the reliability of the decisions made and the risks associated with the data throughout its lifecycle [1].

Data monitoring can cover a variety of areas, such as:

- Audit trails and event logs.
- Access controls.
- Incidents and their resolutions.

Auditing.

Maintaining appropriate levels of control is crucial for systems. The effectiveness of data reliability controls should be evaluated through routine audits or self-inspections [2]. These audits should detect potential data reliability failures within an organization's systems.

Auditing systematically examines processes, procedures, and data to ensure they comply with established standards, specifications, and best practices. It helps verify the effectiveness of reliability measures, assesses the accuracy of data collection and reporting, and identifies areas for improvement. Audits can be conducted periodically or in response to specific events, such as a failure or a change in the operating environment. For instance, in medicinal manufacturing, data on the composition of a drug, the results of quality tests, or the records of manufacturing processes can be audited to ensure compliance with regulatory standards and the product's reliability.

Regarding auditing data, the regulated user [3] should conduct a risk assessment to identify all Current Good Manufacturing Practices (CGMP)-relevant electronic data generated by computer systems and assess the criticality of the data. Once identified, critical data should be audited by the regulated user and verified to determine whether operations were performed correctly and whether any changes (modifications, deletions, or overwriting) have been made to electronic raw data. Additionally, it should be verified whether any relevant unreported data was generated. All changes should be duly authorized.

Detailed documentation of audit processes and findings is essential for ensuring accountability and facilitating continuous improvement. Compliance with the principles and responsibilities should be verified during periodic site audits when outsourcing activities are performed. This should also include reviewing procedures and data, such as raw data and metadata, paper records, electronic data, audit trails, and any other related data held by the relevant contract acceptor identified in the risk assessment.

Audit procedures or other controls should be in place to guarantee data quality [4].

Integration in Reliability Programs.

When conducted regularly and effectively, data monitoring and auditing are integral to continuously improving reliability programs and provide a sense of reassurance. By analyzing data and conducting audits, organizations can refine their processes and enhance system reliability, ensuring the highest standards of performance and dependability.

In data monitoring and auditing, integration plays a crucial role in optimizing the effectiveness of reliability programs.

Data monitoring is pivotal in providing real-time insights when reliability issues occur. This timely information enables us to take immediate corrective actions, thereby enhancing the reliability of our system.

Auditing ensures compliance with industry-specific reliability requirements in industries subject to regulatory standards. Regular audits help organizations demonstrate adherence to standards and regulations.

- *Data Monitoring Integration.*

   Integration involves the deployment of sensors, instruments, and software tools to collect real-time data. This data is collected from various sources, including equipment sensors, production processes, and environmental conditions.

   It allows for the automation of data monitoring processes. Automated systems can continuously collect, process, and analyze data, providing timely insights into the health and performance of critical assets.

- *Integration with Control System.*

   Data monitoring systems can be integrated with control systems, enabling a closed-loop approach where real-time data adjusts processes or operations to maintain optimal reliability and efficiency.

- *Auditing Integration.*

   Integration in auditing involves the orderly review of processes, procedures, and documentation related to reliability. It ensures that audits are structured to cover all relevant aspects of the reliability program.

Integration in auditing fosters a collaborative approach, encouraging teams from different departments and functional areas to work together. As part of this team effort, auditing teams may closely collaborate with operations, maintenance, and engineering teams to gather diverse perspectives and insights during the audit process. Your contribution to this collaborative effort is crucial, making you an integral part of our team.

Auditing processes are integrated with industry standards and regulatory requirements to ensure the organization complies with relevant guidelines and regulations. This integration helps mitigate legal and regulatory risks.

- *Data Analysis and Reporting Integration.*

    Unified analytics platforms can help organizations consolidate data, which facilitates comprehensive analysis. Identifying patterns, trends, and anomalies can help identify potential reliability risks.

    Integrated data monitoring systems often include reporting tools that facilitate easy communication of insights to stakeholders. This ensures that relevant information is disseminated efficiently to support decision-making and action planning.

- *Root Cause Analysis Integration.*

    Integration is critical to ensuring clear traceability from data anomalies to their root causes. When reliability problems are detected through data monitoring, integration enables a seamless transition to root cause analysis through the auditing process.

    Integration also promotes collaboration between data analysts, engineers, and auditors during the root cause analysis phase. This collaborative approach guarantees a more comprehensive investigation and a more effective resolution of underlying issues.

- *Continuous Improvement Integration.*

    Integrating data monitoring, auditing, and improvement processes creates feedback loops contributing to continuously improving reliability programs. Lessons learned from audits and data analysis can be applied to adapt strategies in response to the evolving nature of reliability challenges. This adaptability supports long-term success in maintaining and enhancing reliability.

- *Documentation and Knowledge Management Integration.*

  Integration involves creating a central repository for documentation related to data monitoring, audit findings, and improvement initiatives. This repository ensures relevant stakeholders have easy access to information.

Reliability programs benefit from integration, which allows for a comprehensive and coordinated approach to data monitoring and auditing. By integrating these components, organizations can enhance their capacity to identify and mitigate reliability risks, foster collaboration across functional boundaries, and continually refine their processes and systems.

Risk Mitigation.

Data monitoring and auditing are essential for organizations to proactively identify potential issues and reduce the likelihood of future failures. Reliability programs help organizations take preventive actions based on historical data and audit findings.

Risk mitigation is a critical element of data monitoring and auditing, which involves identifying, assessing, and addressing potential risks associated with the reliability of systems, processes, or products.

A comprehensive risk mitigation strategy must include data monitoring and auditing to identify potential issues early and proactively address risks through a systematic review of processes and procedures.

How is risk mitigation addressed through data monitoring and auditing?

Early Detection of Anomalies (Data Monitoring).

- *Identification of Potential Risks.*

  Organizations can detect potential risks to reliability by continuously monitoring data for real-time anomalies or deviations from expected performance.

- *Timely Response.*

  Early detection and correction of anomalies can prevent reliability issues.

Root Cause Analysis (Data Monitoring and Auditing).

- *Investigation of Failures [5].*

  Data monitoring provides insights into conditions that lead to reliability issues. Auditing complements this by investigating the root causes of failures.

- *Addressing Underlying Issues.*

  Organizations can prevent similar failures by addressing root causes.

Continuous Improvement (Data Monitoring and Auditing).

- *Feedback Loop.*

  Data monitoring and auditing create a feedback loop for continuous improvement. Regular analysis of data and audits helps identify areas for enhancement in processes, procedures, and reliability measures.

- *Adaptive Strategies.*

  Organizations can enhance the reliability of their systems by implementing iterative enhancements based on data monitoring and auditing.

Performance Benchmarking (Auditing).

- *Comparison with Standards.*

  Auditing involves evaluating systems and processes to ensure compliance with established standards and best practices. It helps to identify areas of underperformance and reduce non-compliance risk.

Predictive Maintenance (Data Monitoring).

- *Proactive Maintenance.*

  Data monitoring enables organizations to monitor the condition and performance of their assets in real-time. By analyzing trends and patterns, organizations can implement predictive maintenance strategies, proactively addressing potential issues before they result in failures, reducing the risk of unexpected downtime.

Documentation and Accountability (Auditing).

- *Documentation of Processes.*

    Audit trails provide documented evidence to ensure accountability and track decision-making in response to identified risks.

- *Continuous Compliance.*

    Regular audits help organizations comply with industry regulations and standards, mitigating the risk of legal or regulatory consequences associated with non-compliance.

Training and Skill Development (Auditing).

- *Identifying Skill Gaps.*

    Audit results can highlight skill gaps and training needs. Addressing these through training programs helps build a competent workforce that effectively manages reliability risks.

Benefits.

Data monitoring and auditing processes play a vital role in ensuring the ongoing quality, accuracy, and integrity of data within an organization by:

- allowing organizations to detect data quality issues in real-time or near-real-time. By continuously observing data, anomalies, errors, or deviations from established standards can be identified promptly. Early detection enables organizations to address issues before they escalate and impact business processes.

- Proactively address potential problems before they adversely affect decision-making or operational processes. Automated alert systems can notify relevant stakeholders when predefined thresholds or data quality rules are breached, enabling swift intervention and resolution.

- Ensuring compliance with regulatory requirements, industry standards, and internal data governance policies. Audits systematically examine data processes, structures, and quality, helping organizations demonstrate adherence to data-related regulations and standards.

- Identifying the root causes of data quality issues. By conducting a comprehensive assessment, organizations can understand the underlying factors contributing to data inaccuracies, inconsistencies, or incompleteness. This knowledge is crucial for implementing targeted improvements.

- Documenting the processes, findings, corrective actions, and recommendations for improvement. This documentation is a transparent record of the organization's commitment to data quality. It also provides a basis for communication with internal and external stakeholders, including regulatory bodies and customers.

- Contributing to a culture of continuous improvement. Insights gained from monitoring activities and audit results can be used to refine data processes over time. Organizations can iteratively enhance data quality measures based on lessons learned from monitoring and auditing experiences.

- Monitoring helps mitigate risks associated with poor data quality. By identifying and addressing data issues early on, organizations reduce the likelihood of making decisions based on inaccurate or incomplete information. This, in turn, minimizes the potential negative impact on business operations and outcomes.

- Aligning with the principles of data governance. These processes contribute to establishing and enforcing data quality standards, ensuring that data is managed consistently and per organizational policies.

- Contributing to building trust among stakeholders, including internal teams, executives, customers, and regulatory bodies. Stakeholders can have confidence in the reliability and accuracy of the data used for decision-making and reporting.

- Identifying areas for user education and accountability. Users can be educated on the importance of accurate data entry, adherence to data quality standards, and their role in maintaining data integrity.

Summary.

Risk mitigation in data monitoring and auditing involves:

- Taking a proactive approach to identifying.
- Analyzing.
- We are addressing potential risks to the reliability of systems and processes.

Using insights from real-time data monitoring and systematic audits, organizations can implement measures to improve reliability, prevent failures, and continuously enhance operational performance.

Data monitoring and auditing are essential for proactive system, process, or product reliability management. They help identify issues, implement preventive measures, and facilitate continuous improvement for sustained performance and dependability of critical assets.

References.

[1] MHRA, *"GxP Data Integrity Guidance and Definitions,"* March 2018.

[2] EudraLex, *The Rule Governing Medicinal Products in the European Union, Volume 4 EU Good Manufacturing Practice (GMP) Medicinal Products for Human and Veterinary Use, Chapter 9: Self Inspections,* 2001. (https://health.ec.europa.eu/document/download/07195 808-d02e-4d7a-b8f4- f84a83278b62_en?filename=cap9_en.pdf)

[3] Regulated user—The regulated Good Practice entity operates a computer system and its applications, files, and data (PIC/S PI 011-3).

[4] Heads of Medicines Agencies (HMA), *"Data Quality Framework EU Medicines Regulation,"* October 2023.

[5] WHO, *"Addressing data reliability issues,"* in Guidance on sound data and record management practices, 2016, pp. 189.

Chapter 13
Data Lifecycle Management

Introduction.

Data undergoes a lifecycle from initial generation and recording through processing (including transformation or migration), utilization, retention, archiving, and retrieval [1]. Refer to Figure 13-1 for a sample pictorial view of a data lifecycle.

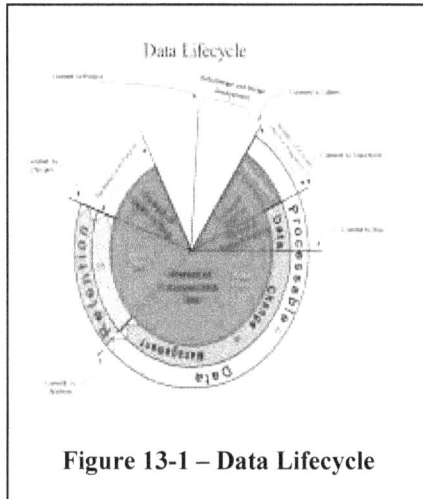

Figure 13-1 – Data Lifecycle

Data lifecycle management (DLM) is a pivotal concept in data management. It is a comprehensive approach that guides data throughout its lifespan, from its creation or acquisition to its archival and disposal. The DLM includes defining policies and procedures for data retention that comply with legal requirements and the typical stages in the data lifecycle.

DLM is crucial in ensuring that data is handled efficiently and securely. It also ensures compliance with relevant regulations and organizational policies, making it an indispensable part of data management.

The data lifecycle typically involves several significant stages, which we will discuss in detail in the following sections. These stages are data capture, storage, processing and analysis, usage and access, archiving, backup and disaster recovery, retention and compliance, and deletion and purging.

DLM Stages.

The data lifecycle typically consists of several key stages: data capture, storage, processing and analysis, usage and access, archiving, backup and disaster recovery, retention and compliance, and deletion and purging.

Data Capture or Ingestion.

Data capture is the initial step in the data lifecycle and is at the top as it sets the foundation for all subsequent data management processes. Data is captured, generated, or acquired through various sources, such as user inputs, sensors, applications, or external data feeds.

Capturing data and associated metadata (data about the data) during this stage is essential to facilitate later management and retrieval.

Data capture actions include verifying, recording, and ensuring the data is wholly and accurately captured. The steps that confirm what was collected were planned to be collected. These actions are crucial for maintaining data integrity and reliability.

Refer to Figure 13-1, Period to Capture.

Some controls for collecting data include [1]:

- The interface between the originating system, data acquisition, and recording systems should be qualified to ensure data accuracy (21 CRF 211.68(b) or EU Annex 11 p5 [2] (Rev 1)).

- Collected data can be saved into memory in a format that is not vulnerable to manipulation, loss, or change.

- The system software should incorporate checks to ensure the completeness of the data acquired and any relevant metadata associated with the data (EU Annex 11 p5 (Rev 1)).

Data Processing and Analysis.

During this stage, data is collected and verified. It is like a "Work in Progress" similar to draft documents. Refer to Figure 13-1, Period of Transformation.

The data is often transformed, cleaned, and analyzed for valuable insights, making this stage a potential goldmine and an exciting opportunity for improving decision-making and business operations.

This stage involves data preparation, integration, and the application of analytics and machine learning algorithms.

Data Stored.

Data is stored in various repositories, including databases, file systems, cloud storage, or data warehouses. Saving the data in storage indicates that the saved data is committed to being used.

Storage solutions should be chosen based on data type, volume, access requirements, and cost considerations.

Security controls must be established for all electronic storage devices and networks to protect data storage. This ensures your data is safe and secure and adheres to the highest data protection standards.

Refer to Figure 13-1, Active Phase.

Data Usage and Access.

During this stage, the data is used. Authorized users or systems access and utilize the data for various purposes, such as reporting, decision-making, or application support. In this stage, your data comes to life, providing valuable insights for your business operations.

Access control mechanisms are not just important; they are crucial to ensure data security and compliance with privacy regulations during the data usage and access stage.

During this stage, there are two phases.

- Active Phase—The data is currently being used. Any modifications to the data must be recorded at the time of modification. Refer to Figure 13-1, Commit to Use.

- Inactive Phase—Data is offline and not readily available. During this phase, the data is inactive, superseded, replaced, and withdrawn. The data must be kept to meet retention schedule requirements and maintain the read/view attributes. It is periodically backed up and secure from alteration, unintentional erasures, or loss. Refer to Figure 13-1, Commit to Archive.

During the Data Processing stage through the Active Phase, the data is typically processable and editable from when it is collected until retention.

Data Archiving.

Not all data remains actively used throughout its entire lifecycle. While not frequently accessed, some data may still need to be retained for compliance, legal, or historical purposes.

Archiving involves moving data to lower-cost, long-term storage solutions while ensuring it remains accessible when needed.

Refer to the Inactive Phase in Figure 13-1.

Data Backup and Disaster Recovery.

Regular backups are crucial for protecting against data loss resulting from hardware failures, corruption, or disasters.

Disaster recovery plans outline procedures for restoring data in the event of a catastrophic failure.

In Figure 13-1, refer to the Period of Access and Use.

Data Retention and Compliance.

Organizations must adhere to data retention policies, which dictate the duration for which specific data types should be retained. This adherence is not just a requirement; it is a necessity to ensure data integrity and compliance with regulations like GDPR, HIPAA, GMPs, or industry-specific standards.

Compliance with regulations such as GDPR, HIPAA, GMPs, or industry-specific standards is crucial, as it can significantly impact data handling and storage practices.

In Figure 13-1, refer to the Period of Access and Use.

Data Deletion or Purging.

To mitigate privacy and security risks, data should be securely deleted at the end of its useful life or as required by retention policies.

Proper data erasure methods are crucial to prevent data breaches.

Figure 13-1 refers to the Period of Destruction.

Data Disposal.

When data reaches the end of its lifecycle and is no longer needed, physical storage media should be disposed of securely to prevent data recovery.

Figure 13-1 refers to the Period of Destruction.

Monitoring and Auditing.

Continuous monitoring ensures data integrity, security, and compliance with policies and regulations.

Audits help identify and rectify issues in the DLM process.

Data Governance.

Data governance encompasses the policies, procedures, and roles responsible for overseeing and managing data throughout its lifecycle.

It ensures data quality, privacy, and security are maintained.

Refer to Chapter 10.

Benefits.

Implementing an effective Data Loss Management (DLM) within a data reliability program can provide several benefits.

Data Quality Assurance.

DLM maintains data quality throughout its lifecycle by employing standards and processes for correct data collection, transformation, and storage. These standards and processes enable organizations to consistently uphold the accuracy and reliability of their data.

Timely Access to Relevant Data.

DLM enables organizations to identify and prioritize data based on its relevance and importance at different stages of its lifecycle. It ensures that users have timely access to the most pertinent data for decision-making and analysis.

Resource Optimization.

Efficient DLM helps optimize resources by allocating storage and processing capacities based on data needs. It prevents unnecessary resource usage on less critical or outdated data.

Compliance and Regulatory Adherence.

DLM helps organizations comply with data protection regulations and industry standards by defining clear policies for data retention, privacy, and disposal.

Cost Reduction.

Proper DLM practices can minimize storage costs associated with unnecessary or redundant data. Organizations can identify and eliminate obsolete data, reducing the overall storage footprint.

Risk Mitigation.

Proper data management can save costs by minimizing storage associated with redundant data. Organizations can eliminate obsolete data, thereby reducing overall storage requirements.

Data Governance Support.

DLM provides a structured approach to enforce data governance policies related to quality, security, and compliance.

Improved Decision-Making.

Access to reliable, up-to-date data is essential for making informed decisions. DLM ensures decision-makers have access to accurate information, improving the quality of strategic decisions.

Efficient Data Archiving and Retrieval

DLM enables efficient storage and retrieval of historical data. Archived data remains accessible for compliance and analysis, while active data is optimized for performance.

Enhanced Collaboration.

DLM promotes collaboration by providing a structured approach to data sharing and collaboration tools. It ensures that teams work with the most current and reliable data, fostering effective collaboration across the organization.

Adaptability to Changing Business Needs.

DLM allows organizations to adapt to changing business needs by providing flexibility in managing data. DLM practices can be adjusted as business requirements evolve to align with new priorities and objectives.

Summary.

DLM is essential to any comprehensive data reliability program. It offers several benefits, including improved data quality, efficient resource utilization, adherence to compliance, and enhanced decision-making. Effective DLM ensures that data is treated as a valuable asset, managed effectively, and remains reliable in its entire lifecycle.

Organizations that implement effective Data Lifecycle Management (DLM) can optimize their data storage costs, reduce compliance risks, enhance data security, and maximize the value of their data assets. Effective DLM requires collaboration among IT, data management teams, legal departments, and business stakeholders. Together, they can develop and enforce policies and practices that align with the organization's goals and regulatory requirements.

References.

[1]MHRA, *"GxP Data Integrity Guidance and Definitions,"* March 2018.

[2]Computerized systems. In: The rules governing medicinal products in the European Union. Volume 4: Good manufacturing practice (GMP) guidelines: Annex 11, June 2011.

Additional Readings.

- López, O., *"Data Lifecycle and its Integrity,* (Book Publishing Pros, Los Angeles, CA, 1st ed, 2024), September 2024.

Chapter 14
Continuous Improvement

Introduction.

Continuous Improvement (CI) in the context of a Data Reliability Program is not just a process, but a strategic mission. It is an ongoing commitment to enhancing and optimizing data reliability within an organization, a mission in which each of you, with your unique skills and expertise, plays a crucial role.

Data reliability is crucial; it is the backbone of making informed decisions. A Data Reliability Program is the guardian that ensures data is accurate, consistent, and trustworthy. In this context, CI is not just a process; it is a mission to uphold the reliability of the data.

Components of Continuous Improvement in a Data Reliability Program.

The following are the essential elements of a CI program for ensuring data reliability.

- *Data Quality Assessment.*

Regularly assess the quality of data to identify any issues or anomalies. The data quality assessment evaluates the accuracy, completeness, consistency, and timeliness of the data. Establish metrics and key performance indicators (KPIs) to measure data quality.

- *Feedback Mechanisms.*

Establish feedback loops to gather input on data quality. Use surveys, support tickets, and meetings.

- *Root Cause Analysis.*

Conducting thorough root-cause analyses is crucial for understanding the underlying reasons behind data issues. By addressing the root causes, similar issues can be prevented from recurring.

- *Process Optimization.*

It is essential to continually review and optimize data processes, including data collection, transformation, storage, and distribution. The optimization process helps identify inefficiencies and bottlenecks, thereby enhancing the overall reliability of data flows.

- *Automated Monitoring.*

Automated monitoring and alerting systems should be implemented as a proactive measure to detect real-time anomalies or deviations in data quality. This proactive approach provides reassurance that issues can be identified and resolved before they escalate, ensuring the robustness of our data reliability program.

- *Training and Education.*

Invest in training programs to improve the workforce's data literacy. Educate teams on the importance of data reliability, proper data handling practices, and the use of tools to ensure accurate and consistent data.

- *Technology Upgrades.*

It is essential to stay current with technological advancements and upgrade data infrastructure and tools as needed. New technologies can provide improved data reliability features and more efficient data processing capabilities.

- *Documentation and Standardization.*

Maintain thorough documentation of data sources, definitions, and processes. Standardize data formats and definitions for consistency across the organization.

- *Collaboration and Communication.*

Foster collaboration among departments in data management by organizing regular meetings, sharing best practices, and encouraging open communication. Your role in this is vital, as it ensures reliable data and insights are shared across the organization, fostering a data-driven culture.

- *Benchmarking.*

Comparing data reliability practices to industry benchmarks and best practices involves evaluating your current practices against established standards and identifying areas for improvement. This provides valuable insights for improvement and helps organizations maintain a competitive edge in data quality.

Benefits.

Continuous Improvement in a Data Reliability Program is not just a process; it is a strategic investment that yields immediate and long-term benefits. It has a positive impact on decision-making, operational efficiency, risk management, and overall organizational success. Your efforts in Continuous Improvement are not just beneficial; they are invaluable. For instance, [provide an example of a successful CI implementation in a data-driven organization].

Here are some key advantages to consider.

- *Enhanced Data Accuracy.*

CI processes help identify, rectify, and prevent errors in data collection, entry, and processing. Regular reviews and adjustments increase accuracy, ensuring decision-makers rely on trustworthy data.

- *Increased Data Quality.*

Data quality [1] can be improved by refining data collection methods and validation processes, as well as promptly addressing data quality issues to prevent errors from propagating throughout the system.

- *Timely Detection of Anomalies.*

Regular monitoring and analysis enable the early detection of anomalies or outliers in datasets. Quickly identifying discrepancies enables timely investigation and correction, thereby minimizing the impact on decision-making.

- *Optimized Data Infrastructure.*

Optimizing data infrastructure and systems through CIs, including regular updates and enhancements to databases, data storage, and processing capabilities, leads to a more efficient and reliable data ecosystem.

- *Adaptability to Changing Requirements.*

The business environment and data requirements are dynamic. CI ensures that data processes adapt to changing needs and evolving industry standards. Flexibility in data management allows organizations to stay relevant and responsive to emerging challenges.

- *Improved Decision-Making.*

Reliable and accurate data are crucial for making educated decisions. CI contributes to the availability of high-quality data, supporting better strategic and operational decisions.

- *Cost Reduction.*

Minimizing errors and optimizing data workflows can save costs by proactively addressing data issues and improving processes. Reducing costs can help organizations avoid the expenses associated with correcting mistakes and managing the consequences of unreliable data.

- *Enhanced Stakeholder Trust.*

Reliable data fosters trust with customers, partners, and teams, thereby enhancing confidence in decision-making and goal attainment.

- *Compliance with Standards.*

Adhering to compliance standards is crucial for avoiding legal issues and maintaining data integrity. CI ensures that data management practices align with industry standards and regulatory requirements.

Summary.

Continuous Improvement in a Data Reliability Program is not a one-time task; it is an ongoing commitment. It involves continuous process refinement, issue resolution, and optimization of the overall data ecosystem. Your work in Continuous Improvement ensures that data remains reliable, accurate, and valuable for decision-making, demonstrating your commitment and dedication to the process.

CI is crucial for maintaining high data quality, adaptability, and trustworthiness in a data reliability program. It contributes to better decision-making and organizational success. In summary, CI involves an ongoing commitment to refining processes, addressing issues, and optimizing the overall data ecosystem to ensure that data remains reliable, accurate, and valuable for decision-making.

Reference.

[1]López, O., "*Introduction to Data Quality*," Journal of Validation Technology, April 2020.

Chapter 15
External Data Sources

Introduction

In the Data Reliability Program, External Data Sources refer to any data obtained from outside the organization or system where the program is implemented.

Concepts

Incorporating external data sources is crucial yet challenging for organizations that rely on diverse datasets to make informed decisions. The Data Reliability Program was developed to address these challenges by implementing processes and standards to validate and clean the data, ensuring data accuracy [1] from external sources.

The Data Reliability Program plays a pivotal role in ensuring the quality of the data sources that feed into the systems, thereby maintaining the reliability of the data. This robust system assures the data analysts and scientists, reinforcing the importance of their work.

Managing External Data Sources is a critical factor of the Data Reliability Program. It involves various steps, such as regular audits (Chapter 12), data validation [2], and documentation of data sources (Chapter 9). Organizations need to establish protocols for handling discrepancies or errors in external data. External data sources should be reliable, and their reliability should be monitored. Confidence in these sources can be established by instituting data quality rules at the external data sources.

Effective management of external data sources is not just a task but a necessity for enhancing the overall reliability of an organization's data. This leads to more accurate analyses, better decision-making, and increased trust in the information used for various purposes within the organization.

External sources may also include:

- *Third-Party Databases.*

Data obtained from external databases is not directly managed by the organization.

- *Application Programming Interfaces (APIs).*

Data is exchanged between software applications through Application Programming Interfaces (APIs) to access external systems or services.

- *Publicly Available Data.*

Information collected from public sources such as government databases, public records, or open data initiatives is publicly accessible.

- *Sensor Data.*

Data is gathered from external sensors, Internet of Things (IoT) devices, or monitoring tools not part of the company's internal systems.

- *Partner Data.*

Information shared by business partners and other organizations with which the Data Reliability Program interacts.

Benefits.

Integrating external data sources into the Data Reliability Program brings many benefits, enhancing the robustness and comprehensiveness of the data ecosystem. This optimistic outlook can inspire data professionals to explore new possibilities and improve their data management strategies.

Here are some significant benefits.

- *Enhanced Data Completeness.*

Data completeness refers to the extent to which all required data is present in a dataset. External Data Sources contribute to data completeness by providing additional information that may not be available within the organization's internal systems. This contributes to a more comprehensive and complete dataset, allowing a more holistic analysis of the subject matter.

- *Diversification of Data.*

Organizations can gain a deeper understanding of trends, patterns, and correlations by diversifying their datasets with data from external sources.

- *Real-Time and Timely Insights.*

Accessing up-to-date information through External Data Sources, especially those obtained through APIs or real-time feeds, is particularly beneficial for scenarios where timely insights are crucial, such as market trends, social media sentiments, or weather conditions.

- *Broader Context and Validation.*

External data sources can verify and cross-check internal data, improving accuracy and reliability while minimizing reliance on biased or incomplete datasets.

- *Strategic Decision-Making.*

A more diverse and comprehensive dataset from external sources can provide valuable insights for strategic decision-making. For instance, external data can offer a broader perspective and deeper insights into market research, competitive analysis, and trend forecasting, leading to more informed and effective decisions.

- *Innovation and Agility.*

Leveraging external data sources enables organizations to adapt quickly to changing conditions, identify emerging trends and opportunities, and make informed, agile decisions.

- *Efficient Resource Utilization.*

Organizations can save resources by avoiding the collection of data that is already available externally. This approach is beneficial when high-quality data can be obtained from external sources without extensive internal data collection processes. By doing so, organizations can optimize their efforts and use resources more efficiently.

- *Global Perspective.*

External Data Sources are crucial in providing a global perspective, especially when dealing with data beyond the organization's geographic or operational boundaries. This broader context can enlighten data professionals about the global factors that influence their work, fostering a sense of understanding and adaptability.

Summary.

While the benefits of External Data Sources are significant, organizations must implement robust processes within their data reliability programs to ensure the accuracy, reliability, and ethical use of external data. Proper data validation, documentation, and ongoing monitoring are crucial for effectively managing external data within a data reliability framework.

References.

[1]Data accuracy refers to the extent to which data accurately represents real-life entities.

[2]Data validation ensures that a program or system processes accurate and complete data by examining it to determine whether it is accurate, complete, consistent, unambiguous, and reasonable. It is performed by implementing the Data Observation process. The data is checked against validation rules or constraints, such as data type, length, range, or format, to ensure the reliability of input and stored data. It is equivalent to the built-in checks (EU Annex 11, p. 5, Rev. 2011) or I/O checks (US FDA CPG 7132a.07). (https://www.amazon.com/Data-Lifecycle-Integrity-Orlando-Lopez/dp/191743880X?ref_=ast_author_dp&th=1&psc=1)

Chapter 16
Reporting and Communication

Introduction.

Reporting and communication refer to the processes and practices involved in presenting and disseminating reliable data insights to relevant stakeholders in the context of the Data Reliability Program. These are essential for managing, monitoring, and improving data quality in a data reliability program.

Effectively reporting and communicating data reliability findings are crucial to ensuring that decision-makers and other stakeholders can trust and understand the information derived from the organization's data.

In the context of data reliability, reporting refers to the process of creating and sharing information about the reliability, quality, and performance of data. It involves presenting metrics, key performance indicators (KPIs), and insights that help stakeholders understand the effectiveness of the data reliability program.

Concepts.

The Data Reliability Program relies on effective reporting and communication. Understanding and prioritizing the following aspects are essential to ensure the program's success. This includes the active participation of stakeholders, who play a vital and valued role in interpreting and applying the data. Their involvement is critical to the program's success, providing context and insights that data professionals may not have.

- *Clear and Transparent Reporting.*

The reports produced under the Data Reliability Program must be clear, concise, and easily understandable. The reports must contain critical discoveries, insights, and the status of the data's reliability. Clear communication is essential for stakeholders to understand the implications of the data and the associated confidence level.

- *Documentation of Data Sources and Methods.*

It is important to include detailed documentation of data sources, such as databases, APIs, and data collection tools; collection methods, such as surveys, automated data collection, and manual data entry; and any transformations or processing steps applied to the data, such as data cleaning, normalization, and aggregation, in reports. This documentation is crucial in establishing the reliability of the data and enables stakeholders to trace the origin and processing of the information.

- *Data Quality Metrics.*

The reporting process should comprise data quality metrics for accuracy, completeness, consistency, and timeliness. Accuracy refers to how close the data is to the truth. Completeness measures how much of the data is present. Consistency checks if the data is uniform. Timeliness ensures the data is up-to-date. These metrics help stakeholders understand the reliability of the data.

- *Visualization Techniques.*

Utilizing effective data visualization techniques is crucial for conveying complex information clearly and concisely. For instance, graphs can show trends over time, charts can compare different data points, and dashboards can offer a comprehensive view of data reliability findings and trends.

- *Frequency and Timeliness.*

Regular reporting keeps stakeholders informed about the status of data reliability. Timely reports are essential for decision-making.

- *Targeted Audiences.*

Tailoring reports to specific audiences is crucial. Customizing reports to address the diverse needs and concerns of various stakeholders enhances the impact of communication.

- *Communication Protocols for Anomalies or Issues.*

Establishing clear communication protocols for data anomalies or issues requires a well-defined process for communicating discrepancies or unexpected findings, potential implications, and corrective actions.

- *Engagement and Collaboration.*

Foster engagement and collaboration between data professionals and stakeholders. It includes facilitating a two-way communication channel where stakeholders can provide feedback, ask questions, and contribute insights that enhance the overall understanding of data reliability and accuracy.

- *Training and Education.*

Stakeholders can enhance their data literacy by leveraging training and educational resources that explain the data reliability program and its associated processes.

- *Continuous Improvement.*

It is vital to view reporting and communication as iterative processes. Regularly assess and adjust their effectiveness based on feedback and changing stakeholder needs. Continuous improvement ensures alignment with organizational goals.

By emphasizing transparent reporting and effective communication within the Data Reliability Program, organizations can establish trust in their data, empower stakeholders to make informed decisions, and cultivate a data-driven culture.

Benefits.

The following are some benefits of reporting and communication in the context of a data reliability program.

- *Transparency.*

Organizations can increase transparency by reporting their data reliability efforts, progress, challenges, and outcomes, which can help build trust among stakeholders, including employees, customers, and investors.

- *Accountability.*

Regular reporting establishes accountability within an organization. When teams are required to report on data reliability metrics and issues, they are more likely to take ownership of their responsibilities, leading to improved data quality.

- *Continuous Improvement.*

Organizations can make better decisions by analyzing reports that provide insights into areas for improvement, enabling them to enhance data reliability continually.

- *Risk Mitigation.*

Organizations can prevent data quality issues from impacting business operations by promptly communicating data issues and risks.

- *Decision-Making Support.*

Having accurate and reliable data is essential for informed decision-making. Reporting enables decision-makers to access up-to-date and trustworthy information, empowering them to make strategic choices that align with organizational goals.

- *Efficient Problem Resolution.*

Effective communication is crucial for efficiently resolving data discrepancies and errors, enabling teams to collaborate and identify the root causes of these issues.

- *Alignment with Business Goals.*

Reporting on metrics related to data reliability helps to ensure alignment between data management practices and overall business goals, supporting strategic success.

- *Compliance and Regulation.*

Many industries are subject to regulatory requirements governing the quality and reliability of data. Reporting helps organizations demonstrate compliance with these regulations, thereby reducing the risk of legal and financial consequences.

- *User Empowerment.*

Clear and comprehensive communication about data reliability is not just a necessity but a powerful tool for empowering end-users. By helping them understand and trust the data they work with, we can enhance their confidence and control over their work. This empowerment can improve productivity, decision-making, and a more data-driven culture. Educational initiatives can be an integral part of a communication strategy to enhance organizational data literacy further.

- *Feedback Loop.*

Continuous learning is a vital part of our data reliability program. We foster this through a feedback loop created by reporting and communication. By gathering stakeholder feedback, we can adapt our data reliability processes to address evolving needs and challenges. This ensures that everyone is part of an evolving, engaging process.

Summary.

Establishing a robust reporting and communication system is crucial to maintaining dependable data. Regular reports are a formality and a proactive tool for managing data quality, reliability, and program performance. Effective communication ensures that all stakeholders are well-informed and engaged in efforts to enhance data reliability. By integrating these components, an organization can succeed and constantly enhance its data reliability program.

Reporting and communication are integral to a data reliability program, supporting transparency, accountability, and continuous improvement in data management practices. Their importance cannot be overstated, as they are the pillars that uphold the reliability and trustworthiness of our data.

Chapter 17
Compliance and Regulation

Introduction

In data management [1] and business operations, compliance entails ensuring that an organization adheres to all applicable laws, regulations, and ethical frameworks relevant to its activities.

Compliance is not just a requirement but a crucial element in the data management process. It is the key to maintaining data reliability, security, and privacy.

Your role in ensuring this cannot be overstated. You are not just a part of the team, but a vital component in upholding these standards and ensuring they are maintained. Your contribution is invaluable and integral to the success of our compliance efforts.

Concepts.

Understanding the critical aspects of compliance and regulations in a Data Reliability Program context is not only important but also empowering. Your knowledge and expertise in this area are invaluable, enabling you to make informed decisions and contribute significantly to the organization's data management.

- *Data Privacy Laws.*

Understanding and complying with data privacy regulations, such as the EU General Data Protection Regulation (GDPR) and the California Consumer Privacy Act (CCPA), as well as other regional laws, is not only significant but also a significant responsibility in data management. Your knowledge and expertise in this area are invaluable.

- *Industry-Specific Regulations.*

Different industries have specific regulations that govern data reliability. For instance, the healthcare industry is bound to comply with the Health Insurance Portability and Accountability Act (HIPAA). In contrast, the financial sector may be subject to regulations like the Sarbanes-Oxley Act (SOX).

Medicinal manufacturing is subject to strict regulations set by health authorities worldwide. GMPs are principles, guidelines, and rules that establish the standards for manufacturing, processing, packaging, and distribution of pharmaceuticals, biologicals, food, and medical devices. The primary objective of GMPs is to ensure that products are consistently produced and controlled in compliance with quality standards, with a focus on safety, efficacy, and regulatory requirements.

Data reliability is critical in global medicinal manufacturing. It refers to the accuracy, consistency, and trustworthiness of the data generated throughout the various stages of pharmaceutical production and distribution, ensuring the safety, efficacy, and quality of medicinal products.

Documentation and record-keeping are essential aspects of Good Manufacturing Practice (GMPs). It includes creating and maintaining detailed records of all aspects of the manufacturing process, including manufacturing batch records and records of critical activities.

Data reliability is important; it is essential for complying with GMPs, regulatory submissions, and audits. As a data manager, you are responsible for ensuring the accuracy and completeness of the data you collect and use, as required by regulations.

- *Data Security Standards.*

Adhering to data security standards, such as ISO/IEC 27001 [2], is crucial to protecting sensitive information. These standards provide guidelines for implementing security controls and safeguarding data against unauthorized access or breaches, which are essential for data reliability.

- *Data Governance Frameworks.*

Compliance often necessitates a robust data governance framework, which entails defining roles and responsibilities, establishing data quality standards, and aligning data management practices with organizational objectives.

Refer to Chapter 10.

- *Record-Keeping Requirements.*

Accurate data processing records, including data collection, consent mechanisms, and data retention duration, must be maintained for compliance. This documentation is often needed for audits and regulatory inspections.

- *Consent Management.*

Obtaining and managing consent properly from individuals is crucial for ensuring compliance with data collection and processing.

- *Data Accuracy and Reliable.*

Data accuracy is the degree to which data reflects the valid values or facts it represents [3]. All data should be precise, complete, and accurate, reflecting the actual events that occurred.

Data is reliable if its content can be trusted as a complete and accurate representation of the transaction, activities, or facts it attests to. It can be depended upon during subsequent transactions and activities [4].

Organizations must ensure accuracy and completeness. [5]. Furthermore, the reliability of the data they collect and use is required by regulations.

- *Data Breach Notification.*

Compliance may require organizations to establish procedures for detecting and responding to data breaches. It includes timely notification to regulatory authorities and affected individuals, as mandated by data breach notification laws.

- *Training and Awareness Programs.*

Training employees on data protection policies and regulations fosters a culture of compliance.

- *Regular Audits and Assessments.*

Conducting regular audits and assessments of data management practices is crucial to ensuring compliance. These audits and assessments involve evaluating processes, controls, and documentation to identify areas for improvement and address potential non-compliance issues.

Benefits.

In the context of the Data Reliability Program, Compliance and Regulation refer to the adherence to legal and regulatory frameworks governing data collection, processing, and use.

Ensuring compliance with relevant laws and regulations is not just a requirement but a pathway to several benefits within the Data Reliability Program. These benefits provide reassurance and confidence in the value of our compliance efforts.

- *Data Reliability and Accuracy.*

Implementing measures to ensure data reliability and accuracy is crucial for compliance with regulations. Regulatory requirements in the medicinal manufacturing environment aim to ensure patient safety, product quality, and data integrity [6].

Data validation checks, audit trails, and documentation practices must be implemented to ensure the reliability of data in computer systems.

- *Risk Mitigation.*

Adhering to compliance standards can help organizations reduce legal and reputational risks associated with data-related activities. These measures can include safeguards against unauthorized access, data breaches, and other potential threats to the reliability of the data.

- *Enhanced Data Security.*

Regulatory requirements often include guidelines for data security and protection. Compliance measures can involve implementing robust data security protocols, such as encryption, access controls, and regular security audits, to safeguard data from unauthorized access or breaches.

- *Trust and Transparency.*

Compliance with regulations builds trust among stakeholders, including customers, partners, and regulatory authorities. It achieves this by demonstrating a commitment to adhering to established rules and regulations, thereby enhancing transparency and reinforcing the reliability of the organization's data practices.

- *Legal Compliance.*

Organizations must comply with data protection laws, privacy regulations, and other legal requirements to ensure that they operate within the boundaries defined by the law. Legal compliance is critical in regions with stringent data protection regulations, such as the GDPR in the European Union or HIPAA in the United States.

- *Ethical Data Practices.*

Compliance with ethical guidelines and regulations promotes responsible and ethical data practices. These practices include obtaining informed consent for data collection, ensuring fair and lawful processing, and respecting individuals' rights over their data.

- *Global Operations Alignment.*

For organizations with a global presence, compliance with various international regulations ensures alignment with diverse legal frameworks. This alignment is crucial for managing data across various jurisdictions and ensuring a consistent approach to data reliability.

- *Avoidance of Legal Consequences.*

Non-compliance with data regulations can result in severe legal consequences, including substantial fines, sanctions, and legal actions. These consequences can have a significant impact on the organization's financial health and reputation. Organizations must integrate compliance measures into their Data Reliability Program to avoid such pitfalls.

- *Framework for Data Governance.*

Establishing a robust data governance framework often necessitates adherence to regulatory compliance. Data governance encompasses creating policies, procedures, and documentation that govern the management, processing, and utilization of data within the organization. A well-structured data governance framework ensures compliance, enhances data reliability and transparency, and fosters stakeholder trust.

Refer to Chapter 10.

- *Stakeholder Confidence.*

Compliance with regulations fosters confidence among stakeholders, including customers, investors, and business partners. Stakeholders' confidence in the organization's data practices establishes the organization's credibility and can positively impact relationships with external parties.

- *Continuous Improvement.*

Organizations must stay informed about evolving regulations to ensure ongoing compliance with them. Commitment to continuous improvement ensures adaptability to changes in the regulatory landscape for the Data Reliability Program.

Summary.

Organizations must comply with various laws and regulations; failing to do so can result in legal consequences, financial penalties, and reputational damage. To avoid such adverse effects, compliance is often monitored and enforced through audits, inspections, and assessments. Therefore, organizations implement compliance programs and initiatives to establish a culture of responsibility and ensure that their operations align with applicable laws and regulations.

To remain compliant, organizations must stay updated with relevant laws and standards, implement appropriate measures, and continuously monitor and adapt their data practices.

Integrating compliance and regulation into the Data Reliability Program enables organizations to meet legal requirements, enhances data reliability, and fosters the establishment of a trustworthy and responsible data environment.

References.

[1]National Medical Products Association (NMPA (former CFDA)), *"Drug Data Management Practices Guidance,"* December 2020.

[2]ISO/IEC 27001: 2022, *"Information technology— Security techniques — Information security management systems — Requirements."*

[3]EMA, *"EMA Questions and answers: Good manufacturing practice Data Integrity,"* August 2016.

[4]United States National Archives and Records Administration (https://www.archives.gov/).

[5]Data completeness is a property that encompasses all necessary components of the entity in question. Data completeness measures the number of data elements or values present in a dataset, excluding those with missing or null values.

[6]MHRA, *"GxP Data Integrity Guidance and Definitions,"* March 2018.

Chapter 18
Data Recovery and Disaster Planning

Introduction.

Data recovery and disaster planning are not just components but the backbone of a comprehensive data reliability program. Their role is to ensure that an organization can recover its data effectively in the event of unforeseen incidents or disasters.

> *Procedures: A Necessity for Data Retention procedures should be in place to ensure that essential information remains complete and retrievable throughout the specified retention period.*
>
> **Universal Electronic Records Management (ERM) Requirements Ver 3.0**

Data Recovery.

Data recovery is the process of recovering data that has been lost, damaged, or rendered inaccessible due to issues with storage systems or backups.

Even with robust preventive measures in place, data loss can still occur due to various reasons. Data recovery mechanisms are crucial in restoring lost data and minimizing downtime [1].

It is crucial to have a recovery procedure in place in case of a breakdown [2]. Regular checks for these procedures are necessary to ensure the system's return to its previous state.

Effective data recovery and disaster planning are crucial for data management professionals, IT managers, and compliance officers in regulated industries. These arrangements must be designed to permit recovery and readability of the data and metadata throughout the required retention period. In the case of archiving data, this process should be verified, and for legacy systems, the ability to review data should be ensured [3].

Ensuring complete and timely data recovery during a disaster should also be considered (PIC/S).

When computer systems perform medical tasks related to data generation, processing, and reporting, specific training should be given. This training should include backup, restoration, and disaster recovery [4].

In outsourcing data services, the vendor must define in a service level agreement (SLA) how it will notify the Regulated Company of executing a Disaster Recovery Plan [1].

The critical components of data recovery include:

- *Regular Backups.*

Implementing a regular and automated backup strategy is a proactive step that ensures copies of critical data are always available for recovery.

Backups for recovery purposes do not replace the need for the long-term retention of data and metadata in its final form for verification of the process or activity [3].

The US FDA 21 CFR Part 211.68 [5] provides specific backup requirements. It requires that "backup data is exact and complete," and "secure from alteration, inadvertent erasures, or loss," and that "output from the computer … be checked for accuracy." As a result of these requirements, the backup file should contain the data, including associated metadata, and be in the original format or a format compatible with the original format. Temporary backup copies (e.g., in case of a computer crash or other interruption) would not satisfy the requirement in § 211.68(b) to maintain a backup data file [6].

- *Redundancy.*

Having redundant systems and storage is not just a strategy; it is a safety net that provides a sense of reassurance and security. It helps minimize the impact of hardware failures and provides a backup source for data retrieval, ensuring a secure data environment.

- *Data Versioning.*

Maintaining multiple versions of data is not just a practice; it is a strategy that instills a sense of control and confidence. It can help recover from accidental changes or corruptions, preserving data integrity and ensuring a secure data environment.

Disaster Planning.

Disaster planning involves creating and implementing strategies to mitigate the impact of unforeseen events that can lead to data loss or system downtime.

Disasters can encompass both natural events, such as earthquakes, floods, and fires, as well as human-made events, including cyberattacks or power outages. Planning for these contingencies is crucial to ensure business continuity and data reliability.

Backup allows for provisions to recover data files or software, restart processing, or use alternative computer equipment in the event of a system failure or disaster.

The critical components of data recovery include:

- *Risk Assessment.*

Identifying potential risks and vulnerabilities allows organizations to develop targeted plans for specific scenarios.

- *Business Continuity Plan (BCP).*

Business continuity refers to the control measures that ensure business operations remain secure in the event of system failure or disruption, such as implementing a manual or alternative system to maintain operational continuity.

The business continuity process includes control measures that ensure the continuity of support for critical processes in the event of a system breakdown, such as implementing a manual or alternative system to maintain operations.

At the lowest level, business continuity applies to the accidental deletion or corruption of a file; in such cases, a procedure should be in place for restoring the most recently backed-up copy. At the other extreme is a disaster, such as the destruction of hardware, software, and electronic records files, necessitating a transition back to a paper-based system until the disaster is fully recovered from.

BCP outlines procedures ensuring essential business functions can continue in the face of a disaster. It includes considerations for data recovery, system restoration, and communication plans.

The BCP shall detail the precautions taken to minimize the effects of a disaster, enabling the organization to either maintain or quickly resume critical functions, with a particular focus on disaster prevention, such as providing redundancy for critical systems and infrastructure.

Section 9.8.6 in the Russian Data Integrity and Computer System Validation Guidelines [1] provides an extensive discussion of Business Continuity Plans (BCPs).

- *Incident Response Plan (IRP).*

A detailed plan specifies actions to be taken immediately after an incident occurs. The IRP includes isolating affected systems, notifying stakeholders, and initiating recovery.

- *Offsite Storage.*

Storing backups and critical data in off-site locations ensures data availability even if the primary site is compromised.

Benefits.

Data Recovery and Disaster Planning play a crucial role in the Data Reliability Program, offering several benefits to organizations in ensuring the availability, integrity, and reliability of their data.

Here are the key advantages:

- *Minimized Data Loss.*

Effective data recovery and disaster planning can significantly reduce the likelihood of losing valuable information due to unforeseen events, such as hardware malfunctions, system crashes, cyberattacks, or natural calamities. Organizations can successfully retrieve and restore lost or corrupted data by implementing robust recovery mechanisms, thereby ensuring the safety and security of their data.

- Business Continuity.

Effective disaster planning is crucial for business continuity. It involves implementing backup systems, redundant infrastructure, and recovery processes to ensure the organization can continue functioning during and after disruptive events.

- *Enhanced Data Availability.*

Data recovery measures can ensure data availability by implementing backup solutions, redundant servers, and failover mechanisms to keep data accessible even when primary systems are compromised or unavailable.

- *Reduced Downtime.*

Quick recovery from data incidents helps minimize downtime. The ability to restore data promptly enables the organization to resume normal operations quickly, thereby minimizing the impact on productivity and service delivery.

- *Protection Against Cyber Threats.*

Organizations must have comprehensive data recovery and disaster plans in light of increasing cyber threats. Regularly backing up data and having a well-defined recovery process can help organizations minimize the damage caused by cyber incidents.

- *Data Integrity Preservation.*

Preserving data integrity is critical in disaster planning. Disaster recovery planning includes recovering lost data and ensuring its accuracy, consistency, and corruption.

- *Compliance with Data Protection Regulations.*

Organizations must take measures to safeguard and ensure the availability of data to comply with data protection regulations. Companies can meet regulatory data integrity and availability requirements by implementing data recovery and disaster planning.

- *Customer Trust and Reputation.*

Quickly recovering from data incidents is crucial for maintaining customer trust and protecting an organization's reputation. Demonstrating a commitment to data reliability through effective disaster planning fosters confidence among customers and stakeholders, thereby enhancing the organization's reputation.

- *Cost Savings.*

Although implementing data recovery and disaster planning measures requires an initial investment, it can lead to substantial long-term cost savings. It minimizes the financial impact of downtime, lost productivity, and potential data reconstruction efforts by enabling rapid recovery.

- *Scalability and Flexibility.*

Organizations can adjust their data recovery strategies to match evolving business needs. Reliable, scalable recovery solutions can be modified as data volumes and operations change.

- *Employee Productivity.*

Quick data recovery supports employee productivity. When critical data is restored promptly after a data loss, employees can resume their tasks more efficiently.

Summary.

Organizations must ensure the reliability of their data. A successful data reliability program must have two critical components: data recovery and disaster planning. These components protect an organization's data, enabling it to recover quickly and efficiently in the event of challenges or disruptions. A well-designed program should also include measures to prevent data loss, regular testing, and continuous improvement to enhance data reliability and accuracy.

Data recovery and disaster planning are integral components of the Data Reliability Program. They provide a safety net for organizations to recover from unexpected events, minimize data loss, and maintain the integrity and availability of crucial information.

References.

[1]Russian Federal State Institute of Drugs and Good Practices (FSI SID&GP), *"Data Integrity and Validation of Computerized Systems (Rev 1)"*, July 2022.

[2]TGA, *"Australian code of good manufacturing practice for human blood and blood components, human tissues and human cellular therapy products,"* April 2013.

[3]MHRA, *"GxP Data Integrity Guidance and Definitions,"* March 2018.

[4]WHO, *"Guideline on Data Integrity."* (TRS No.1033, Annex 4) March 2021.

[5]US FDA 21 CFR Part 211 -- Current Good Manufacturing Practice for Finished Pharmaceuticals. (n.d.).

https://www.ecfr.gov/current/title-21/chapter-I/subchapter-C/part-211.

[6]US FDA, *"Data integrity and compliance with drug CGMP - Questions and Answers,"* December 2018.

Chapter 19
Performance Metrics and Key Performance Indicators

Introduction.

In the context of a Data Reliability Program, KPIs and measurable metrics play a vital role as quantifiable indicators used to assess the effectiveness, performance, and quality of data-related processes and outcomes. These metrics provide a basis for measuring progress, identifying areas for improvement, and ensuring that the objectives of the data reliability initiative are met.

The behavior-driven performance indicators of the regulated entity[OBJ] should not be underestimated.

Measurable Metrics.

The following outlines some key measurable metrics within the context of a data reliability program.

- *Data Accuracy Metrics.*

The accuracy rate, a key metric, measures the correctness and precision of the data. It assesses the percentage of accurate data within the overall dataset, significantly ensuring data reliability.

Example: Percentage of data records with accurate information, error rates in data entry, or discrepancies between data sources.

Formula: (Correct Data in dataset / Total Data in the dataset) * 100

- *Completeness Metrics.*

Completeness is the extent to which data is complete without missing values or gaps.

Example: Percentage of completeness in key datasets, missing data rates, or adherence to data entry requirements.

Formula: (Complete Data Entries / Total Data Entries) * 100

- *Consistency Metrics.*

Consistency is the uniformity of data across different sources, databases, or systems.

Example: Percentage of consistency in data formats, coding schemes, or data alignment across different databases.

Formula: (Consistent Data Entries / Total Data Entries) * 100

- *Timeliness Metrics.*

Timeliness assesses the relevance and currency of data by measuring the time it takes for data to be collected, processed, and made available for use.

Examples include time lags in data updates, adherence to data reporting timelines, or the age of data beyond the required timeframe.

Formula: (Number of Timely Entries / Total Entries) * 100

- *Error Rate Metrics.*

The error rates quantify errors within the data, including data entry errors, processing errors, or discrepancies between expected and actual values.

Example: Overall error rate, error rates in specific data fields, or frequency of data correction activities.

Formula: (Error Data Entries / Total Data Entries) * 100

- *Data Governance Adherence Metrics.*

The data governance adherence assesses the organization's adherence to data governance policies and practices.

Example: Compliance with data quality standards, adherence to data management processes, or the effectiveness of data stewardship activities.

Formula: (Adherence to Data Governance Policies / Total Data Entries) * 100

- *Data Quality Index.*

The data quality index composite metric combines data quality aspects (accuracy [1], suitability [2], conformity [3], completeness [4], consistency [5], integrity [6], validity [7], timeliness [8], and consistency with the intended use) into a single index for an overall assessment.

It is a holistic score that combines various aspects of data quality, providing an overall measure of data reliability and accuracy.

Example: A weighted average of individual data quality metrics to provide a holistic view of data quality [9].

Formula: (Sum of Quality Scores / Number of Quality Aspects)

- *Data Profiling Metrics.*

Data profiling metrics refer to the quantitative and qualitative measures used to assess a dataset's quality, consistency, and completeness. These metrics help data analysts and scientists gain insights into the data's characteristics and patterns, which is crucial for data cleaning, integration, and analysis.

Examples are the frequency of data profiling activities and identifying data anomalies or trends in data quality over time.

- *User Satisfaction Metrics.*

User satisfaction metrics are measurements used to assess the level of user satisfaction with a product, service, or experience. These metrics are crucial for understanding how well a product meets the needs and expectations of its users, as well as for identifying areas for improvement. User satisfaction metrics can vary depending on the context and the type of product or service being evaluated.

Example: Surveys or feedback mechanisms to gauge user satisfaction, response times to user queries, or user-reported data issues.

- *Cost of Poor Data Quality Metrics.*

The cost of poor data quality metrics refers to the measurements used to quantify the financial and operational impacts of low-quality data within an organization. Poor data quality can lead to various issues, including inaccurate decision-making, inefficiencies, compliance violations, and lost opportunities. Organizations must understand the costs associated with data quality issues to justify investments in quality improvement initiatives and prioritize efforts to address the underlying causes.

Example: Costs of data-related errors, costs of data correction activities, or costs associated with business process disruptions due to poor data quality.

- *Data Security and Privacy Compliance Metrics.*

Data security and privacy compliance metrics evaluate an organization's adherence to relevant laws, regulations, standards, and internal policies that govern the protection of sensitive data and privacy rights. These metrics enable organizations to measure their compliance efforts, identify areas of non-compliance, and mitigate risks associated with data breaches, unauthorized access, and privacy violations.

Example: Compliance with data protection laws, frequency of security audits, or incidents of data breaches.

Benefits.

The above KPIs can provide valuable insights into the effectiveness of a data reliability program, guiding organizations in identifying areas for improvement to ensure high-quality, reliable data for informed decision-making and analysis.

Utilizing performance metrics and KPIs in a data reliability program context can provide several benefits. These tools can provide valuable insights into the effectiveness of your data reliability program, guide you in identifying areas for improvement, and ensure the production of high-quality, reliable data for informed decision-making and analysis.

- *Measurement of Data Quality.*

  Tracking data accuracy, completeness, consistency, and timeliness provides a quantifiable measure of data quality in organizations.

- *Identification of Data Issues.*

  Performance metrics and KPIs easily detect data anomalies, errors, or inconsistencies. Organizations can establish thresholds for acceptable performance levels to flag deviations and address underlying issues promptly.

- *Continuous Improvement.*

  Organizations can track progress by establishing performance metrics and key performance indicators (KPIs). Regular monitoring enables the identification of areas for improvement in data reliability processes and the implementation of necessary changes to enhance overall performance.

- *Alignment with Business Objectives.*

  Performance metrics and KPIs are most effective when closely tied to an organization's strategic goals and objectives. Selecting performance metrics and KPIs that contribute directly to desirable business outcomes is essential to ensure that data reliability efforts align with broader organizational priorities. These may include increased efficiency, cost reduction, or improved decision-making. By selecting the right KPIs, companies can more effectively measure their progress toward achieving their strategic goals and objectives.

- *Enhanced Decision-Making.*

  Tracking performance metrics and key performance indicators (KPIs) related to data reliability can enhance decision-making. These tools provide the necessary data and insights to make informed decisions, enhancing confidence in data-related choices.

- *Resource Allocation.*

  Allocating resources effectively requires the use of performance metrics and key performance indicators (KPIs). Organizations can address issues and improve data reliability by identifying poor data quality or performance bottlenecks.

- *Stakeholder Communication and Transparency.*

  Using performance metrics and KPIs to communicate the effectiveness of the data reliability program to stakeholders across the organization fosters trust, accountability, and collaboration among different teams and departments.

- *Risk Mitigation.*

  Having unreliable data can lead to significant risks for organizations, including financial losses, compliance violations, and damage to their reputation. One way to mitigate these risks is to track performance metrics and key performance indicators (KPIs). By doing so, businesses can proactively identify and address data quality issues before they become more significant problems.

Summary.

Performance metrics and key performance indicators (KPIs) are essential for evaluating and improving data reliability programs.

Aligning measurable metrics with the program's specific objectives and goals is essential when defining a data reliability program. Refer to "Alignment with Organizational Objectives" in Chapter 3.

These metrics serve as valuable tools for monitoring progress, demonstrating the impact of data reliability efforts, and driving continuous improvement initiatives within the organization. Regularly tracking and analyzing these metrics can provide insights into the effectiveness of data reliability measures and guide informed decision-making.

By measuring critical aspects of data quality and performance, organizations can identify areas for improvement, align data reliability efforts with strategic objectives, and make more informed decisions, ultimately driving better business outcomes.

References.

[1]Data accuracy is how data correctly represents "real-life" entities. To be correct, a data value must be the right value and represented in a consistent and unambiguous form.

[2]Data suitability refers to the appropriateness and fitness of a dataset for a particular purpose or analysis.

[3]Conformity refers to data adhering to specific definitions, such as its type, size, and format.

[4]Data completeness refers to the extent to which all required data elements or values are present in a dataset without missing or null values.

[5]Data consistency refers to data accuracy, reliability, and coherence within a system or database.

[6]Data integrity is the property that data has not been retrieved or altered without authorization since creation and until disposal (NIST SP 800-57P1, IEEE, ISO-17025, INFOSEC, 44 USC 3542, 36 CFR Part 1236, and others standards).

[7]Data validity refers to whether the data contained within that object conforms to whether the data contained within that object meets the expected criteria, rules, and constraints of data accuracy, correctness, and fitness.

[8]Data timeliness refers to the degree to which data is current and up-to-date about the point in time when it is needed for analysis, decision-making, or other business processes.

[9]Lopez, O., *"Are Data Quality and ALCOA attributes equivalent?"* GMP Journal, November 2023.

Chapter 20
Feedback and Iteration

Introduction.

Feedback refers to the information or response an individual or system provides about its performance, behavior, or output. It is vital in facilitating learning, improving, and making necessary adjustments. Feedback can be shared in different ways, such as verbal communication, written comments, numerical ratings, gestures, or signals.

Iteration refers to repeating steps or actions multiple times to achieve a desired outcome, refine a product, or improve a solution. It is fundamental in problem-solving, design, development, and many other fields.

Continuous improvement and adaptability of a Data Reliability Program are achieved through feedback and iteration.

Concepts.

For instance, feedback can be gathered from data analysts about the accuracy of data sources, and this feedback can be used to iterate on data collection methods. Similarly, user feedback on the usability of data management tools can lead to iterative improvements in the tools' design and functionality.

- *Continuous Improvement.*

By collecting feedback from users, data analysts, and other stakeholders, organizations can identify areas for improvement and make necessary adjustments. This can lead to enhanced data quality and reliability, as issues and errors are identified and addressed through iterative improvements.

- *User Satisfaction.*

It is crucial to ask end-user feedback to assess the quality and reliability of data. User feedback can help identify specific issues, errors, or inconsistencies that may not be immediately noticeable to data management teams. Improving data based on user feedback can lead to better user satisfaction and trust in the data.

- *Performance Evaluation.*

Regular feedback on the performance of data reliability measures helps organizations evaluate the effectiveness of their data management processes. This includes assessing data accuracy, the efficiency of data processing workflows, and the overall reliability of data sources.

- *Identifying Data Issues.*

Feedback mechanisms allow users to report data issues, anomalies, or discrepancies, serving as an early warning system for potential data reliability problems.

- *Data Governance Enhancement.*

Iterative feedback loops improve data governance policies by adjusting frameworks based on data quality feedback.

- *Training and Education.*

Providing feedback on the effectiveness of training and educational programs within an organization can help tailor these initiatives to meet users' needs better. By understanding where users struggle with data-related tasks, organizations can provide targeted training and improve overall data literacy.

- *Adaptability to Changing Requirements.*

Iterative feedback loops help organizations align data reliability practices with goals and objectives as business requirements evolve.

- *Technology Optimization.*

Organizations commonly use various technologies to manage data. Feedback on the performance of these technologies helps optimize toolsets and select the most effective solutions for ensuring data reliability, thus ensuring that the technology stack meets the organization's evolving needs.

- *Risk Management.*

Feedback can identify and address potential data-related risks. Understanding user concerns helps organizations mitigate risk and avoid data issues.

- *Agile Data Management.*

An iterative approach that incorporates feedback aligns with agile principles and enables organizations to respond quickly to changing requirements and emerging issues. This adaptability is essential in dynamic business environments.

Benefits.

Feedback and iteration offer numerous benefits that improve data management practices' enhancement, adaptability, and sustained improvement in a data reliability program.

Some key benefits are:

- *Continuous Improvement.*

Feedback loops facilitate continuous improvement. Gathering feedback from users, data analysts, and other stakeholders allows organizations to identify areas where data reliability can be enhanced, leading to ongoing refinements in processes and procedures.

- *User-Centric Data Quality.*

Gathering feedback from end-users provides insights into their experiences with the data, which can help prioritize improvements that directly impact user satisfaction and trust in the reliability of the data.

- *Early Issue Detection.*

Early detection of data issues, anomalies, and inaccuracies through iterative feedback helps organizations swiftly address problems, minimizing their impact on business operations and decision-making.

- *Alignment with Business Needs.*

Regular feedback ensures that data reliability practices remain aligned with evolving business needs. This adaptability is crucial as organizational objectives and priorities change over time, ensuring that data management efforts support current business goals.

- *Increased Data Literacy.*

Targeted resources and support can enhance employee data literacy and improve data understanding and usage. Feedback identifies challenges to tailor programs.

- *Efficient Resource Allocation.*

Through iterative feedback, organizations can optimize resource allocation for data reliability initiatives. By understanding which areas require more attention or improvement, they can allocate resources effectively and focus on the most critical aspects of data management.

- *Risk Mitigation.*

Regular feedback enables organizations to identify and mitigate risks to data reliability, preventing potential breaches and compliance violations.

- *Agility in Response to Change.*

An iterative feedback-based approach aligns with agile principles, enabling organizations to quickly respond to changes in the business environment, technology landscape, or data sources. This agility is crucial for staying relevant and practical.

- *Enhanced Data Governance.*

Feedback improves data governance policies. Adjust frameworks based on feedback to ensure effective, enforceable, and supportive policies that meet data reliability goals.

- *Cultural Shift towards Data Quality.*

A feedback-driven approach can foster a culture that values and prioritizes data quality. Users' and stakeholders' active participation in providing feedback promotes a strong sense of ownership and responsibility for data quality throughout the organization, enhancing their engagement and commitment.

- *Optimized Technology Stack.*

Feedback on the performance of data management technologies helps organizations optimize their technology stack [1]. This feedback ensures the tools and systems are well-suited to the organization's needs and efficiently support data reliability efforts.

Summary.

In summary, a Data Reliability Program benefits from feedback and iteration by fostering a culture of continual improvement. The feedback and iterations enable organizations to enhance data quality, adapt to changing requirements, and effectively address emerging challenges. Regularly seeking and acting upon feedback contributes to data management practices' overall success and resilience within an organization's decision-making and business outcomes.

Feedback and iteration are not just integral to the success of a data reliability program; they are the driving forces behind it. They enable organizations to respond to user needs, promptly detect and address issues, and align with business goals. Ultimately, they foster a culture of continuous improvement and adaptability in data management practice, inspiring and motivating all involved.

Reference.

[1]A technology stack refers to the combination of programming languages, frameworks, libraries, tools, and software developers use to build and maintain a software application.

Chapter 21
Scalability and Future Readiness

Introduction.

The key features of a data reliability program, scalability, and future readiness play crucial roles in the rapidly changing data management and analytics environment.

Scalability.

Scalability refers to the capacity of a system, process, or organization to effectively handle a growing amount of work, data, or demand. As data sources and usage patterns evolve, a scalable data reliability program must be able to adapt to changes without causing significant disruptions. Scalability involves handling larger datasets, supporting more concurrent users, and seamlessly integrating new data sources.

Scalability is not just a feature, but a cornerstone in maintaining reliability as the scale of data processing and storage requirements grows over time. It ensures that the system can handle the increasing demands without compromising its performance or efficiency, providing a sense of reassurance about the program's robustness.

Future Readiness.

Future readiness is critical, ensuring that systems and processes are designed with emerging technologies, industry trends, and potential changes in data requirements in mind. In a Data Reliability Program context, future readiness guarantees that the infrastructure can evolve and adopt new technologies and methodologies as they become available or necessary. This includes designing systems that can easily integrate with new tools, data storage solutions, processing techniques, and security measures, and having a plan in place to implement these changes when necessary.

The data landscape is constantly evolving, with ongoing advancements in technologies and methodologies. A future-ready Data Reliability Program can swiftly adapt to new tools, data storage solutions, processing techniques, and security measures. This adaptability can assist organizations in staying competitive, compliant, and resilient despite ever-changing data challenges.

Integration of Scalability and Future Readiness.

- *Design Principle.*

Architects should adopt modular and flexible architectures when developing a Data Reliability Program [1], leverage cloud-based solutions, and implement best data modeling and storage practices to promote scalability and future readiness.

- *Technology Stack.*

Choosing a technology stack [2] A solution that can handle scalability and future requirements, such as compatibility with emerging data processing frameworks and integration with machine learning tools, is essential. This can be done by using distributed databases and cloud-based storage.

- *Continuous Monitoring and Optimization.*

Regularly monitoring system performance, identifying potential scalability bottlenecks, and optimizing processes ensure that the Data Reliability Program remains effective as data volumes and usage patterns evolve.

Benefits.

In a Data Reliability Program context, scalability ensures that the data infrastructure can accommodate increasing volumes of data and growing user requirements without compromising performance, reliability, or efficiency.

As data reliability programs often deal with large datasets, scalability ensures the program can efficiently process and manage growing amounts of data without compromising performance.

It allows the program to accommodate many users or data consumers without experiencing bottlenecks or slowdowns.

Organizations can future-proof their data infrastructure by designing the data reliability program to be scalable, ensuring it can adapt to changing business needs and data demands over time.

Readiness in a data reliability program is not just about being prepared but about being proactive and responsive. The system is designed to promptly detect, address, and recover from potential issues, maintaining data integrity and reliability. This stress on proactivity instills confidence in the program's ability to handle potential issues.

A ready data reliability program can detect inconsistencies, errors, or downtimes promptly and take corrective actions, minimizing the impact on data reliability.

Readiness ensures that the program is efficient and adaptable to changes in data sources, formats, or processing requirements. This adaptability is crucial in dynamic environments where data landscapes may evolve rapidly, providing the system with the flexibility and resilience it needs. It assures the audience of the program's future relevance and adaptability.

A ready system is more reliable as it can proactively address potential issues, reducing the likelihood of data quality issues or system failures.

Scalability ensures that the data reliability program can handle growth and changes in data volume and user demands. In contrast, readiness ensures that the program is well-prepared to detect and address issues promptly, maintaining high data reliability. Together, these attributes contribute to the robustness and effectiveness of a data reliability program in ensuring the integrity and availability of critical data.

Summary.

A robust Data Reliability Program should be able to handle greater data demands and be adaptable to new technologies and industry standards. It ensures that an organization's data infrastructure remains reliable, performs well, and stays applicable in the long run.

References.

[1]Data architecture refers to designing and structuring an organization's data assets, including how data is collected, stored, processed, and utilized.

[2]"Technology stack" is a term used to describe a group of software, tools, frameworks, programming languages, libraries, and components that are used to develop and operate a software application or system. The software application or system includes all the layers and components to create and manage a software solution. Remember, integrity is measured by how well we handle challenging and prosperous situations. (Top-of-stack software companies. (n.d.). https://ofdotanur.web.app/1295.html)

Chapter 22
Data Reliability Implementation Program Applicable to Outsourced Activities

Introduction.

The structured Data Reliability Implementation Program (DRIP) is not just a program; it guarantees the accuracy, integrity, and consistency of data generated or managed by third-party vendors or partners in outsourced activities. You can be assured that your data is in safe hands.

This program is not just essential; it is a catalyst for your business. The data quality ensured by DRIP impacts decision-making, regulatory compliance, and drives business performance, keeping you focused on your goals and motivated to achieve them.

Concepts.

When organizations outsource certain activities or functions to external partners, they rely on the data provided by these vendors to make informed decisions, comply with regulations, and support business processes. However, ensuring the reliability of outsourced data can be challenging due to factors such as data quality issues, communication gaps, and differences in data management practices.

The following is a breakdown of the DRIP applicable to outsourced activities.

- *Outsourced Activities.*

Many organizations delegate specific tasks or functions to external vendors or partners to leverage specialized expertise, cost efficiencies, or resource scalability. This document focuses on these outsourced activities, including component manufacturing, product testing, data entry for customer records, data processing for financial reports, analytics for market research, IT services for system maintenance, customer support for product inquiries, etc.

- *Data Reliability.*

Reliable data is essential for making informed decisions, ensuring regulatory compliance, and maintaining customer satisfaction. The DRIP plays a crucial role in this, ensuring that the data generated or managed by third-party entities is trustworthy, accurate, complete, and consistent.

Implementation Program.

A DRIP involves systematically implementing processes, procedures, controls, and measures to uphold data reliability standards in outsourced activities. It encompasses various stages, from vendor selection and qualification to ongoing monitoring, evaluation, and improvement.

The following is a breakdown of critical components and considerations for implementing a DRIP for outsourced activities.

- *Vendor Selection and Qualification.*

Evaluating vendors' capabilities, track records, quality systems, and commitment to data reliability is vital when selecting them. A rigorous selection process can help determine their commitment to providing accurate and dependable data. Therefore, it is recommended that vendors be thoroughly vetted and that their capabilities, quality systems, and track records be assessed before finalizing the selection.

- *Quality Agreements.*

Organizations must have clear and concise documentation outlining their expectations, responsibilities, quality standards, and compliance requirements when entering vendor agreements or contracts. This documentation should be comprehensive and include quality agreements that explain expectations, responsibilities, and procedures for data generation, management, and reporting. Additionally, these agreements should stipulate requirements and controls for data accuracy, completeness, security, and compliance with relevant regulations.

The contract giver and receiver should be actively involved in auditing the system for issuing and controlling true copies [1]. This ensures the process is robust and meets data integrity principles [2].

- *Standard Operating Procedures (SOPs).*

The objective is to create and record standardized protocols for data-related tasks, guaranteeing vendor uniformity and compliance with quality standards. All outsourced data generation or management tasks must be documented using the standardized protocols. Standard Operating Procedures (SOPs) should encompass data collection, recording, storage, retrieval, and transfer processes to ensure vendor consistency and dependability.

- *Training and Communication.*

Provide training and ongoing communication on data reliability requirements, SOPs, and quality standards. Foster open communication channels to address concerns, clarify expectations, and ensure alignment between your organization and vendors regarding data reliability goals. This training ensures vendor personnel understand and comply with data reliability requirements and procedures.

- *Data Integrity Controls.*

Implement technical and procedural controls to prevent unauthorized access, loss, corruption, or data tampering throughout its lifecycle. These controls safeguard data integrity throughout its lifecycle. The controls may include validation of data entry systems, access controls, audit trails, version control mechanisms, and regular interruption.

- *Quality Assurance and Monitoring.*

Establishment of mechanisms for ongoing monitoring of vendor performance, conducting audits, inspections, and assessments to verify compliance with quality standards and regulatory requirements. Conduct periodic audits, inspections, or performance evaluations to assess vendor performance and identify areas for improvement.

- *Risk Management.*

The 'Risk Management' section provides a comprehensive guide on identifying, assessing, and mitigating risks associated with outsourced activities that could impact data reliability. It also guides on implementing contingency planning and corrective actions to ensure data reliability despite potential risks.

- *Continuous Improvement.*

The 'Continuous Improvement' section details how to foster a culture of continuous improvement by regularly reviewing and analyzing data reliability metrics, feedback, and performance indicators. It explains how to use this information to identify opportunities for optimization, corrective actions, and enhancements to the DRIP, as well as controls to enhance data reliability, address issues, and drive continuous improvement.

- *Regulatory Compliance.*

Alignment of the DRIP with relevant regulatory requirements governing data reliability, security, privacy, and outsourcing arrangements in specific industries or jurisdictions. Stay updated on changes to regulations and standards to maintain compliance and adapt the DRIP accordingly.

Benefits.

Implementing a DRIP for your outsourced activities offers numerous benefits, including improved data quality and enhanced trust and credibility. It is a game-changer for your operations.

- *Improved Data Quality.*

The program ensures higher data quality by implementing standardized processes and protocols for data collection, storage, and analysis across outsourced activities. Consistent data quality yields more reliable insights and informed decision-making.

- *Risk Mitigation.*

Outsourcing data-related activities introduces risks, including breaches, errors, or inconsistencies. A robust reliability program is crucial in identifying and mitigating these risks early on, reducing the likelihood of costly data-related issues.

- *Compliance Adherence.*

Many industries are subject to stringent data management and privacy regulatory requirements. A well-designed reliability program ensures that outsourced activities comply with relevant regulations, minimizing the risk of fines or legal consequences.

- *Enhanced Trust and Credibility.*

The DRIP fosters reliable data, a cornerstone in building trust among stakeholders, including customers, investors, and regulatory bodies. Organizations enhance their reputation and credibility by demonstrating a commitment to data reliability through a structured implementation program.

- *Cost Savings.*

Investing in data reliability upfront can result in long-term cost savings. By preventing errors and inconsistencies, organizations avoid the expenses associated with correcting data issues post hoc, such as conducting audits, reanalyzing data, or addressing customer complaints.

- *Streamlined Collaboration.*

Clear guidelines and standards established through the reliability program facilitate collaboration between the organization and its outsourcing partners. Communication is smoother when everyone follows the same protocols, and the likelihood of misunderstandings or conflicts decreases.

- *Continuous Improvement.*

A data reliability program is not static; it should evolve to address changing needs, technologies, and regulations. Organizations can continuously enhance the reliability of outsourced data activities by establishing ongoing monitoring, feedback, and improvement processes.

- *Competitive Advantage.*

In an increasingly data-driven business environment, organizations that can demonstrate the reliability of their data have a competitive edge. Reliable data enables more accurate predictions, better customer insights, and faster decision-making, ultimately driving business success.

Summary.

A DRIP applicable to outsourced activities is essential for maintaining data integrity, mitigating risks, ensuring compliance, and ultimately gaining a competitive advantage in today's data-centric landscape.

It can help organizations rely on accurate and trustworthy data from external sources. The DRIP can support the organization's operations, decision-making processes, and compliance obligations. The program can also enhance transparency, accountability, and confidence in outsourced partnerships while mitigating data quality and integrity risks.

References.

[1]A true copy is an exact copy of an original record, which may be retained in the same or different format in which it was initially generated, e.g., a paper copy of a paper record, an electronic scan of a paper record, or a paper record of electronically generated data (MHRA).

[2] PI 041-1, *"Good Practice for Data Management and Integrity in Regulated GMP/GDP Environments,"* Pharmaceutical Inspection Co-operation Scheme (PIC/S), July 2021.

Additional Reference.

- EudraLex - Volume 4. (2024b, June 18). Public Health. https://health.ec.europa.eu/medicinal-products/eudralex/eudralex-volume-4_en, Chapter 7 - Outsourced activities (January 2013).

Chapter 23
Summary

Implementing a data reliability program provides numerous benefits across industries and operations. These include:

1. Improved Data Quality

Ensures that data is accurate, consistent, complete, and timely that enhances the reliability of insights and decision-making processes.

2. Enhanced Decision-Making

High-quality, reliable data leads to more informed, data-driven decisions, reducing the likelihood of errors or misguided strategies based on inaccurate data.

3. Increased Operational Efficiency

A data reliability program streamlines data processing, reducing time spent cleaning and correcting data and improving overall operational efficiency.

4. Risk Reduction

Minimizes the risks associated with poor data quality, such as incorrect analyses, faulty predictions, and compliance issues, which can result in financial or reputational damage.

5. Regulatory Compliance

Ensures that data management practices meet regulatory requirements for accuracy, traceability, and data security, helping to avoid fines, penalties, and audits.

6. Consistency Across Systems

Provides standardized processes and controls that ensure consistency in data handling across departments or systems, leading to consistency in data reporting and analysis.

7. Cost Savings

Reduces the costs associated with data errors, rework, system failures, and inefficient processes, leading to significant cost savings over time.

8. Trust and Credibility

Builds trust among stakeholders, partners, and customers by ensuring the reliability of the data used in decision-making, forecasting, and reporting.

9. Scalability

Ensures that as data volumes grow, systems can handle and maintain high-quality data at scale, supporting business expansion and more complex analytics.

10. Continuous Improvement

Establishes a feedback loop that continuously monitors and improves data reliability, ensuring that data quality standards evolve with business needs and technological advances.

In summary, a data reliability program enhances data quality, decision-making, efficiency, and regulatory compliance while reducing risks and costs, ultimately leading to more trustworthy and scalable data systems.

Appendix I
Glossary of Terms

For additional terms, refer to the Glossary of Computerized Systems and Software Development Terminology[1]; A Globally Harmonized Glossary of Terms for Communicating Computer Validation Key Practices[2], EudraLex - Volume 4 Good Manufacturing Practice (GMP) Guidelines – Glossary[3], US FDA Digital Health and Artificial Intelligence Glossary – Educational Resource[4], and the MHRA, 'GXP' Data Integrity Guidance and Definitions (Rev 1), March 2018.

For this glossary, the terms and definitions given in 9000-3 and ISO 12207 are applicable. In the event of a conflict in terms and definitions, the terms and definitions specified in this glossary and the references in the first paragraph above apply.

---

[1] FDA, "*Glossary of Computerized System and Software Development Terminology*," Division of Field Investigations, Office of Regional Operations, Office of Regulatory Affairs, Food and Drug Administration, August 1995.

[2] Herr, Robert R. and Wyrick, Michael L., "*A Globally Harmonized Glossary of Terms for Communicating Computer Validation Key Practices*," PDA Journal of Pharmaceutical Science and Technology, March/April 1999.

[3] http://ec.europa.eu/health/files/eudralex/vol-4/pdfs-en/glos4en200408_en.pdf

[4] https://www.fda.gov/science-research/artificial-intelligence-and-medical-products/fda-digital-health-and-artificial-intelligence-glossary-educational-resource?utm_medium=email&utm_source=govdelivery

Abstraction.

This fundamental software engineering principle enables understanding the application's design and complexity management.

Acceptance Criteria.

A system or component must satisfy the criteria to be accepted by a user, customer, or other authorized entity (IEEE).

Acceptance Test.

Testing is conducted to determine whether a system satisfies its acceptance criteria and enables the customer to determine whether to accept the system (IEEE).

Access.

The ability or opportunity to gain knowledge of stored information (DoD 5015.2-STD).

Access Method.

1. The portion of a computer's operating system responsible for formatting data sets and their direction to specific storage devices. 2. In local-area networks, the technique or program code is used to arbitrate the use of the communications medium by granting access selectively to individual stations.

Accountability.

The obligation or willingness to accept the consequences of one's actions.

Accuracy.

It refers to whether the data values stored for an object are correct. To be correct, a data value must be the right value and represented in a consistent and unambiguous form.

Data is accurate when it reflects the activity or measurement performed (EMA, "EMA Questions and Answers: Good Manufacturing Practice Data Integrity," Aug 2016).

Acquirer.

An organization that acquires or procures a system, software product or software service from a supplier (ISO 12207:1995[5]).

Active Pharmaceutical Ingredient (API) / Drug Substance.

Any substance or mixture of substances intended to be used in the manufacture of a drug (medicinal) product / finished pharmaceutical product (FPP) / a pharmaceutical dosage form and that, when used in the production of a drug, becomes an active ingredient of the drug product. Such substances are intended to furnish pharmacological activity or other direct effect in the diagnosis, cure, mitigation, treatment, or prevention of disease or to affect the structure and function of the body (EU GMP Guide, Part II 2014; ICH Q7; TRS 957 Annex 2, TRS 1025 Annex 7, WHO; FDA Guidance for Industry cGMP for Phase 1 Investigational Drugs).

---

[5] Note: The 1995 revision is not the most recent version.

The unformulated drug substance may subsequently be formulated with excipients to produce the dosage form (ICH Q1A).

Any substance or mixture of substances intended to be used in the manufacture of a pharmaceutical dosage form and that, when so used, becomes an active ingredient of that pharmaceutical dosage form/drug. Such substances are intended to furnish pharmacological activity or other direct effects in the diagnosis, cure, mitigation, treatment, or prevention of disease or to affect the structure and function of the body (TRS 986 Annex 2, TRS 1025 Annex 7, WHO).

Any substance or mixture of substances to which a finished medicinal product's effect is adjudged or acts as such (PIC/S PE 010-4).

Any component intended to furnish pharmacological activity or another direct effect in the diagnosis, cure, mitigation, treatment, or prevention of disease or to affect the structure function of the body of man or other animals. The term includes those components that may undergo chemical change in the manufacture of the drug product and be present in the drug product in a modified form intended to furnish the specified activity or effect (21 CFR Part 210, FDA).

Application.

Software installed on a defined platform/hardware providing specific functionality (EMA Annex 11).

Application Developer.

See Software Developer.

Application Server.

The application server is a modern form of platform middleware. It is system software that resides between the operating system (OS) on one side, the external resources (such as a database management system (DBMS), communications and Internet services) on another side and the users' applications on the third side. The function of the application server is to act as a host (or container) for the user's business logic while facilitating access to and performance of the business application. The application server must perform despite the variable and competing traffic of client requests, hardware and software failures, the distributed nature of the larger-scale applications, and the potential heterogeneity of data and processing resources required to fulfil the business requirements of the applications.

Approver(s).

In configuration management, the approver is the person(s) responsible for evaluating the reviewers' recommendations of deliverable documentation, deciding whether to proceed with a proposed change and initiating the implementation of a change request.

Archive.

Long-term, permanent retention of completed data and relevant metadata in its final form to construct the process or activity.

Assessment.

A subject matter expert or IT Quality and Compliance investigates processes, systems, or platforms. An assessment does not need to be independent in contrast to an audit.

Attributable.

Data / e-records can be assigned to the task's individual (EMA, "EMA Questions and answers: Good manufacturing practice Data Integrity," Aug 2016).

Audit.

An independent examination of a software product, software process, or set of software processes to assess compliance with specifications, standards, contractual agreements, or other criteria (IEEE).

Auditor.

In configuration management, the auditor is responsible for reviewing the steps taken during a development or change management process to ensure that the appropriate procedures have been followed.

Audit Trail.

An electronic means of auditing the interactions with records within an electronic system so that any access to the system can be documented as it occurs for identifying unauthorized actions about the records, e.g., modification, deletion, or addition (DOD 5015.2-STD) (2) GMP audit trails are recorded metadata recorded the change or deletion of GMP relevant data) (MHRA).

Authentication.

Verifying a user, process, or device's identity is often a prerequisite to allowing access to resources in an information system (NIST Special Publication 800-18).

Authentic.

The property of being genuine and being able to be verified and trusted; confidence in the validity of a transmission, a message, or message originator. See authentication (NIST Special Publication 800-18).

Authority.

Power to influence or command thoughts, opinions or behaviors of others.

Automated Systems.

It includes a broad range of systems, including, but not limited to, automated manufacturing equipment, automated laboratory equipment, process control, manufacturing execution, clinical trials data management, and document management systems. The automated system comprises the hardware, software, network components, controlled functions, and associated documentation. Automated systems are sometimes called computerized systems (PICS CSV PI 011-3[6]).

Availability.

We ensure timely and reliable access to and use of information (44 U.S.C., SEC. 3542).

---

[6] PI 011-3. "Good Practices for Computerised Systems in Regulated "GXP" Environments", Pharmaceutical Inspection Co-operation Scheme (PIC/S), September 2007.

Backup.

A copy of current (editable) data, metadata and system configuration settings (variable settings related to an analytical run) is maintained for disaster recovery (MHRA).

Baseline.

An agreed description of the attributes of a product at a point in time serves as a basis for defining change. A "change" is moving from a baseline to the next revision.

Bespoke Computerized System.

A computerized system is individually designed to suit a specific business process (EMA Annex 11).

Best Practices.

Practices are established by experience and common sense.

Biometrics.

These are methods of identifying a person based on physical measurements of an individual's physical characteristics or repeatable actions. Some examples of biometrics include identifying a user based on a physical signature, fingerprints, and so on.

Business Continuity Plan.

A plan describes how business processes will continue, respond or recover during a disruption. The plan will include preparedness to meet and address emergencies and threats based on the business' prioritization of those business processes.

Business Process.

A set of structured activities or tasks that produce a specific service for a particular customer or customers. It is often visualized as a flowchart of activities with decision points (CEFIC).

Calibration.

Set of operations that establish, under specified conditions, the relationship between values of quantities indicated by a measuring instrument or measuring system, or values represented by a material measure or a reference material, and the corresponding values realized by standards (PICS CSV PI 011-3).

Centrally Managed-Security System.

Computer system authentication with a centralized domain. These systems use the regulated entity network user security configuration.

Capture.

Place an object under records management control for disposition and access purposes. Objects are not necessarily moved from the system they reside in when captured. Records can be imported from other sources, manually entered, or linked to their systems (36 CFR 1236.20).

Certificate.

Certificates are used to verify the identity of an individual, organization, Web server, or hardware device. They also ensure non-repudiation in business transactions and enable confidentiality using public-key encryption.

Certification Authority.

As part of public critical infrastructure (PKI), an authority in a network that issues and manages from a Certificate Server security credentials and public key for message encryption and decryption (NARA).

Certified Copy.

(1) A copy of original information that has been verified, as indicated by a dated signature, as an exact copy having all the same attributes and information as the original (Source: FDA, Electronic Source Data in Clinical Investigations, September 2013) (2) A copy of original information that has been verified as an exact (accurate and complete) copy having all the same attributes and information as the original. The copy may be verified by a dated signature or a validated electronic process (Source: CDISC (Clinical Data Interchange Standards Consortium) Clinical Research Glossary Version 8.0, December 2009).

CGMP Data System.

CGMP Data System encompasses the data lifecycle elements of generated, processed, reported, checked, used for decision-making, stored, and finally discarded and disposed of data related to an identified CGMP process.

Change.

Any variation or alteration in form, state or quality. It includes additions, deletions, or modifications impacting the hardware or software components that affect operational integrity, service level agreements, or the validated status of applications on the system.

Change Control.

A formal system by which qualified representatives of appropriate disciplines review proposed or actual changes that might affect the validated status of facilities, systems, equipment or processes. The intent is to determine the need for action to ensure and document that the system is maintained in a validated state (EMA Annex 15, Qualification and Validation).

Cipher.

Series of transformations that convert plaintext to cypher text using the Cipher key.

Cipher Key.

The Key Expansion routine uses the secret cryptography key to generate a set of round keys.

Cipher Text.

Data is outputted from the Cipher or inputted to the Inverse Cipher.

Cleanse.

Cleansing of data means any action on data to correct for incorrect values.

Clear Printed.

Apart from the values, the units and the respective context can also be seen in the printout (Journal for GMP and Regulatory Affairs, "Q&As on Annex 11", Issue 8, April/May 2012).

Cloud Computing.

It uses a network of remote servers hosted on the Internet to store, manage, and process data rather than a local server or a personal computer.

Cloud Services.

Refers to technology that allows users to access and use shared data and computing services via the Internet or a Virtual Private Network (VPN). It gives users access to resources without having to build infrastructure to support these resources within their environment or network. E-records can reside in a cloud environment hosted by a 3rd service provider (e.g., DaaS) (NARA).

Code Audit.

An independent source code review by a person, team, or tool to verify compliance with software design documentation and programming standards. Correctness and efficiency may also be evaluated (IEEE).

Code of Federal Regulations.

The codification of the general and permanent rules published in the Federal Register by the executive departments and agencies of the Federal Government.

Code Inspection.

A manual (formal) testing (error detection) technique where the programmer reads source code, statement by statement, to a group who ask questions analyzing the program logic, analyzing the code concerning a checklist of historically common programming errors, and analyzing its compliance with coding standards. This technique can also be applied to other software and configuration items (Myers/NBS).

Code Review.

A meeting at which software code is presented to project personnel, managers, users, customers, or other interested parties for comment or approval (IEEE).

Code Walkthrough.

A manual testing (error detection) technique where program (source code) logic (structure) is traced manually (mentally) by a group with a small set of test cases, while the state of program variables is manually monitored to analyze the programmer's logic and assumptions (FDA Glossary of Computerized System and Software Development Technology (8/95), FDA).

Commercial of the Shelf Software.

Software commercially available, whose fitness for use is demonstrated by a broad spectrum of users (EMA Annex 11).

Commissioning.

Refer to Site Acceptance Testing (SAT).

Competent.

Having the necessary experience and/or training to perform the job adequately.

Competent Authority.

In the European Union (EU), a Competent Authority belongs to the government of a Member State of the EU. It is responsible for transposing the requirements of European regulations into national legislation.

Completeness.

The property that all necessary parts of the entity in question are included. The completeness of a product is often used to extract that the product has met all requirements.

Complexity.

In the context of this book, complexity means the degree to which a system or component has a design or implementation that is difficult to understand and verify.

Compliance.

Compliance covers adhering to application-related standards or conventions, regulations, in-laws, and similar prescriptions and fulfilling regulatory requirements.

Compliant System.

A system that meets applicable guidelines and predicate rule requirements.

Computer.

(1) A functional unit that can perform substantial computations, including numerous arithmetic and logical operations, without human intervention (2) Hardware components and associated software design to perform specific functions.

Computer System.

(1) A system that includes data input, electronic processing, and information output will be used for reporting or automatic control (PICS CSV PI 011-3). (2) A functional

unit consisting of one or more computers associated with peripheral input and output devices and associated software that uses shared storage for all or part of a program and also for all or part of the data necessary for the execution of the program; executes user-written or user-designated programs; performs user-designated data manipulation, including arithmetic operations and logic operations; and that can execute programs that modify themselves during their execution. A computer system may be a stand-alone unit or consist of several interconnected units (ANSI).

Computer Systems Validation.

(1) The formal assessment and reporting of quality and performance measures for all the life-cycle stages of software and system development: implementation, qualification and acceptance, operation, modification, re-qualification, maintenance and retirement. This should enable both the regulated user and competent authority to have a high level of confidence in the integrity of both the processes executed within the controlling computer system(s) and in those processes controlled by and/or linked to the computer system(s), within the prescribed operating environment(s) (PICS CSV PI 011-3[7]). (2) Documented evidence provides a high degree of assurance that a computerized system analyses, controls, and records data correctly and that data processing complies with predetermined specifications (WHO).

---

[7] PI 011-3. *"Good Practices for Computerised Systems in Regulated "GXP" Environments"*, Pharmaceutical Inspection Co-operation Scheme (PIC/S), September 2007.

Computerized Process.

A process where a computer controls some or all the actions.

Computerized System.

(1) A system controlled partially or totally by a computer. (2) All the components necessary to capture, process, transfer, store, display and manage information, including (but not limited to) hardware, software, personnel and documentation (Health Canada GMPs, GUI0001). (3) See Automated Systems.

(1) Refer to Computer Systems Validation[8]. (2) establishing and documenting that the specified requirements of a computerized system can be consistently fulfilled from design until decommissioning or transition to a new system (ICH E6(R2), section 1.65).

Concurrent Validation.

Sometimes, a drug product or medical device may be manufactured individually or on a one-time basis. As it relates to those situations, prospective or retrospective validation may need more applicability. The data obtained during the manufacturing and assembly process may be used with product understanding to demonstrate that the instant run yielded a finished product meeting all its specifications and quality characteristics (FDA).

---

[8] PI 011-3. *"Good Practices for Computerised Systems in Regulated "GXP" Environments"*, Pharmaceutical Inspection Co-operation Scheme (PIC/S), September 2007.

Confidentiality.

Preserving authorized restrictions on information access and disclosure, including means for protecting personal privacy and proprietary information (44 U.S.C., SEC. 3542).

Configurable Software.

Application software, sometimes for general purposes, is written for various industries or users in a manner that permits users to modify the program to meet their individual needs (FDA).

Configuration Item.

The entity within a configuration that satisfied-use use function and that can be uniquely identified as a given reference point (ISO 9000-3).

Configuration Specification.

The Configuration   Specification details   the configuration parameters and how these settings address the URS (Pharm Out) requirements.

Contemporaneous E-records.

Data / e-records are created when the activity is performed (EMA, "EMA Questions and Answers: Good Manufacturing Practice Data Integrity," August 2016).

Contract Acceptor.

The entity agrees to provide the contract giver with a service, product, project or study according to the giver's specified requirements.

Contract Giver.

An entity is responsible for evaluating the ability of a contract acceptor to deliver work successfully.

Control System.

Included in this classification are Supervisory Control and Data Acquisition Systems (SCADA), Distributed Control Systems (DCS), Statistical Process Control systems (SPC), Programmable Logic Controllers (PLCs), intelligent electronic devices, and computer systems that control manufacturing equipment or receive data directly from manufacturing equipment PLCs.

Consistency.

The property of logical coherency among constituent parts. Consistency may also be expressed as adherence to a given set of rules.

Correctness.

The extent to which software is free from design and coding defects, i.e., fault-free. It is also the extent to which software meets its specified requirements and user objectives.

Compliance Policy Guide.

Compliance Policy Guides (CPGs) are primarily for FDA staff and assist them in evaluating and enforcing industry regulations. Many details and interpretations are found there that need to be covered by existing FDA laws, regulations, or guidance.

Criticality.

In the context of this book, criticality means the regulatory impact on a system or component. See Critical System.

Critical.

Describes a process step, condition, test requirement, or other relevant parameter or item that must be controlled within predetermined criteria to ensure the product/process meets its specification.

Critical Electronic Records.

This book interprets critical e-records as those that pose a high risk to product quality or patient safety (ISPE GAMP COP Annex 11—Interpretation, July/August 2011).

Critical Data.

Critical data poses a high risk to product quality, efficacy, or patient safety (ISPE GAMP COP Annex 11—Interpretation, July/August 2011).

Critical Deficiency.

A deficiency in practice or process that has produced, or may result in, a significant risk of producing a product that is harmful to the user. It occurs when it is observed that the manufacturer has engaged in fraud, misrepresentation or falsification of products or data (TGA, Code of GMPs, 2013).

Critical Process Parameter.

A parameter which, if not controlled, will contribute to the variability of the end product (Health Canada GUI-0029).

Critical Requirement.

A requirement that, if not met, harms any of the following: patient safety, product quality, requirements satisfying health authority regulation, cGxP data integrity or security.

Critical Step.

It is a parameter that must be within an appropriate limit, range, or distribution to ensure the subject's safety or quality ty of the product of data (MHRA).

Critical Systems.

Structural, mechanical, or electrical systems that can impact the processing parameters and attributes of the finished product or regulatory study. Critical systems may include utilities, process equipment and systems (PDA Glossary).

Systems that directly or indirectly influence patient safety, product quality and data integrity.

Cryptography or cryptology.

It is the practice and study of techniques for secure communication in the presence of third parties called adversaries (http://searchsoftwarequality.techtarget.com/definition/cryptography).

Custom Built Software.

Also known as a Bespoke System, Custom-Built Software is software produced for a customer, specifically to order, to meet a defined set of user requirements (GAMP).

Customized Computerized System.

See Bespoke Computerized System.

Data.

(1) Data, or the contents of a record, may be defined as measurable or descriptive attributes of a physical entity, process, or event. (ISPE/PDA, "Technical Report: Good Electronic Records Management (GERM)," July 2002) (2) All original records and accurate copies of original records, including source data and metadata and all subsequent transformations and reports of these data, are generated or recorded at the time of the GXP activity and allow complete reconstruction and evaluation of the GXP activity (MHRA).

Data Architecture.

Data architecture refers to the design and structure of an organization's assets, including how data is collected, stored, processed, and utilized.

Database.

In electronic records, data consisting of at least one file or a group of integrated files is usually stored in one location and made available to several users simultaneously for various applications (36 CFR 1234.2, reference (ii)).

Databases refer to structured repositories of indexed information that allow information retrieval, analysis, and output (NARA).

Database Field.

It is a place for a piece of information in a record or file.

Data Accuracy.

(1) This is a dimension of data quality. Data accuracy is how data correctly represents "real-life" entities. (2) Accuracy in attribute data pertains to the precision and correctness of the information, ensuring that the qualitative characteristics and properties are measured and represented with high quality and relevance. (What Does Attribute Data Mean? https://www.bizmanualz.com/library/what-does-attribute-data-mean)

Data Analytics.

Data analytics involves gathering, retaining, handling, and interpreting data from diverse sources to obtain valuable insights to help make better business decisions.

Data Auditability.

Changes to a set of data need to be traceable. A history of updates is essential to track what, when, and by whom data edits were made.

Data Authenticity.

Data authenticity refers to the quality or state of being genuine, trustworthy, and accurate in digital information.

Data Base Management System (DBMS).

A software system is used to access and retrieve data stored in a database (36 CFR 1234.2, reference (ii)).

Data Catalog.

A data catalog is a centralized repository and management system for metadata and information about an organization's data assets. It is a critical component of data management and governance initiatives, helping users discover, understand, and effectively use the organization's data resources.

Data Collection.

The process of gathering and measuring information on variables of interest.

Data Completeness.

Completeness is the property that all necessary parts of the entity in question are included.

Data Confidentiality.

The state exists when data is held in confidence and protected from unauthorized disclosure. Misuse of data by those authorized to use it for limited purposes violates confidentiality (FIBS).

Data Conformity.

Conformity refers to data adhering to specific definitions, such as its type, size, and format.

Data Consistency.

(1) Data consistency is one dimension of data quality. Data consistency refers to data accuracy, reliability, and coherence within a system or database. (2) Consistency ensures that the information maintains its significance and relevance across different contexts. (What Does Attribute Data Mean? https://www.bizmanualz.com/library/what-does-attribute-data-mean)

Data Degradation.

Data degradation is the deterioration in stored data's accuracy, completeness, consistency, and reliability.

Data Elements.

(1) Individual GxP data items that are part of raw data or metadata (CEFIC). (2) A data element is a data unit with a precise meaning or semantics. As such, the option of a data element should include a definition, a unit, and, where relevant, the process by which the data element was generated.

Data Engineering Lifecycle.

The data engineering lifecycle comprises stages that turn raw data ingredients into valuable end products, ready for consumption by analysts, data scientists, machine learning engineers, and others.

Data Fidelity.

Fidelity in the context of a data object refers to the degree to which the data accurately represents or reflects the real-world phenomenon or information it is meant to capture. Fidelity measures how closely the data object aligns with the actual state of the real-world entity, event, or concept it is intended to represent. Fidelity is closely related to the concept of data accuracy.

Data Flow.

A diagram that maps the flow of information of any process or system (inputs, outputs, storage points, and routes) between each destination (CEFIC).

Data Governance.

The sum of arrangements to ensure that data, irrespective of the format in which it is generated, are recorded, processed, retained, and used to ensure a complete, consistent, and accurate record throughout the data lifecycle.

Data Handling.

Ensuring data is stored, archived, or disposed of in a safe and secure data cycle.

Data Heritage.

Data heritage represents information about the source of the data (DataManagementU).

Data Integrity.

(1) Data/e-records integrity is the property that data has not been unauthorized-ly altered since created and until disposal (NIST SP 800-57P1).

(2) The degree to which a system or component prevents unauthorized access to, or modification of, computer programs or data (IEEE). (3) Data integrity is the degree to which data/e-records are secure and traceable and that these characteristics of the data/e-records are maintained throughout the data life cycle.

Data Lake.

The data lake is a centralized repository for the organization's data. It stores raw data, processed data, and analytical data.

Data Lifecycle.

Data life spans all phases, from generation and recording through processing (including analysis, transformation, or migration), us, data retention, archive/retrieval, and destruction (MHRA).

Data Lineage.

Data lineage represents information about everything that has "happened" to the data. Whether it was moved from one system to another, transformed, aggregated, etc., ETL (extraction, transformation, and load) tools can capture this metadata electronically (DataManagementU).

Data Mart.

A data mart is a structure/access pattern specific to data warehouse environments to retrieve client-facing data.

Data Migration.

Data migration transfers data between storage types, formats, or computer systems. It is crucial for any system implementation, upgrade, or consolidation (Wikipedia).

Data Pipeline.

A data pipeline is a set of processes and tools for ingesting, processing, transforming, and moving data from one or more sources to a destination for storage, analysis, or other purposes.

Datapoint class.

A data point's class is the category or label assigned to it. In machine learning, data points are often categorized into different classes or groups based on their characteristics.

Data Process Mapping.

A visual representation of data creation and movement through the business process, including documentation of the systems used, is generated.

Data Provenance.

Data provenance is the confidence of the data source systems. Instituting data quality rules at the source enhances this confidence.

Data Obfuscation.

Data masking or obfuscation is modifying sensitive data so that it is of no or little value to unauthorized intruders while still being usable by software or authorized personnel (Wikipedia).

Data Ownership.

It refers to the possession of and responsibility for information.

Data Quality.

Data quality is considered accurate, auditable, conforming to requirements template, consistent, with integrity, provenance, and value, making data both correct and helpful valuable (IPS, Publication 11-3, "American National Dictionary for Information Systems," Windrowed, July 1979).

Data Reliability.

Data is reliable if its content can be trusted as a complete and accurate representation of the transaction, activities, or facts to which it attests, and it can be depended upon during subsequent transactions and activities (NARA)

Data Reasonability.

This is a data quality dimension. It consists of data patterns meeting expectations.

Data Relevance.

Relevance in attribute data emphasizes the significance and applicability of the qualitative attributes and properties to specific contexts, ensuring that the information is meaningful and valuable for understanding and application.

Data Selection.

The process of determining the appropriate data type, source, and suitable instruments to collect data.

Data Suitability.

Data suitability refers to the appropriateness and fitness of a dataset for a particular purpose or analysis.

Dataset.

A dataset is a structured data collection associated with a unique body of work.

Data Source.

(1) Origin where data is collected. (2) Data set sustained by a specified organization, the data holder. The data trigger creates a record in the data source and the data model used in the data source (EMA/HMA).

Data Standards.

A set of rules about how a particular data type should be structured, defined, formatted, or exchanged between computer systems. Data standards make submissions predictable and consistent and have a form that an information technology system or a scientific tool can use.

Data Steward.

The person or group manages the development, approval, and use of data within a specified functional area, ensuring that it can be used to satisfy data requirements throughout the organization (DoD 8320.1-M-1, "Data Standardization Procedures," April 1998).

Data Stewardship.

Data stewardship is having data stewards work with an organization's data and metadata to ensure their quality, accuracy, formats, and domain values are properly defined and understood across the enterprise.

Data Stewardship's role is to ensure that organizational data and metadata meet quality, accuracy, format, and value criteria and that data is properly defined and understood (standardized) across the enterprise.

Data Timeliness.

One data quality dimension is timeliness. Data timeliness refers to the degree to which data is current and up-to-date about the point in time when it is needed for analysis, decision-making, or other business processes.

Data Transformation.

Data extraction, cleansing, and integration (e.g., into a Common 201 Data Model (CDM)).

Data Trustworthiness.

From a record management perspective, reliability, authenticity, integrity, and usability are the main characteristics of trustworthy data (NARA). Trustworthy data meets specific standards of quality and integrity, ensuring users can confidently rely on it.

Data Uniqueness.

One of the dimensions of data quality. Data uniqueness means no entity exists more than once within a data set.

Data Warehousing.

An architected, periodic, coordinated process of copying from numerous sources into an optimized environment capable of analytical and informational processing.

Data Validity.

Data validity refers to data accuracy, correctness, and fitness. This is an essential aspect of data quality, as it ensures that the values within the data are consistent with the defined domain of values, types, and formats. This means the data object is free from errors, inconsistencies, or inaccuracies that could negatively impact decision-making, analysis, or system functionality.

Decommissioning.

A planned, systematic process to disassemble and retire from service a facility system and equipment without altering the integrity (validation state) of any other facility, system, or equipment previously connected to the facility, system, or equipment being decommissioned. The decommissioning is done via inspection, testing, and documentation.

Decryption.

The transformation of unintelligible data ("ciphertext") into original data ("clear text").

Delete.

The process of permanently removing, erasing, or obliterating recorded information from a medium, especially an electronic medium.

Deliverable.

A tangible or intangible object produced due to project execution is part of an obligation. In Validation Projects, Deliverables are usually documented.

Derived Data.

Data originally in one form was converted to another using some automated process.

Design Qualification.

The documented verification that the proposed design of the facilities, systems, and equipment is suitable for the intended purpose is also known as Design Verification (EMA Annex 15, Validation and Qualification).

Design Specification.

A specification documents how a system will be built (NIST).

Developer.

An organization that performs development activities (including requirements analysis, design, testing through acceptance) during the software lifecycle process.

Development.

The software lifecycle process contains requirements analysis, design, coding, integration, testing, installation, and support for acceptance of software products (ISO 9000-3).

Deviation.

When a system does not act as expected.

Digital.

About data (signals) in discrete (separate/pulse form) integral values.

Digital Certificate.

A digital certificate (a.k.a. also known as a public key or identity certificate) is a credential issued by a trusted authority. An entity can present a digital certificate to prove its identity or right to access information. It links a public-key value to a set of information identifying the entity associated with using the corresponding private key. Certificates are authenticated, issued, and managed by a trusted third party called a CA. See also Public-key Certificates.

Digital Preservation.

Digital preservation consists of the processes to ensure the continued accessibility of digital materials.

Digital Signature Standard (DSS).

A National Institute of Standards and Technology (NIST) standard for digital signatures authenticates both a message and the signer. DSS has a security level comparable to RSA (Rivest-Shamir-Adleman) cryptography, with 1,024-bit keys.

Disaster Recovery.

The activities required to restore one or more computer systems to their valid state in response to a significant hardware or software failure or destruction of facilities.

Disaster Recovery Plan.

The written and approved plan is associated with disaster recovery.

Discrepancy.

Any problem or entry into the Problem Reporting System. Includes all bugs and may include design issues.

Destruction.

In records management, the primary type of disposal action is destroying records. Methods of destroying records include selling or salvaging the record medium and burning, pulping, shredding, macerating, or discarding them with other waste materials.

Disposition.

Disposition means actions taken after they are no longer in office space to conduct current business (41 CFR 201-4 and RM Handbook, references (kk) and (w)).

Documentation.

1) Manuals, written procedures or policies, records, or reports that provide information concerning the uses, maintenance, or validation of a process or system involving either hardware or software. This material may be presented from electronic media. Documents include but are not limited to Standard Operating Procedures (SOPs), Technical Operating Procedures (TOPs), manuals, logs, system development documents, test plans, scripts and results, plans, protocols, and reports. Refer to Documentation and Documentation, the Glossary of Computerized System and Software Development Terminology level, August 1995.

2) Any written or pictorial information describing, defining, specifying, reporting, or certifying activities, requirements, procedures, or results (ANSI N45.2.10-1982).

Note: In software engineering, documentation is considered software. It is controlled by the same controls associated with typical software.

Efficacy.

The measurement of a medicine's desired effect under ideal conditions, such as in a clinical trial.

EFG 11.

The German Expert Group for Computer Systems (EFG 11) deals with all issues relating to the use of computer systems in facilities and companies subject to surveillance under the German Medicines Act.

Electronic Archive.

The designated electronic storage device in which electronic records are retained for their long-term preservation (SAG, "A Guide to Archiving of Electronic Records," February 2014).

Electronic Record (E-record).

Information recorded electronically requires a computer system to access or process it (SAG, "A Guide to Archiving of Electronic Records," February 2014).

In this book, based on the MHRA definitions, raw data and data are considered e-records. The term e-records will be used when referring to electronic raw data and data.

Electronic Record Lifecycle.

All phases in the life of the electronic record, from initial generation and recording through processing (including transformation or migration), use of electronic records retention, archive/retrieval, and destruction

Electronic Records Management.

Electronic records management (ERM) is the management of electronic files and documents as records.

Electronic Source Data.

Data was initially recorded electronically (Source: FDA, Use of Electronic Health Records Data in Clinical Investigations, September 2018).

Electronic Storage Device.

Hard drives and any fixed or portable storage media (e.g., network drives, data servers, cloud storage, USB jump/flash drives, and other peripherals).

Electronic System.

Electronic system means systems, including hardware and software, that produce e-records (US FDA, "Electronic Systems, Electronic Records, and Electronic Signatures in Clinical Investigations Questions and Answers Guidance for Industry," March 2023 (Draft)).

End User.

Personnel who use the validated computer system.

Emergency Change.

A change to a validated system is necessary to eliminate an error condition that prevents the system's use and interrupts the business function.

Emulation.

Emulation refers to mimicking a piece of hardware or software in software so that other processes think that the original equipment/function is still available in its original form. Emulation is a way of preserving the functionality and access to digital information that might otherwise be lost due to technological obsolescence.

Encryption.

(1) The process of converting information into a code or cipher so people cannot read it. A secret key, or password, is required to decrypt (decode) the information. (2) Transformation of confidential plaintext into ciphertext to protect it. An encryption algorithm combines plaintext with other values called keys or ciphers, making the data unintelligible (45 CFR 142.304).

Entity.

A software or hardware product that can be individually qualified or validated.

Establish.

In this book, the word establish means defining, documenting, and implementing.

Evaluation.

A systematic determination of the extent to which an entity meets its specified criteria.

Exchange Format.

A data format for converting from one file or database structure to another. For example, XML is commonly used as a data exchange format.

Expected Result.

What should a system do when a particular action is performed?

Extract.

"Extract" refers to pulling data out of a source.

Extract, transform load (ETL).

It is a repeatable process of moving data from a source, such as an application, to a destination, usually a data warehouse. It converts data from one format to another and adds the standardized dictionary if applicable. It is a type of data pipeline.

Factory Acceptance Test.

An acceptance test in the supplier's factory usually involves the customer (IEEE).

Failure Analysis.

It is the process of collecting and analyzing data to determine the cause of a failure. One software-based fault location technique is Automatic Test Pattern Generation.

FDA Guidance Documents.

FDA guidance documents represent the FDA's current thinking on a subject. These documents do not create or confer any rights for or on any person and do not operate to bind FDA or the public. An alternative approach may be used if such an approach satisfies the requirements of the applicable statutes, regulations, or both.

Federal Register.

A daily issuance of the US government provides a uniform system for making the regulations and legal notices issued by federal agencies available.

Field Devices.

Hardware devices typically located in the field at or near the process are needed to bring information to the computer or to implement a computer-driven control action. Devices include sensors, analytical instruments, transducers, and valves.

File.

An arrangement of records. The term is used to denote papers, photographs, photographic copies, maps, machine-readable information, or other recorded information regardless of physical form or characteristics, accumulated or maintained in filing equipment, boxes, or machine-readable media, or on shelves, and occupying an office or storage space (Noun) (41 CFR 201-4 and 36 CFR 1220.14, references (kk)) and (11)).

File Format.

A file format is a standard way to encode data for storage in a computer file. File formats are usually specific to the kind of information they store. For instance, a file format, "xlsx," is specific to storing Excel spreadsheets. Instead, a file format, "jpg," stores images. These are usually independent of the terminologies but may be incorporated within an overall data standard.

File Management.

The process and act of creating an organized structure in which you store information for easy retrieval.

File Server.

A file server is a computer containing files available to all users connected to a local-area network (LAN). In some LANs, a microcomputer is designated as the file server; in others, it is a computer with a large disk drive and specialized software. Some file servers offer other resources, such as gateways and protocol conversion.

Final Rule.

The regulation is finalized for implementation, published in the FR (preamble and codified), and codified in the CFR.

Format.

The format refers to the computer file format described by a formal or vendor standard or specification for electronic records. For non-electronic records, the format refers to its physical form, e.g., paper, microfilm, video, etc.

Function.

A set of specified, ordered actions that are part of a process.

Functional Requirements.

This specification describes how the system must technically operate to meet the requirements document.

Functional Testing.

Test data can be applied derived from the specified functional requirements without regard to the final program structure.

GAP.

A gap is the difference between current capabilities and future potential or needs.

GMP.

Good Manufacturing Practice (GMP) is the part of quality assurance that ensures products are consistently produced and controlled by quality standards appropriate to their intended use (Commission Directive 2003/94/EC).

Current Good Manufacturing Practice (CGMP) refers to requirements in the Federal Food, Drug, and Cosmetic Act (FD&C Act), section 501(a)(2)(B), for all drugs and active pharmaceutical ingredients (APIs). The term includes applicable requirements for finished human and animal drugs under 21 CFR parts 210 and 211. For biologics, the term includes additional applicable requirements under 21 CFR parts 600-680 (US FDA).

GMP Controls.

Set of controls that assure consistently continued process performance and product quality.

GMP Data.

The GMP-relevant data describe the development of a batch and provide information on processes that directly or indirectly influence the quality of the medicinal product or impact the risk for patients. This data and information, whether critical to product quality and/or critical to risk related to its integrity, should have been evaluated as part of a data assessment (AIM of EFG 11," Monitoring of Computerized Systems," (Germany), August 2022).

GMP Regulated Activities.

The manufacturing-related activities established in the primary legislation compiled in Volume 1 and Volume 5 of the publication "The rules governing medicinal products in the European Union, US FDA 21 CFR Part 211, "Current Good Manufacturing Practice in Manufacturing, Processing, Packing or Holding of Drugs; General and Current Good Manufacturing Practice for Finished Pharmaceuticals" or any predicate rule applicable to medicinal products for the referenced country.

Good Documentation Practices.

In the context of these guidelines, good documentation practices collectively and individually ensure that documentation, whether paper or electronic, is secure, attributable, legible, traceable, permanent, contemporaneously recorded, original, and accurate (WHO).

Guidelines.

A document guiding the scientific or regulatory aspects of developing medicines and applications for marketing authorization. Although guidelines are not legally binding, applicants must justify deviations (EMA).

Guidelines are departmental policies and recommended standards or statements derived from legislation. They do not have the force of law or regulation.

GxP Application.

Software entities with a specific user-defined business purpose must meet the requirements of the corresponding GxP regulation.

GxP Computerized Systems.

A computer system that performs a regulated operation must be formally controlled under a GXP international life science requirement.

GxP Regulation.

A global abbreviation intended to cover GMP, GCP, GLP, and other regulated applications in context.

The underlying international life science requirements, such as those outlined in the US FD&C Act, US PHS Act, FDA regulations, EU Directives, Japanese MHL.W regulations, Australia TGA, or other applicable national legislation under which a company operates (GAMP Good Practice Guide, IT Infrastructure Control and Compliance, ISPE 2005).

Hash-based Message Authentication Code (HMAC).

A hash-based message authentication code (HMAC) is a message authentication code that uses a cryptographic key with a hash function. Hash-based message authentication code (HMAC) provides the server and the client each with a private key that is readable and known only to that specific server.

An electronic record, data, or signature can be displayed in a viewable form, e.g., on paper or a computer screen, and has meaning (words in a written language).

Hybrid Systems.

Hybrid computer systems include combinations of paper records (or other non-electronic media) and electronic records, paper records, electronic signatures, or handwritten signatures executed to electronic records.

Ingestion.

The process that accepts electronic records for archiving (SAG, "A Guide to Archiving of Electronic Records," February 2014).

Information.

Facts provided or learned about something or someone.

Information security.

It is a set of strategies for managing the processes, tools, and policies necessary to prevent, detect, document, and counter digital and non-digital information threats. Infosec's responsibilities include establishing business processes that protect information assets regardless of how the information is formatted or whether it is in transit, being processed, or at rest in storage.

Information Technology.

Any equipment or interconnected system or subsystem of equipment used in the automatic acquisition, storage, manipulation, management, movement, control, display, switching, interchange, transmission, or reception of data or information by the executive agency. For purposes of the preceding sentence, equipment is used by an executive agency if the equipment is used by the executive agency directly or is used by a contractor under a contract with the executive agency which (i) requires the use of such equipment or (ii) requires the use, to a significant extent, of such equipment in the performance of a service or the furnishing of a product. Information technology includes computers, ancillary equipment, software, firmware, similar procedures, services (including support services), and related resources (40 U.S.C., SEC. 1401).

Infrastructure.

The hardware and software, such as networking software and operation systems, allow the application to function (EMA Annex 11).

Interface.

A shared boundary. To interact or communicate with another system component (ANSI/IEEE).

Impact of change.

The impact of change is the change's effect on the GxP computer system. The components by which the impact of change is evaluated may include, but are not limited to, business considerations, resource requirements and availability, application of appropriate regulatory agency requirements, and criticality of the system.

Inspection.

(1) A manual testing technique in which program documents (specifications (requirements, design), source code, or user manuals) are examined in a very formal and disciplined manner to discover any errors, violations of standards, or other problems. Checklists are typical vehicles used to accomplish this process. (2) A visual examination of a software product to detect and identify software anomalies, including errors and deviations from standards and

specifications. Inspections are peer examinations led by impartial facilitators trained in inspection techniques. Determination of remedial or investigative action for an anomaly is a mandatory element of a software inspection, although the solution should not be determined in the inspection meeting. (3) An independent assessment of facilities and processes a regulatory authority performs to determine if the regulated facility meets regulatory cGMP requirements.

Installation Qualification.

Establish confidence that process equipment and ancillary systems can consistently operate within established limits and tolerances (FDA).

Integration Testing.

The orderly progression of testing in which software elements, hardware elements, or both are combined and tested until all inter-module communication links have been integrated.

Integrity.

(1) Guarding against improper information modification or destruction and ensuring information non-repudiation and authenticity (44 U.S.C., Sec. 3542). (2) Protection against unauthorized changes to information. (3) Condition existing when data is unchanged from its source and has not been accidentally or maliciously modified, altered, or destroyed (National Information System Security (INFOSEC) Glossary). (4) The degree to which a system or component prevents unauthorized

access to or modification of computer programs or data (ANSI/IEEE).

Intended Use.

(1) Use of a product, process, or service by the manufacturer's specifications, instructions, and information (ANSI/AAMI/ISO 14971). (2) Refer to the objective intent of the persons legally responsible for the labeling of labeling. Such persons' expressions determine the intent shown by the circumstances surrounding the distribution of the article. This objective intent may, for example, be shown by labeling claims, advertising matters, or oral or written statements by such persons or their representatives. It may be shown by the circumstances that the article is, with the knowledge of such persons or their representatives, offered and used for a purpose for which it is neither labeled nor advertised. The intended uses of an article may change after it has been introduced into interstate commerce by its manufacturer. If, for example, a packer, distributor, or seller intends an article for different uses than those intended by the person from whom he received the devices, US FDA Draft Guidance for Industry and Food and Drug Administration Staff - Mobile Medical Applications, July 2011.

IT Infrastructure.

The hardware and software, such as networking software and operation systems, allow the application to function (EMA Annex 11).

Key Practices.

Processes essential for computer validation include tools, workflow, and people (PDA).

Legacy Systems.

Production of computer systems operating on older computer hardware or based on older software applications. Sometimes, the vendor may no longer support the hardware or software (2) These are regarded as systems that have been established and used for considerable time. For various reasons, they may be generally characterized by a need for adequate compliance-related documentation and records about the development and commissioning stage of the system. Additionally, because of their age, there may be no records of a formal approach to validating the system (PICS CSV PI 011-3[9]).

Legible.

Data can be read by eye or electronically and retained permanently (EMA, "EMA Questions and answers: Good manufacturing practice Data Integrity," Aug 2016.).

Lifecycle Model.

A framework containing the processes, activities, and tasks involved in developing, operating, and maintaining a software product, spanning the system's life from defining its requirements to terminating its use (ISO 9000-3).

Lifecycle (record).

A record's lifecycle is the period from its creation to its final disposition. There are four stages in a record's lifecycle:

---

[9] PI 011-3. *"Good Practices for Computerised Systems in Regulated "GXP" Environments"*, Pharmaceutical Inspection Co-operation Scheme (PIC/S), September 2007.

creation, Maintenance, Retention Management, and Disposal.

Limited Security System.

Computer systems with limited security functionality, such as but not limited to non-individual accounts, a limited number of users, and security based on group passwords.

Living Document.

A document (or collection of documents) is revised throughout a computer system's life. Only the most recent version(s) is effective and supersedes prior versions.

Load.

"Load" is about inserting the data into the destination.

Locally Managed-Security System.

A computer system is locally authenticated (e.g., with a local domain or a stand-alone system), in which the security process is performed. These systems use equipment-specific user security configurations and do not use the regulated entity network user security configuration.

Logically Secure and Controlled Environment.

A computing environment controlled by policies, procedures, and technology deters direct or remote unauthorized access that could damage computer components, production applications, and/or data.

Lifecycle.

All phases in the system's life, from initial requirements until retirement, including design, specification, programming, testing, installation, operation, and maintenance (EMA Annex 11)

Lifecycle Model.

A framework containing the processes, activities, and tasks involved in developing, operating, and maintaining a software product, spanning the system's life from defining its requirements to terminating its use (ISO 9000-3).

Machine Learning.

Machine learning is a subset of artificial intelligence that allows systems to learn from data and improve performance over time without being explicitly programmed.

Machine Learning Algorithm.

A Machine Learning algorithm is a mathematical and computational process that enables computers to learn patterns, relationships, and insights from data and then use that knowledge to make predictions, decisions, or classifications without being explicitly programmed to perform the task.

A machine learning algorithm takes data as input, analyzes it, and outputs a model that can perform a specific task, such as predicting future trends, classifying objects, or detecting anomalies. The algorithm "learns" from the data by adjusting internal parameters (like weights) to improve its accuracy over time.

Machine Learning Application.

A machine learning application is the practical use of machine learning algorithms and models to solve real-world problems by enabling systems to learn from data without being explicitly programmed. These applications use statistical techniques and data-driven approaches to allow systems to automatically improve their performance on a task as they process more data.

Machine Learning Architecture.

Machine Learning Architecture refers to components' structured design and framework for developing, training, deploying, and managing machine learning models. It encompasses the various layers, tools, algorithms, and infrastructure that work together to enable a machine-learning system to function effectively. A well-defined architecture helps ensure that machine learning systems are scalable, efficient, maintainable, and easily integrated into existing workflows or environments.

Machine learning architecture typically comprises multiple components that interact with tasks such as data ingestion, model training, deployment, and monitoring.

Machine Learning Engineers.

A machine learning engineer is a specialized role that bridges the gap between data science and software engineering. They are responsible for designing, building, and maintaining machine learning systems that can learn from data and make predictions or decisions.

Machine Learning Governance.

Governance of a machine learning system involves setting up policies, frameworks, and controls to ensure the ethical, legal, and practical use of machine learning models.

Machine Learning Infrastructure.

Machine learning infrastructure refers to the underlying systems, tools, and platforms that support machine learning model development, deployment, and management. It is essentially the foundation on which AI applications are built.

Machine Learning Model.

A machine learning model is a mathematical or computational structure designed to make predictions or decisions based on data. The model learns patterns, relationships, or structures from historical data (training data) and uses that knowledge to make inferences or predictions on new, unseen data.

A machine learning model is a program or function that processes input data and produces an output, typically a prediction, classification, or recommendation, based on the patterns it has learned from previous data.

Machine Learning Model Artifacts.

Machine learning model artifacts refer to the collection of files and components that encapsulate a trained model, making it usable for inference or further development. These artifacts are generated after the model has been trained and represent the model's "output" that can be deployed or transferred across environments.

Machine Learning Pipeline.

A machine learning pipeline is a sequence of steps or stages in building and deploying a machine learning model. It is a systematic approach to ensure reproducibility, efficiency, and scalability in the model development process.

Machine Learning Platform.

A machine learning platform is a software environment that provides tools and services to streamline the development, deployment, and management of machine learning models. These platforms simplify the complex process of building and maintaining AI applications, making them accessible to a broader range of developers, data scientists, and analysts.

Machine Learning Practitioners.

Machine learning practitioners design, build, test, and deploy machine learning models and systems. They work with large data sets to derive insights, make predictions, or automate decision-making processes. Machine Learning practitioners typically possess expertise in data science, computer science, mathematics, and statistics, leveraging this knowledge to apply machine learning techniques to solve real-world problems.

Machine Learning Process.

The machine learning process refers to the sequence of steps or stages involved in developing, training, evaluating, and deploying machine learning models. The structured approach guides data scientists and machine learning engineers in solving real-world problems by leveraging data to create predictive models.

The process typically includes stages like data collection, preprocessing, model training, evaluation, and deployment, with iterative refinements at each step. Refer to Machine Learning System Lifecycle.

Machine Learning Risk.

Machine Learning Risk refers to the potential negative consequences or unintended outcomes arising from deploying or using a machine learning model. These risks can range from financial losses to ethical concerns.

Machine Learning System.

A machine learning system is a computational system that learns from data and improves performance on a specific task over time without being explicitly programmed.

Machine Learning System Lifecycle.

The lifecycle of a machine learning system is a cyclical process comprising multiple stages, each with its own specific tasks and objectives.

Machine Learning Training Data.

In machine learning, training data is the dataset from which the model learns. It is essentially the foundation upon which a machine-learning model is built.

Machine Learning Trustworthy.

A trustworthy machine learning system is reliable, fair, accountable, and transparent. These qualities ensure that AI systems are deployed responsibly and ethically.

Machine Learning Workloads.

Machine Learning workloads refer to the specific computational tasks involved in developing, training, testing, and deploying machine learning models. These workloads consist of various processes that utilize large amounts of data, computational power, and storage resources to create intelligent systems capable of learning from data, making predictions, or automating decisions.

Maintainer.

An organization that performs maintenance activities (ISO 12207:2008).

Major Change.

A change to a validated system that reviewers determine to require the execution of extensive validation activities.

Management.

We are planning, organizing, coordinating, and controlling the use of resources to achieve goals.

Manufacture.

All operations related to the purchase of materials and products, Production, Quality Control, release, storage, and dispatch of medicinal products and the related controls.

Manufacturer.

An entity that engages in CGMP activities, including implementation of oversight and controls over the manufacture of drugs to ensure quality.

Manufacturing.

All operations of receipt of materials, production, packaging, repackaging, labeling, relabeling, quality control, release, storage, and distribution of medicinal products and the related controls.

Manufacturing Systems.

Elements of pharmaceutical and biopharmaceutical manufacturing capability, including manufacturing systems, facility equipment, process equipment, supporting utilities, associated process monitoring and control systems, and automation systems, can potentially affect product quality and patient safety (ASTM E 2500 – 07).

Mapping.

The process of creating data element linkages between two distinct data models.

May.

This word, or the adjective "OPTIONAL," means an item is truly optional. A statement using "may" for permissible actions.

Medicinal Manufacturing Regulatory Environment.

The medicinal manufacturing regulatory environment encompasses the set of regulations, guidelines, and standards governing pharmaceutical product production, quality control, and distribution. It includes Pharmaceuticals, Biotechnology, Active Pharmaceutical Ingredients (APIs), Radiopharmaceuticals, Herbal Medicines, and Traditional Medicines.

Metadata.

Data describing stored data: that is, data describing the structure, data elements, interrelationships, and other characteristics of electronic records (DOD 5015.2-STD). Data that describe the attributes of other data and provide context and meaning. Typically, these data describe the structure, elements, interrelationships, and other data characteristics. It also permits data to be attributable to an individual (MHRA).

Migration.

The act of moving records from one system to another.

Minor Change.

A change to a validated system that reviewers determine to require the execution of only targeted qualification and validation activities.

Model.

A model is an abstract representation of a given object in any form (including mathematical, symbolic, graphical, or descriptive) representing a particular aspect of that physical system. In this book, the DI model describes, assesses, and/or predicts data/e-records integrity controls in a drug manufacturing regulatory environment.

Module Testing.

Refer to Testing, Unit in the Glossary of Computerized System and Software Development Terminology, August 1995.

Native file format.

It is a method used by the computer operating system or file management to arrange data.

NEMA Enclosure.

Hardware enclosures (usually cabinets) provide different mechanical and environmental protection levels to the devices installed.

Non-Conformance.

A departure from minimum requirements specified in a contract, specification, drawing, or other approved product description or service.

Non-Custom Purchased Software Package.

A generally available, marketed software product performs specific data collection, manipulation, output, or archiving functions. Refer to Configurable, off-the-shelf software in the Glossary of Computerized System and Software Development Terminology, August 1995.

Non-Repudiation.

Strong and substantial evidence of the message signer's identity and message integrity is enough to prevent a party from successfully denying the message's origin, submission, or delivery and the integrity of its contents.

Objective Evidence.

Qualitative or quantitative information is records or statements of fact about the quality of an item or service or the existence of a quality system element, which is based on observation, measurement, or test and can be verified.

Operator.

An organization that operates the system (ISO 12207:1995).

Operating Environment.

All outside influences interface with the computer system (GAMP).

Ongoing Evaluation.

A term used to describe the dynamic process employed after a system's initial validation that can assist in maintaining a computer system in a validated state.

Operational Testing.

Refer to Operational Qualification in the Glossary of Computerized System and Software Development Terminology, August 1995.

Operating System.

Operating systems are software that controls the execution of programs and provides services such as resource allocation, scheduling, input/output control, and data management. They are usually predominantly software, but partial or complete hardware implementations are possible (ISO).

Original Record.

(1) Data as the file or format in which it was initially generated, preserving the integrity (accuracy, completeness, content, and meaning) of the record, e.g., original paper record of manual observation or data file from a computer system

(MHRA) (2) Data is in the same format as it was initially generated, or as a 'verified copy,' which retains content and meaning (EMA, "EMA Questions and answers: Good manufacturing practice Data Integrity," Aug 2016).

Part 11 Records.

Records that are required to be maintained under predicate rule requirements and that are maintained in electronic format in place of paper format, or records that are required to be maintained under predicate rules, that are maintained in electronic format in addition to paper format, and that are relied on to perform regulated activities. Part 11 records include records submitted to the FDA under predicate rules (even if such records are not explicitly identified in Agency regulations) in electronic format (assuming the records have been identified in docket number 92S-0251 as the types of submissions the Agency accepts in electronic format) (FDA Guidance: Part 11 Scope and Application).

Password.

A character string authenticates an identity. Knowledge of the password associated with a user ID is considered proof of authorization to use the capabilities associated with that user ID (CSC-STD-002-85).

Packaged Software.

Software provided and maintained by a vendor/supplier can provide general business functionality or system services. Refer to Configurable, off-the-shelf software in the Glossary of Computerized System and Software Development Terminology, August 1995.

Periodic Review.

A documented assessment of a computer system's documentation, procedures, records, and performance to determine whether it is still in a validated state and what actions, if any, are necessary to restore its validated state (PDA). The review is performed at regular intervals. The timing of intervals is left flexible.

Persisted Data/E-record.

They persisted E-records - E-records residing in the diverse data warehouses acquired from a source system(s).

Person.

In the context of regulatory compliance, 'Person' refers to an individual or an organization with legal rights and duties, a concept that is fundamental to understanding the regulatory landscape.

Personal Identification Number.

A Personal Identification Number (PIN) is an alphanumeric code or password used to authenticate an individual's identity, a crucial aspect of data security in electronic records management.

Physical Environment.

The physical environment of a computer system encompasses its physical location, such as the data center, and the environmental parameters, including temperature and humidity, in which the system operates.

Planned Change.

An intentional change to a validated system for which an implementation and evaluation program is predetermined.

Policy.

A directive usually specifies what is to be accomplished.

Preamble.

Analysis preceding a proposed or final rule that clarifies the intention of the rulemaking and any ambiguities regarding the rule. Responses to comments on a proposed rule are published in the preamble preceding the final rule. Preambles are published only in the FR and do not have a binding effect.

Predicate Regulations.

Federal Food, Drug, and Cosmetic Act, the Public Health Service Act, or any FDA Regulation, except for 21 CFR Part 11. Predicate regulations address the research, production, and control of FDA-regulated articles.

Preservation.

They ensure that electronic records in the archive remain accessible by applying appropriate preservation policies and processes. In the context of electronic archiving, this means maintenance of the authenticity and integrity of e-records (SAG, "A Guide to Archiving of Electronic Records," February 2014).

Primary Record.

The record, which takes precedence in cases collected or retained concurrently by multiple methods, fails to concur (MHRA).

Principles.

A foundation of beliefs, truths, and so on, upon which others are based.

Procedural Controls.

(1) Written and approved procedures providing appropriate instructions for each development, operations, maintenance, and security aspect applicable to computer technologies. Procedural controls should have QA/QC controls equivalent to the applicable predicate regulations in regulated operations (2) A directive specifies how certain activities are to be accomplished. PMA CSVC

Process.

(1) A set of specified, ordered actions required to achieve a defined result.

(2) a set of interrelated interacting activities that transform input into outputs (ISO 9000-3).

Process Owner.

The person is responsible for the business process (EMA Annex 11).

Process Mapping.

Activities involved in defining what a business entity does, who is responsible, to what standard a business process should be completed, and how the success of a business process can be determined (CEFIC).

Process System.

The combination of the process equipment, support systems (such as utilities), and procedures used to execute a process.

Processable Electronic Records.

Records in native file formats can be read, analyzed, interpreted, and manipulated by current and future hardware and software that can read the native file structure.

Processing Environment.

The environment in which the e-records were initially created (ISPE/PDA, "Technical Report: Good Electronic Records Management (GERM)," July 2002).

Product.

A product is a finished dosage form (21 CFR §210.3(b)(4)) or a finished device (21 CFR §820.3).

Production Environment.

The operational environment in which the system is being used for its intended purpose, i.e., not in a test or development environment.

Production Verification (PV).

Documented verification that the integrated system performs as intended in its production environment. PV is the execution of selected Performance Qualification (PQ) tests in the production environment using production data.

Project.

A project is an activity that achieves specific objectives through defining tasks and effective use of resources.

Project Management.

Project management is the application of knowledge, skills, tools, and techniques to project activities to meet the project requirements (ANSI).

Prospective Validation.

Validation is conducted before the distribution of either a new product or a product made under a revised manufacturing process, where the revisions may affect the product's characteristics (FDA).

Public-key Certificate.

A public key certificate (a.k.a. a digital certificate or identity certificate) is an electronic representation of an identification or passport issued by a certification authority (CA) to a PKI user, stating identification information, validity period, the holder's public key, the identity and digital signature of the issuer, and the purpose for which it is issued (GERM)

Qualification.

(1) Proving that equipment works correctly leads to the expected results. The word validation is sometimes widened to incorporate the concept of qualification (PIC/S). (2) Qualification demonstrates whether a computer system and associated controlled process/operation, procedural controls, and documentation can fulfill specified requirements. (3) demonstrating whether an entity can fulfill specified requirements (ISO 8402: 1994, 2.13.1). (4) Describes

verification of system functionality (Notice to sponsors on validation and qualification of computerized systems used in clinical trials EMA/INS/GCP/467532/2019). (5) proving that equipment works correctly and consistently produces the expected results. Qualification is part of, but not limited to, a validation process, i.e., installation qualification (IQ), operational qualification (OQ), and performance qualification (PQ) (Draft API GMP Guide, September 1997 (Draft)).

Qualification Protocol.

A prospective experimental plan stating how the qualification will be conducted, including test parameters, product characteristics, production equipment, and decision points on what constitutes an acceptable test. When executed, a protocol is intended to produce documented evidence that a system or subsystem performs as required.

Quality and Technical Records.

Registered evidence about activities on the QMS and/or the process of performing tests (e.g., worksheets, logbooks, control graphs, documentation of equipment qualification, test requests, test reports, reports from audits, training records, records of corrective and preventive actions, and so on) (OMLC - Management of Documents and Records (Rephrased)).

Qualification Reports.

These test reports evaluate the conduct and results of the qualification on a computer system.

Quality.

The totality of features and characteristics of a product or service that bears on its ability to satisfy given needs.

Quality Assurance.

All planned, and systematic activities are implemented within the quality system and demonstrated as needed to provide adequate confidence that an entity will fulfill quality requirements.

Quality Management.

All activities of the overall management function determine the quality policy, objectives, and responsibilities and implement them through quality planning, quality control, quality assurance, and quality improvement within the quality system.

Quality Records (internal and external).

Registered evidence on Official Medicines Control Laboratories (OMCLs) activities on the QMS and/or the process of performing tests (e.g., worksheets, logbooks, control graphs, documentation of equipment qualification, test requests, test reports, reports from audits, training records, records of corrective and preventive actions, and so on). A form or template containing data is considered a record. (EU OMLC Quality Management Guideline on Management of Documents and Records, January 2016)

Quality System.

To establish policy and objectives and to achieve those objectives to direct and control an organization regarding quality (ISO 9000:2015).

Raw Data.

All data on which quality decisions are based should be defined as raw data. It includes data that is used to generate other records (Source: Volume 4, EU Good Manufacturing Practice Medicinal Products for Human and Veterinary Use, Chapter 4: Documentation)

Original records and documentation, retained in the format in which they were initially generated (i.e., paper or electronic) or as a "true copy". The printout constitutes the raw data for essential electronic equipment, which does not store data. Raw data must be contemporaneously and accurately recorded permanently (MHRA). The raw data must be permanent, protected against unauthorized modification, written to a durable storage location contemporaneously, and must reflect the actual observation.

Any laboratory worksheets, records, memoranda, notes, or exact copies thereof that are the result of original observations and activities of a nonclinical laboratory study and are necessary for the reconstruction and evaluation of the report of that study. Suppose exact transcripts of raw data have been prepared (e.g., tapes which have been transcribed verbatim, dated, and verified accurate by signature). In that case, the exact copy or transcript may be substituted for the source as raw data. Raw data may include photographs, microfilm or microfiche copies, computer printouts, magnetic media, dictated observations, and recorded data from automated instruments (Source: US FDA 21 CFR 58.3(k)).

Record.

A collection of related data treated as a unit (GERM).

As a crucial piece of evidence, the record demonstrates various actions taken to ensure compliance with instructions. These actions include activities, events, investigations, and, in the case of manufactured batches, a history of each product batch, including its distribution. Records also encompass the raw data used to generate other records; regulated users should define which data will be used as raw data for electronic records. At the very least, all data on which quality decisions are based should be defined as raw data (Eudralex Vol 4 Ch 4). This underscores the pivotal role of record management in ensuring the reliability and integrity of our operations.

A record consists of information detailing the business transaction regardless of medium. Records include all books, papers, maps, photographs, machine-readable materials, and other documentary materials, regardless of physical form or characteristics, made or received by an Agency of the United States Government under Federal law or in connection with the transaction of public business and preserved or appropriate for preservation by that Agency or its legitimate successor as evidence of the organization, functions, policies, decisions, procedures, operations, or other activities of the Government or because of the value of data in the record (44 U.S.C. 3301, reference (bb)).

Record Keeping.

The management field is responsible for the efficient and systematic control of the creation, receipt, maintenance, use, and disposition of records, including the processes for capturing and maintaining evidence of and information about business activities and transactions in the form of records (ISO 15489: 2001).

Rerecord Management.

The planning, controlling, directing, organizing, training, promoting, and other managerial activities involving the lifecycle of information, including creation, maintenance (use, storage, retrieval), and disposal, regardless of media. Record management procedures are used to achieve adequate and proper documentation of Federal policies and transactions and effective and economical management of Agency/organizational operations (44 U.S.C. 2901).

Record Owner.

"Record Owner" means a person or organization who can determine the contents and use of the data collected, stored, processed, or disseminated by that party, regardless of whether the data was acquired from another owner or collected directly from the provider.

Record Retention Period.

The length of time the electronic record is to be retained, as mandated by the record type's requirement, based on regulations or documented policies.

Record Retention Schedule.

A list of record types with the required storage conditions and defined retention periods. The time (retention) periods are established based on regulatory, legal, and tax compliance requirements, operational needs, and historical value.

Reengineering.

We are examining and altering an existing system to reconstitute it in a new form. This may include reverse engineering (analyzing a system and producing a representation at a higher level of abstraction, such as design from code), restructuring (transforming a system from one representation to another at the same level of abstraction), documentation (analyzing a system and producing user or support documentation), forward engineering (using software products derived from an existing system, together with new requirements, to produce a new system), retargeting (transforming a system to install it on a different target system), and translation (transforming source code from one language to another or from one version of a language to another) (DOD-STD-498).

Regression Testing.

Regression testing tests computer program changes to ensure the older programming works with the new ones. Regression testing is a normal part of the program development process and, in larger companies, is done by code testing specialists. Test department coders develop code test scenarios and exercises that will test new code units after they have been written. These test cases form what becomes the test bucket. Before a new software product is released, the old test cases are run against the new version to ensure all the old capabilities still work. They might not work because changing or adding new code to a program can quickly introduce errors into code that is not intended to be changed.

Regulated Data.

(1) Information used for a regulated purpose or to support a regulated process (GAMP). (2) Data used for GMP purposes as required by the Rules GMP related to operations that may affect patient safety and product quality (Russian SIDGP Data Integrity Guidance (August 2018).

Regulated Electronic Records.

It is a regulated record maintained in electronic format.

Regulated Entity.

In this book, the regulated entity is the excellent practice entity responsible for operating a computerized system and the applications, files, and data (PIC/S PI 011-3). See regulated user.

Regulated Operations.

Process/business operations carried out on a regulated agency product are covered in a predicated rule.

Regulated Record.

It is a record required to be maintained or submitted by GxP regulations.

Regulated User.

The regulated Good Practice entity operates a computerized system, including the applications, files, and data (PIC/S PI 011-3). See Also 'User' and 'Operator.'

Regulations.

Regulations are rules for following and enforcing the law. US FDA enforces the regulations contained in Title 21 CFR.

Regulatory Agencies.

Bodies have the statutory power to regulate. The expression "regulatory authorities" includes reviewing submitted product data and conducting inspections.

Regulatory Authorities.

Bodies have the statutory power to regulate. The expression "regulatory authorities" includes reviewing submitted product data and conducting inspections.

Regulatory Data.

Regulatory data is the bioanalytical data, animal health data, preclinical data (cell-based and animal-based laboratory data), spontaneous adverse drug reporting data, and chemical and manufacturing control data

Regulatory Requirements.

Any part of a law, ordinance, decree, or other regulation applies to the regulated article.

Release.

A version of a configuration item made available for a specific purpose (ISO 9000-3)

The ability of a system or component to perform its required functions under stated conditions for a specified period (American National Standards Institute/The Institute of Electrical and Electronics Engineers, Inc (IEEE) Std 610.12-1990, IEEE Standard Glossary of Software Engineering Terminology).

Reliability.

A record is reliable if its content can be trusted as a complete and accurate representation of the transaction, activities, or facts to which it attests, and it can be depended upon during subsequent transactions and activities (NARA)

Reliable Records.

Records that are a complete and accurate representation of the transactions, activities, or facts to which they attest and can be depended upon during subsequent transactions or activities.

Remediate.

This book discusses software, hardware, and/or procedural changes that can be employed to bring a system into compliance with the applicable GxP rule.

Remediation Plan.

A documented approach to bringing existing computer systems into compliance with the regulation/s.

Replacement.

Implement a new, compliant system after the retirement of an existing system.

Reports.

Document the conduct of exercises, projects, or investigations, with results, conclusions, and recommendations (Eudralex Vol 4 Ch 4). A report containing regulated data is considered a regulated record.

Repository for Electronic Records.

A direct access device on which the electronic records and metadata are stored.

Re-qualification.

Repetition of the qualification process or a specific portion thereof.

Requirement.

A condition or capability must be met or possessed by a system or system component to satisfy a contract, standard, specification, or other formally imposed document. The set of all requirements forms the basis for the subsequent development of the system or system component (ANSI/IEEE).

Responsibility.

The state of being held to answer for one's conduct and obligations.

Retention Environment.

The environment is used for subsequent safekeeping and preservation of the e-records (GERM)

Retention Period.

The time is specified for preserving data on a data medium (ISO).

The duration for which records are retained. Retention periods are defined in a retention schedule document. These retention schedules are based on business and country-specific regulatory and legal requirements.

Retirement Phase.

The period in the SLC in which plans are made and executed to decommission or remove a computer technology from operational use.

Retrospective Evaluation.

It establishes documented evidence that a system does what it purports to do based on an analysis of historical information. It evaluates a computer system currently operating against standard validation practices and procedures. The evaluation determines the reliability, accuracy, and completeness of a system.

Retrospective Validation.

See Retrospective Evaluation.

Revision.

Different versions of the same document. It can also be used for software, firmware, and hardware boards. It implies a fully tested, functional, and released unit/component/document.

Risk.

A measure of the extent to which a potential circumstance or event threatens an organization, and typically a function of the following:

a. The adverse impacts that would arise if the circumstance or event occurs; and

b. The likelihood of occurrence. The likelihood is influenced by the ease of exploit(s) required and the frequency with which an exploit or like-objects are attacked (K. Dempsey, P. Eav and G. Moore, "Automation Support for Security Control Assessments Volume 1: Overview," Draft NISTIR 8011, February 2016).

Risk Assessment.

A comprehensive evaluation of the risk and its associated impact.

Risk Management.

The tasks and plans that help avoid risk and help minimize damage.

Review.

A process or meeting during which a software product is presented to project personnel, managers, users, customers, user representatives, or other interested parties for comment or approval (IEEE).

Software as a service (SaaS).

SaaS is software owned, delivered, and managed remotely by one or more providers. The provider delivers software based on one set of standard code and data definitions in a one-to-many model by all contracted customers at any time on a pay-for-use basis or as a subscription based on use metrics.

SAT.

Inspection and/or dynamic testing of the systems or significant system components to support the qualification of an equipment system conducted and documented at the manufacturing site.

Secure Repository.

A repository or application that, by specific country laws and regulations, permits users to store records securely and limits the ability to edit and delete documents.

Secure Socket Layer.

Secure sockets layer (SSL) is a networking protocol designed to secure connections between web clients and servers over an insecure network, such as the Internet.

Security Controls.

The management, operational, and technical controls (i.e., safeguards or countermeasures) prescribed for an information system to protect the confidentiality, integrity, and availability of the system and its information.

Self-inspection.

An audit is carried out by people from within the organization to ensure compliance with GMP and regulatory requirements.

Sensor Data.

Sensor data (a.k.a. transient data) is the output of a device that detects and responds to some input from the physical environment.

Segregation of Duties.

A process that divides roles and responsibilities so that a single individual cannot subvert a critical process.

Service Provider.

An organization supplying services to one or more internal or external customers (ITIL Service Design, 2011 Edition).

Service Level Agreement.

Any outsourced activity covered by the GMP Guide should be appropriately defined, agreed upon, and controlled to avoid misunderstandings that could result in a product or operation of unsatisfactory quality. A written Contract between the Contract Giver and the Contract Acceptor must establish the duties of each party (Volume 4 EU GMP Guide, Part I Chapter 7 Outsourced Activities).

Shall.

They express a binding provision per regulatory requirements. Statements that use "shall" can be traced to a regulatory requirement and must be followed to comply with such requirements (RFC 2119, RFC Key Words, March 1997).

Should.

They are used to express a non-mandatory provision. Statements that use "should" are best practices, recommended activities, or options to perform activities to be considered to achieve quality project results. Other methods may be used if it can be demonstrated that they are equivalent (RFC 2119, RFC Key Words, March 1997).

SIPOC Diagram.

It is a tool for identifying all significant process elements represented by a high-level process map.

Signature, Handwritten.

The individual's scripted name or legal mark was handwritten by that individual and executed or adopted to authenticate a writing in a permanent form (21 CFR 11.3(8)).

Site.

In this book, "Site" indicates where local guidelines, standards, procedures, and organizations underpin a global policy.

Site Acceptance Test.

An acceptance test at the customer's site usually involves the customer (IEEE).

Software Developer.

A person or organization that designs software and writes the programs. Software development includes the user interface design, program architecture, and source code

programming   (TechWeb   Network,
http://www.techweb.com/encyclopedia/).

Software Development Standards.

Written policies or procedures that describe practices a programmer or software developer should follow in creating, debugging, and verifying software.

Software Item.

Identifiable part of a software product (ISO 9000-3).

Software Product.

Set of computer programs, procedures, and possibly associated documentation and data (ISO-90003).

Software Quality Assurance.

Software quality assurance (SQA) ensures that the software product meets and complies with the organization's established and standardized quality specifications. SQA is a set of activities that verifies that everyone involved with the project has correctly implemented all procedures and processes.

SQA works parallel to software development, an ongoing activity applied throughout the software development life cycle. Instead of making quality checks after completion, software quality assurance checks for quality issues in each development phase.

Source Authentication.

Source authentication refers to the data having a verifiable source with well-documented evidence or reliable witnesses.

Source Code.

The human-readable version of the list of instructions (programs) enables a computer to perform a task.

Source Data.

All information in original records and certified copies of original records of clinical findings, observations, or other activities in a clinical trial necessary for the reconstruction and evaluation of the trial. Source data are in source documents (original records or certified copies) (Source: EMA/INS/GCP/454280/2010 GCP Inspectors Working Group (GCP IWG). Reflection paper on expectations for electronic source data and data transcribed to electronic data collection)

All information in original records and certified copies of original records of clinical findings, observations, or other activities (in a clinical investigation) used for the reconstruction and evaluation of the trial. Source data are in source documents (original records or certified copies) (Source: FDA, Electronic Source Data in Clinical Investigations, September 2013).

Source System.

A source system is the origin of the data used in the data engineering lifecycle (Reis, J. and Housley, M., "Fundamentals of Data Engineering," O'Reilly Media, Inc., Sebastopol, CA., July 2022.).

Specification.

A document that specifies, in a complete, precise, verifiable manner, the requirements, design, behaviors, or other characteristics of a system or component and, often, the procedures for determining whether these provisions have been satisfied (IEEE)

Stakeholder.

In this book, anyone with a stake in the project's successful outcome – system owner(s), business managers, regulated end-users, quality assurance, software engineers, support people, etc.

Static Analysis.

(1) Analysis of a program performed without executing the program (NBS). (2) evaluating a system or component based on its form, structure, content, and documentation (IEEE).

Standard Instrument Software.

These are driven by non-user-programmable firmware. They are configurable (GAMP)

Standard Operation Procedures.

See Procedural Controls.

Standard Software Packages.

A complete and documented set of programs supplied to several users for a generic application or function (ISO/IEC 2382-20:1990).

Structured Data.

Structured data refers to data stored in defined fields. Categories for structured data include database formats, spreadsheets, statistical data resulting from quantitative research and analysis, and scientific data collected by instrumentation tools during the scientific process.

Subject Matter Experts.

Individuals with specific expertise and responsibility in a particular area or field (ASTM, E 2500 – 07 Standard Guide for Specification, Design, and Verification of Pharmaceutical and Biopharmaceutical Manufacturing Systems and Equipment).

Supplier.

An organization that enters into a contract with the acquirer to supply a system, software product, or software service under the terms of the contract (ISO 12207:1995).

System.

(1) People, machines, and methods organized to accomplish specific functions (ANSI). (2) A composite of personnel, procedures, materials, tools, equipment, facilities, and software at any level of complexity. The elements of this composite entity are used together in the intended operational or support environment to perform a given task or achieve a specific purpose, support, or mission

requirement (DOD). (3) A group of related objects designed to perform or control specified actions.

System Backup.

Data and programs are stored on separate media separate from the originating system.

System Documentation.

The collection of documents that describe the requirements, capabilities, limitations, design, operation, and maintenance of an information processing system. See specification, test documentation, and user's guide (ISO).

System Integrity.

Quality is the quality of a system when it operationally performs its intended function free from unauthorized manipulation (NIST SP 800-33, Withdrawn: August 2018).

System-level Software.

Software that provides an application's underlying or supporting foundation may comprise the operating system, security tools, file management, database management, layered products, scripts, middleware, and LAN device operating system software.

System Lifecycle.

All phases in the system's life, from initial requirements until retirement, including design, specification, programming, testing, installation, operation, and maintenance (EMA Annex 11).

System Owner.

The person is responsible for the availability and maintenance of a computerized system and the security of the data residing on that system (EMA Annex 11).

System Retirement.

The removal of a system from operational usage. Another system may be replaced or removed without being replaced.

System Software.

See Operating System.

System Specification.

In this book, system specifications correspond to requirements, functional, and/or design specifications. For more information, refer to Specification.

System Test.

Process of testing an integrated hardware and software system to verify that it meets its specified requirements.

Technical Records (internal and external).

Registered evidence on Official Medicines Control Laboratories (OMCLs) activities on the QMS and/or the process of performing tests (e.g., worksheets, logbooks, control graphs, documentation of equipment qualification, test requests, test reports, reports from audits, training records, records of corrective and preventive actions, and so on). A form or template containing data is considered a record. (EU OMLC Quality Management Guideline on Management of Documents and Records, January 2016)

Technological Controls.

Are programs enforcing compliance rules?

Technology Stack.

A technology stack refers to the combination of programming languages, frameworks, libraries, tools, and software developers use to build and maintain a software application.

Templates.

Guidelines that outline the essential information for a specific set of equipment (JETT).

Test Report.

A document that presents test results and other information relevant to a test (ISO/IEC Guide 2:2004).

Test Script.

A detailed set of instructions for execution of the test. This typically includes the following:

- Specific identification of the test
- Prerequisites or dependencies
- Test objective
- Test steps or actions
- Requirements or instructions for capturing data (e.g., screen prints, report printing)
- Pass/fail criteria for the entire script.
- Instructions to follow if a non-conformance is encountered.

- Test execution date

- Person(s) executing the test.

- Review date

- Person reviewing the test results.

For each step of the test script, the item tested, the input to that step, and the expected result are indicated before the execution of the test. The actual results obtained during the test steps are recorded on or attached to the test script. Test scripts and results may be managed through computer-based electronic tools. Refer to Test case in the Glossary of Computerized System and Software Development Terminology, August 1995.

Test Non-Conformance.

A non-conformance occurs when the test result is not equal to the expected result or when an unexpected event (such as a loss of power) occurs.

Testing.

Examine a program's behavior by executing the program on sample data sets.

Third Party.

Parties not directly managed by the manufacturing and/or import authorization holder.

Threat.

The potential for a "threat source" to exploit (intentionally) or trigger (accidentally) a specific vulnerability (NIST SP 800-33, Withdrawn: August 2018).

Threat-source.

Either (1) the intent and method of intentionally exploiting a vulnerability or (2) the situation and method that may accidentally trigger a vulnerability (NIST SP 800-33, Withdrawn: August 2018).

Timestamp.

A record mathematically links a piece of data to a time and date.

Traceability.

(1) The degree to which a relationship can be established between two or more products of the development process, especially products having a predecessor-successor or master-subordinate relationship to one another, e.g., the degree to which the requirements and design of a given software component match (IEEE) (2) The degree to which each element in a software development product establishes its reason for existing, e.g., the degree to which each element in a bubble chart references the requirement it satisfies.

Traceability Analysis.

The tracing of (1) Software Requirements Specifications requirements to system requirements in concept documentation, (2) software design descriptions to software requirements specifications and software requirements specifications to software design descriptions,

(3) source code to corresponding design specifications and design specifications to source code. Analyze identified relationships for correctness, consistency, completeness, and accuracy (IEEE).

Traceability Matrix.

A matrix that records the relationship between two or more products, e.g., a matrix that records the relationship between the requirements and the design of a given software component (IEEE).

Training Data.

Training Plan.

Documentation describing the training required for an individual based on their job title or description.

Training Record.

Documentation (electronic or paper) of the training received by an individual that includes, but is not limited to, the individual's name or identifier; the type of training received; the date the training occurred; the trainer's name or identifier; and an indication of the effectiveness of the training (if applicable).

Transfer.

The act or process of moving records from one location to another.

Transform.

"Transform" is about modifying the data to be loaded into the destination.

Transient Memory.

Memory must have a constant power supply, or the stored data will be lost.

Transport Layer Security.

Transport Layer Security is a cryptographic protocol designed to provide communications security over a computer network. The protocol is widely used in applications such as email, instant messaging, and voice-over IP, but its use in securing HTTPS remains the most publicly visible.

True Copy Record.

> (1) An exact copy of an original record, which may be retained in the same or different format in which it was initially generated, e.g., a paper copy of a paper record, an electronic scan of a paper record, or a paper record of electronically generated data (MHRA). (2) Accurate reproduction of the original record regardless of the technology used to create the reproduction (for example, printing, scanning, photocopying, microfilm, or microfiche). A valid copy of an e-record must contain the entire record, including all associated metadata, audit trails, and applicable signatures to preserve content and meaning.

Trust.

In the network security context, trust refers to privacy (the data is not viewable by unauthorized people), integrity (the data stays in its proper form), non-repudiation (the publisher cannot say they did not send it), and authentication (the publisher--and recipient--are who they say they are).

Trustworthiness'.

Trustworthiness is the demonstrated ability and, therefore, the worthiness of an entity to be trusted to satisfy expectations, including satisfying expectations in the face of adversity (NIST.SP.800-160v1r1).

Trustworthy Computer Systems.

Trustworthy computer systems consist of computer infrastructure, applications, and procedures that:

- are reasonably suited to performing their intended functions;

- provide a reasonably reliable level of availability, reliability, and correct operation;

- are reasonably secure from intrusion and misuse; and

- adhere to generally accepted security principles.

Trustworthy Records.

Reliability, authenticity, integrity, and usability are the characteristics used to describe trustworthy records from a record management perspective (NARA)

Unplanned (Emergency) Change.

An unanticipated necessary change to a validated system requires rapid implementation.

Usable Data.

Usable data refers to information that is accessible, understandable, and applicable for its intended purpose.

Usable Records.

Records that can be located, retrieved, presented, and interpreted.

User.

The company or group operating a system (GAMP) (see also 'Regulated User'). The GxP customer, or user organization, contracts a supplier to provide a product. In the context of this document, it is, therefore, not intended to apply only to individuals who use the system and is synonymous with 'Customer' (EU Annex 11)

User Back-up/Alternative Procedures.

A procedure describes the steps to be taken to continue recording and controlling the raw data in case of a computer system interruption or failure.

Unit.

A separately testable element is specified in the design of a computer software element. It is synonymous with the component module (IEEE).

Unit Test.

Test a module for typographic, syntactic, and logical errors to ensure the correct implementation of its design and satisfaction with its requirements.

Usability.

A usable record can be located, retrieved, presented, and interpreted (NARA).

Users.

People or processes accessing a computer system either by direct connections (i.e., via terminals) or indirect connections (i.e., prepare input data or receive output not reviewed for content or classification by a responsible individual).

User ID.

The computer recognizes a sequence of characters and uniquely identifies one person. The UserID is the first form of identification. UserID is also known as a PIN or identification code.

Validated.

It indicates a status to designate that a system or software complies with applicable GMP requirements.

Validation.

By the principles of Good Manufacturing Practice, she proves that any procedure, process, equipment, material, activity, or system leads to the expected results (see also qualification) (PIC/S).

Validation Coordinator.

A person or designee coordinates the validation activities for a specific project or task.

Validation Protocol.

A written plan states how validation will be conducted, including test parameters, product characteristics, production equipment, and decision points on acceptable test results (FDA).

Validation Plan.

A multidisciplinary strategy from which each phase of a validation process is planned, implemented, and documented to ensure that a facility, process, equipment, or system does what it is designed to do. It may also be known as a system or software Quality Plan.

Validation Summary Report.

Documents confirming that the entire project's planned activities have been completed. On acceptance of the Validation Summary Report, the user releases the system for use, possibly with a requirement that continuing monitoring should take place for a specific time (GAMP).

Verification.

(1) The process of determining whether the products of a given phase of the SLC fulfill the requirements established during the previous phase. (2) A systematic approach to verify that manufacturing systems, acting singly or in combination, are fit for intended use, have been properly installed, and are operating correctly. This umbrella term encompasses all approaches to assuring systems are fit for use, such as qualification, commissioning and qualification, verification, system validation, or others (ASTM 5200) (3). Confirmation by examination and provision of objective evidence that specified requirements have been fulfilled (FDA Medical Devices). (4) In design and development, verification concerns examining the result of a given activity to determine conformity with the stated requirement for that activity.

Verification (validation) of Data.

The procedures are carried out to ensure that the data contained in the final report matches original observations. These procedures may apply to raw data, data in case-report forms (in hard copy or electronic form), computer printouts, and statistical analysis and tables (WHO).

Virtual Private Network.

Describes the use of encryption to secure a secure telecommunications route between parties over an insecure or public network, such as the Internet.

Vulnerability.

Weaknesses in system security procedures, design, implementation, internal controls, and so on could be accidentally triggered or intentionally exploited and violate the systems' security policy (NIST SP 800-33, Withdrawn: August 2018).

Walk-through.

A static analysis technique involves a designer or programmer leading members of the development team and other interested parties through a software product. The participants ask questions and comment on possible errors, violations of development standards, and other problems (IEEE).

Warehouse.

A facility or location where things are stored.

Will.

This word denotes one party's declaration of purpose or intent, not a requirement.

Workflows.

Document and records management consists of the requirements that support the integration and automation of document and records management at each point in a records continuum. These workflows automate the collection, storage, management, editing, removal, routing, and categorization of documents within an organization. They can also enable the ability to communicate these various stages and manage records as part of daily work (NARA's Federal Records Management Council)

Work Products.

The intended result of activities or processes (PDA).

Worst Case.

A set of conditions encompassing upper and lower processing limits and circumstances, including those within standard operating procedures, which pose the most excellent chance of process or product failure when compared to ideal conditions. Such conditions do not necessarily induce product or process failure (FDA).

Written.

In electronic records, "written" means "recorded, or documented on media, paper, electronic or another substrate," from which data may be rendered in a human-readable form (EMA GMP Chapter 4, 2011).

Appendix II
Abbreviations and/or Acronyms

2FA	Two-Factor Authentication
ABA	American Bar Association
ACE	Access-control Entry
ACL	Access Control List
ADP	Automated Data Processing
AES	Advanced Encryption Standard
AGIT	ArbeitsGruppe InformationsTechnologie
AGV	Automated Guidance Vehicle
AI	Artificial Intelligence
AiM	Aid Memoire
AKA	Also Known As
ALCOA	Attributable, Legible, Contemporaneous, Original and Accurate
ALCOA+	ALCOA + Complete, Consistent, Enduring and Available
ANDAs	Abbreviated New Drug Applications
ANSI	American National Standard Institute
API	Active Pharmaceutical Ingredients

APIs	Application Programming Interfaces
ANVISA	Agencia Nacional de Vigilancia Sanitaria (Spanish)
	National Health Surveillance Agency (English)
ASEAN	Association of Southeast Asian Nations
ASN.1	Abstract Syntax Notation One
ASTM	American Society for Testing and Materials
BaaS	Backup as a Service
BCP	Business Continuity Plan
BI	Business Intelligence
BPaaS	Business Process as a Service
CA	Certification Authority
CAPA	Corrective and Preventive Actions
CCPA	California Consumer Privacy Act
CDO	Chief Data Officer
CEFIC	Conseil Européen des Fédérations de l'Industrie Chimique
CFDA	China Food & Drug Administration
CFR	Code of Federal Regulation
CGMP	Current Good Manufacturing Practices
CI	Continuous Improvement
CMC	Chemistry, Manufacturing, and Controls

CNSSI	Committee on National Security Systems Instruction
COBIT	Control Objectives for Information and Related Technologies
ISPE GAMP COP	Groups of ISPE Members with a common interest
CPG	US FDA Compliance Policy Guide
CPU	Central Processing Unit
CPV	Continued Process Verification
CRC	Cyclic Redundancy Check
CRL	Certificate Revocation List
CROs	Contract Research Organizations
CSP	Cloud Service Provider
CSV	Computer Systems Validation
DaaS	Data as a Service
DAC	Discretionary Access Control
DACL	Discretionary Access Control List
DCS	Distributed Control System
DED/D	Data Element Dictionary/Directory
DES	Data Encryption Standard
DFD	Data Flow Diagrams
DI	Data Integrity

DIQbD	Data Integrity/Quality by Design
DIRPP	Data Reliability Implementation Program
DLM	Data Lifecycle Management
DM	Data Marts
DMZ	Website's Demilitarized Zone
DN	Distinguished Name
DoD	Department of Defense
DQ	Design Qualification
DRM	Device Master Record
DRIP	Data Reliability Implementation Program
DSA	Digital Signature Algorithm
DSHEA	Dietary Supplement Health and Education Act
DSS	Digital Signature Standard
DTS	Digital Time-Stamping Service
DW	Data Warehouse
EC	European Commission
ECA	European Compliance Academy
EDMS	Electronic Document Management System
EEA	European Economic Area
EEC	European Economic Community

EFG 11	Die Expertenfachgruppe computergestützte Systeme (Germany expert group for computer systems)
EFS	Encrypting File System
EMA	European Medicines Agency
EMEA	European Medicines Agency
ENISA	European Union Agency for Network and Information Security
ERD	Entity-Relationship Diagrams
ERM	Electronic records management
ERP	Enterprise Resource Planning
ETL	Extract, Transform, and Load
ETSI	European Telecommunications Standards Institute
EU	European Union
EVM	Earned Value Management
FAT	Factory Acceptance Test
FD&C Act	US Food Drug and Cosmetic Act.
FDA	Food and Drug Administration
FIPS	Federal Information Processing Standards
FR	US Federal Register
FRMC	Federal Records Management Council

FSI SID&GP	Russian Federal State Institute of Drugs and Good Practices
FTP	File Transfer Protocol
GAMP	Good Automated Manufacturing Practices
GCP	Good Clinical Practices
GDP	Good Documentation Practices
GDPR	General Data Protection Regulation
GEIP	Good E-records Integrity Practices
GERM	Good Electronic Records Management
GLP	Good Laboratory Practices
GMPs	Good Manufacturing Practices
GXP	Refers to the various good practices regulated by the regulatory authorities. These are Good Clinical Practice (GCP), Good Distribution Practice (GDP), Good Laboratory Practice (GLP), Good Manufacturing Practice (GMP), Good Pharmacovigilance Practice (GPP), and other regulated applications in context. GXP can refer to one specific set of practices or any combination of the GXP.
HIPAA	Health Insurance Portability and Accountability Act
HMA	Heads of Medicines Agencies
HMAC	Hash Message Authentication Code
HMI	Human–Machine Interface
IaaS	Infrastructure as a Service

ICH	International Conference for Harmonization of Technical Requirements for Registration of Pharmaceuticals for Human Use
ICS	Industrial Control System
ID	Identification
I/Os	Inputs and outputs
IEC	International Electrotechnical Commission
IEEE	Institute of Electrical & Electronic Engineers
IIS	Internet Information Services
IMDRF	International Medical Device Regulators Forum
IoT	Internet of things
IRP	Incident Response Plan
ISA	International Society of Automation
ISMS	Information Security Management System
ISO	International Organization for Standardization
ISPE	International Society for Pharmaceutical Engineering
IT	Information Technologies
ITF	Integrated Test Facility
ITIL	IT Infrastructure Library
ITSM	IT service management
KMS	Key Management Service
KPI	Key Performance Indicators

LAN	Local Area Network
LIMS	Laboratory Information Management System
MA	Marketing Authorization
MAC	Mandatory Access Control
MDM	Master Data Management
MFA	Multi-Factor Authentication
MES	Manufacturing Execution System
MHRA	Medicines and Healthcare Products Regulatory Agency (United Kingdom Medicines and Medical Devices Regulatory Agency)
MRA	Mutual Recognition Agreements
MTTR	Mean Time to Repair or Mean time to recovery
MTBF	Mean Time Between Failures
NARA	National Archives and Records Administration
NBS	National Bureau of Standards
NDAs	New Drug Applications
NEMA	National Electrical Manufacturers Association
NIST	National Institutes of Standards and Technology
NMPA	National Medical Products Association (former CFDA).
NoSQL	non-SQL
NTP	Network Time Protocol

OECD	Organization for Economic Co-operation and Development
OMCL	Official Medicines Control Laboratories
OLAs	Operational Level Agreements
OSHA	US Occupational Safety & Health Administration
OTC	Over the Counter
OTS	Off-the-Shelf
P&ID	Process and Instrumentation Drawings
PaaS	Platform as a Service
PAI	Pre-Approval Inspections
PAT	Process Analytical Tools
PDA	Parenteral Drug Association
PFD	Process Flow Diagram
PIC/S	Pharmaceutical Inspection Co-Operation Scheme http://www.picscheme.org/
PIN	Personal Identification Number
PKCS	Public-Key Cryptography Standards
PKI	Public Key Infrastructure
PLC	Programmable Logic Controller
PoLP	Principle of Least Privilege
PQS	Pharmaceutical Quality System

P&ID	Process and Instrumentation Drawing
QA	Quality Assurance
QbD	Quality by Design
QC	Quality Control
QMS	Quality Management System
QP	Qualified Person
RAM	Random Access Memory
RBAC	Role-Based Access Control
R&D	Research and Development
RFP	Request for Proposal
RIPEMD	Race Integrity Primitives Evaluation Message Digest
RTU	Remote Terminal Unit
RU	Regulated User
RWQ	NARA Requirements Working Group
SaaS	Software as a Service
SACL	System Access Control List
SAG	Scientific Archivists Group
SAP	Systems, Applications, and Products
SaaS	Software as a service
SAS	The Statistical Analysis System licensed by the SAS Institute, Inc.

SAT	Site Acceptance Test
SCADA	Supervisory Control and Data Acquisition
SCRF	System Control Audit Review Files
SDLC	Software Development Life Cycle
SHA-1	Secure Hash Algorithm 1
SIDGP	Russia Federal State Institute of Drugs and Good Practices
SIPOC	Suppliers, Inputs, Processes, Outputs, Customers
SLA	Service Level Agreement
SLC	System Lifecycle
SME	Subject Matter Experts
SMART	In the context of objectives, this is the abbreviation of specific, measurable, achievable, relevant, and time-bound related objectives.
SOPs	Standard Operating Procedures
SOX	Sarbanes-Oxley Act
SPC	Statistical Process Control
SQA	Software Quality Assurance
SQE	Software Quality Engineering
SQuaRE	Systems and Software Quality Requirements and Evaluation
SSA	US Social Security Administration

SSL	Secure Sockets Layer
SWEBOK	Software Engineering Body of Knowledge
TGA	Australia Therapeutic Goods Administration
TLS	Transport Layer Security
TRS	Technical Report Series
UCs	Underpinning Contracts
UK	United Kingdom
UPS	Uninterruptable Power Supply
US	United States
US FDA	United States Food and Drug Administration
VPN	Virtual Privates Network
WBS	Work Breakdown Structure
WAN	Wide Area Network
WL	Warning Letter
WLAN	Wireless Local Area Network
WHO	World Health Organization
XaaS	Anything as a Service
XML	Extensible Markup Language
ZGL	Central Office of the Germany Federal States for Health Protection for Drugs and Medical Devices

Appendix III
References

1. *Aide-mémoire of German ZLG regarding EU GMP Annex 11nnex 11*, September 2013.

2. *Aide Memoire (Ref. #: 07121202) of the German ZLG* (Central Authority of the Laender for Health Protection).

3. Alanazi, H., Zaidan, B., Zaidan, A., Jalab, H., Shabbir, M. Al-Nabhani, Y., "New Comparative Study Between DES, 3DES, and AES within Nine Factors," *Journal of Computing*, Vol 2, Issue 3, March 2010, ISSN 2151-9617 (152-157).

4. Amy, L. T., "*Automation Systems for Control and Data Acquisition*," ISA, 1992.

5. Appel, K., "*How Far Does Annex 11 Go Beyond Part 11?*" Pharmaceutical Processing, September 2011.

6. APIC, "*GMPs for APIs: "How to do" Document,*" Version 13, January 2020.

7. APV, "*The APV Guideline "Computerized Systems" based on Annex 11 of the EU-GMP Guideline*", Version 1.0, April 1996.

8. ASTM, E 2500 – 20 *Standard Guide for Specification, Design, and Verification of Pharmaceutical and Biopharmaceutical Manufacturing Systems and Equipment*, 2013.

9. Boogaard, P., Haag, T., Reid, C., Rutherford, M., Wakeham, C., "*Data Integrity*," Pharmaceutical Engineering Special Report, March-April 2016.

10. Breslow, L. (1973). Research in a Strategy for Health Improvement. International Journal of Health Services. https://doi.org/10.2190/422y-u3tg-ma4k-b82a

11. Brown, A., *"Selecting Storage Media for Long-Term Preservation,"* The National Archives, DPGN-02, August 2008.

12. Cappucci, W.; Chris Clark, C.; Goossens, T.; Wyn, S., "ISPE GAMP CoP Annex 11 Interpretation", *Pharmaceutical Engineering*, July/August 2011 CEFIC, "Computer Validation Guide," API Committee of CEFIC, January 2003.

13. CEFIC, *"Practical risk-based guide for managing data integrity,"* April 2022 (Version 2).

14. Center for Technology in Government University at Albany, SUNY, *"Practical Tools for Electronic Records Management and Preservation,"* July 1999.

15. Central Office of the German Federal States for Health Protection for Drugs and Medical Devices (ZLG, Germany)," *Monitoring of Computerized Systems*," (AiM EFG 11), August 2022, (https://www.zlg.de/arzneimittel/deutschland/laendergr emien/expertenfachgruppen/efg-11-kurzportrait).

16. Cloud Service Alliance, *"Cloud Control Matrix,"* Rev 3.0.1, July 2014.

17. Cloud Service Alliance, *"Security Guidance for Critical Areas of Focus in Cloud Computing,"* Rev 3.0, November 2011.

18. Committee on National Security Systems Instruction (CNSSI), *"Glossary,"* CNSSI 4009, September 2022.

19. Commission Directive 91/412/EEC, *Laying down the principles and guidelines of good manufacturing practice for veterinary medicinal products*, July 1991.

20. Commission Directive 95/46/EC *of the European Parliament and of the Council of 24 October 1995 on the protection of individuals about the processing of personal data and on the free movement of such data* http://eur-lex.europa.eu/LexUriServ/LexUriServ.do?uri=CELEX:31995L0046:en:HTML.

21. Commission Directive 2003/94/EC, *laying down the principles and guidelines of good manufacturing practice in respect of medicinal products for human use and investigational medicinal products for human use*, October 2003.

22. Commission Directive 2017/1572, *supplementing Directive 2001/83/EC of the European Parliament and of the Council as regards the principles and guidelines of good manufacturing practice for medicinal products for human use*, September 2017.

23. Council of Europe, *"Handbook on European data protection law,"* December 2013.

24. Churchward, D., *Good Manufacturing Practice (GMP) data integrity: a new look at an old topic*, Part 1 of 3, June 2015.

25. Churchward, D., *Good Manufacturing Practice (GMP) data integrity: a new look at an old topic*, Part 2 of 3, July 2015.

26. Churchward, D., *Good Manufacturing Practice (GMP) data integrity: a new look at an old topic*, Part 3 of 3, August 2015.

27. Churchward, D., *"GMP Compliance and Data Integrity,"* paper presented at the PDA/PIC's Quality and Regulations Conference, Brussels, Belgium, June 2015.

28. Cuddy, B., *"EMA's Guidance on Data Integrity,"* presented at the Indian Pharmaceutical Alliance Annual Congress, Mumbai, India, 23-24 February 2017.

29. Department of Defense (DoD) 8320.1-M-1, *"Data Standardization Procedures,"* April 1998.

30. European Compliance Academy (ECA), *"Deletion of Data: Does it have to be regulated in an SOP?"* June 2019, https://www.gmp-compliance.org/gmp-news/deletion-of-data-does-it-have-to-be-regulated-in-a-sop.

31. ECA, *"Ensuring the data integrity of cloud service providers,"* https://www.it-compliance-group.org/icg_news_7259.html, August 2019.

32. ECA, *"GMP Advisor: The GMP Question & Answers Guide,"* April 2014 (Version 1).

33. ECA, *"GMP, GCP, and GDP Data Governance and Data Integrity,"* Rev 3, December 2022.

34. ECA, *IT Compliance Working Group, Shared Platform and Cloud Services Implications for Information*

Governance and Records Management, http://www.it-compliance-group.org/icg_downloads.html.

35. Eglovitch, J., *"How to Remedy Data Integrity Failures: FDA's Step-by-Step Approach."* The Golden Sheet, October 2015.

36. EMA, *"EMA Questions and answers: Good manufacturing practice Data Integrity,"* August 2016.

37. EMA, *"Guideline on computerised systems and electronic data in clinical trials,"* June 2021.

38. EMA/HMA, *"Good Practice Guide Use Metadata Catalogue Real World Data Sources,"* September 2022 (Draft).

39. EMA/INS/GCP/454280/2010, GCP Inspectors Working Group (GCP IWG), *"Reflection paper on expectations for electronic source data and data transcribed to electronic data collection tools in clinical trials,"* August 2010.

40. EMA/PIC/S, *"Concept paper on revising Annex 11 guidelines on Good Manufacturing Practice for medicinal products – Computerised Systems,"* September 2022.

41. EMA, *"Reflection Paper on the Expectations for Electronic Source Documents Used in Clinical Trials,"* August 2010.

42. European Union Agency for Network and Information Security (ENISA), *"Cloud Security Guide for SMEs,"* April 2015.

43. ETSI, *"CLOUD; Cloud private-sector user recommendations,"* November 2011.

44. ETSI, *"Identification of Cloud user needs,"* ETSI SR 003 381 V2.1.1, February 2016.

45. European Compliance Academy (ECA), *"GMP, GCP and GDP Data Governance and Data Integrity,"* Version 3, December 2022.

46. European Commission (EC), *"General Data Protection Regulation (GDPR),"* January 2012 (Proposed regulation to replace EU Data Protection Directive 95/46/EC).

47. EU *Annex III to Guidance for the Conduct of Good Clinical Practice Inspections Computer Systems*, May 2008. http://ec.europa.eu/health/files/eudralex/vol-10/chap4/annex_iii_to_guidance_for_the_conduct_of_g cp_inspections_-_computer_systems_en.pdf

48. EU OMLC, *"Quality management guideline on management of documents and records,"* January 2016.

49. EU, Questions, and Answers: *Good Manufacturing Practice and Good Distribution Practice, Data Integrity*, August 2016, https://www.ema.europa.eu/en/human-regulatory/research-development/compliance/good-manufacturing-practice/guidance-good-manufacturing-practice-good-distribution-practice-questions-answers#data-integrity-(new-august-2016)-section.

50. EU, Questions and Answers: *Good Manufacturing Practice and Good Distribution Practice, Annex 11*, https://www.ema.europa.eu/en/human-regulatory/research-development/compliance/good-

manufacturing-practice/guidance-good-manufacturing-practice-good-distribution-practice-questions-answers#eu-gmp-guide-annexes:-supplementary-requirements:-annex-11:-computerised-systems-section.

51. EudraLex, The Rules Governing Medicinal Products in the European Union, Volume 4, "*EU Guidelines to Good Manufacturing Practice, Medicinal Products for Human and Veterinary Use Part 1, Annex 11 - Computerized Systems,*" June 2011. http://ec.europa.eu/health/files/eudralex/vol-4/annex11_01-2011_en.pdf.

52. EudraLex, The Rules Governing Medicinal Products in the European Union, Volume 4, "*EU Guidelines to Good Manufacturing Practice, Medicinal Products for Human and Veterinary Use, Annex 15 – Validation and Qualification*", October 2015.

53. EudraLex, The Rules Governing Medicinal Products in the European Union, Volume 4, "*EU Guidelines to Good Manufacturing Practice, Medicinal Products for Human and Veterinary Use,*" Annex 16 - Certification by a Qualified Person and Batch Release, April 2016.

54. EudraLex. *The Rules Governing Medicinal Products in the European Union, Volume 4, "EU Guidelines for Good Manufacturing Practices for Medicinal Products for Human and Veterinary Use, Annex 20 - Quality Risk Management*", February 2008.

55. EudraLex, *The Rules Governing Medicinal Products in the European Union, Volume 4, "EU Guidelines to Good Manufacturing Practice, Medicinal Products for Human and Veterinary Use – Glossary,*" February 2013.

56. EudraLex, *The Rule Governing Medicinal Products in the European Union, Volume 4, EU Guidelines for Good Manufacturing Practices for Medicinal Products for Human and Veterinary Use, Part 1, Chapter 2 – Personnel*", February 2014.

57. EudraLex, *The Rules Governing Medicinal Products in the European Union Volume 4, Good Manufacturing Practice, Medicinal Products for Human and Veterinary Use, Chapter 3: Premises and Equipment*, March 2015.

58. EudraLex, *The Rules Governing Medicinal Products in the European Union Volume 4, Good Manufacturing Practice, Medicinal Products for Human and Veterinary Use, Chapter 4: Documentation*, June 2011.

59. EudraLex, *The Rules Governing Medicinal Products in the European Union Volume 4, Good Manufacturing Practice, Medicinal Products for Human and Veterinary Use, Chapter 7: Outsourced Activities*, January 2013.

60. EudraLex, *The Rule Governing Medicinal Products in the European Union, Volume 4 EU Good Manufacturing Practice (GMP) Medicinal Products for Human and Veterinary Use, Chapter 9: Self Inspections*, 2001.

61. European Agencies Agency, Questions and Answers: Good manufacturing practice, "*EU GMP guide annexes: Supplementary requirements: Annex 11: Computerised systems*",
http://www.ema.europa.eu/ema/index.jsp?curl=pages/regulation/general/gmp_q_a.jsp&mid=WC0b01ac058006e06c#section8.

62. Network of official medicines control laboratories (OMLC), *"Validation of Computerised Systems – Core Document,"* PA/PH/OMCL (08) 69 R7, July 2018, (http://www.edqm.eu/medias/fichiers/Validation_of_Computerised_Systems_Core_Document.pdf).

63. Network of official medicines control laboratories (OMLC), *"Validation of Computerised Systems – Annex 2: Validation of Databases (DB), Laboratory Information Management Systems (LIMS) and Electronic Laboratory Notebooks (ELN),"* PA/PH/OMCL (08) 88 R, July 2009.

64. European Medicines Agency (EMA), *"Guidance on good manufacturing practice and distribution practice: Questions and answers - Data Integrity,"* August 2016.

65. European Medicines Agency (EMEA), "*Q&A: Good Manufacturing Practices (GMP)*," February 2011.

66. EWSolutions. (2021, April 14). *"Remain focused on data management fundamentals."* https://www.ewsolutions.com/remain-focused-on-data-management-fundamentals/.

67. Federal Information Processing Standards (FIPS), Publication 11-3, *"American National Dictionary for Information Systems,"* Windrowed, July 1979.

68. FRMC Requirements Working Group, *"IT Tiered Requirements for Records Management,"* May 2023 (Version 1).

69. GAMP® *Good Practice Guide: A Risk-based Approach to Compliant Electronic Records and Signatures*, 2005.

70. GAMP® *Good Practice Guide: Electronic Data Archiving*, 2007.

71. GAMP® *Good Practice Guide: Global Information Systems Control and Compliance - Appendix 2 – Data Management Considerations*, 2005.

72. GAMP® *Good Practice Guide: IT Control and Compliance, International Society of Pharmaceutical Engineering*, Tampa, FL, 2005.

73. GAMP® *Good Practice Guide: Risk-Based Approach to Operation of GXP Computerized Systems*, 2010.

74. GAMP®/ISPE, *A Risk-Based Approach to Compliant GxP Computerized Systems*, International Society for Pharmaceutical Engineering (ISPE), Fifth Edition, July 2022.

75. GAMP®/ISPE, "*Risk Assessment for Use of Automated Systems Supporting Manufacturing Processes – Part 2 – Risk to Records*," Pharmaceutical Engineering, Vol. 23 No. 6, November/December 2003.

76. GAMP®/ISPE, *Records and Data Integrity Guide*, 2017.

77. GAMP®/ISPE, *Risk Assessment for Automated Systems Supporting Manufacturing Process -- Functional Risk*, Pharmaceutical Engineering, May/Jun 2003.

78. GHTF, "*Implementation of risk management principles and activities within a Quality Management System*," May 2005.

79. GMP Journal, "Q&As on Annex 11 (1-4) at the Computer Validation in Mannheim, Germany, in June 2011", Issue 7, October/November 2011.

80. GMP Journal, *"Q&As on Annex 11 (5-11) at the Computer Validation in Mannheim, Germany, in June 2011"*, Issue 8, April/May 2012.

81. GMP Journal, *"Q&As on Annex 11 (12-16) at the Computer Validation in Mannheim, Germany, in June 2011"*, Issue 9, October/November 2012.

82. George J. Grigonis, Jr., Edward J. Subak, Jr., and Michael L. Wyrick, *"Validation Key Practices for Computer Systems Used in Regulated Operations,"* Pharmaceutical Technology, pages 74-98, June 1997.

83. Graham, L., *"Compliance matters, Good laboratory practice,"* Blog MHRA Inspectorate, September 2015.

84. Gupta, A., *"What Is Data Integrity?"* www.linkedin.com, https://www.linkedin.com/pulse/what-data-integrity-ankur-gupta/?trackingId=ZNv6qeB%2FQKydY5etsJM6fw%3D%3D. Accessed 24 July 2022.

85. Hart, S., *"Data Integrity: TGA Expectations,"* paper presented at the PDA conference, Tel Aviv, Israel, July 2015.

86. Heads of Medicines Agencies (HMA), *"Data Quality Framework EU Medicines Regulation,"* October 2023

87. Health Canada, *"Good Manufacturing Practices (GMP) Guidelines for Active Pharmaceutical Ingredients*

(APIs"), *GUI-0104*, *C.02.05*, *Interpretation #15*, February 2022.

88. Health Canada, *"Good Manufacturing Practices (GMP) Guidelines"* - 2018 Edition, Version 3 (GUI-0001).

89. HMA/EMA, *"Data Quality Framework E.U. Medicines Regulation,"* September 2022 (Draft). https://www.ema.europa.eu/en/documents/regulatory-procedural-guideline/data-quality-framework-eu-medicines-regulation_en.pdf.

90. ICH Harmonized Tripartite Guideline, *"Good Manufacturing Practice Guidance for Active Pharmaceutical Ingredients, Q7"*, November 2000.

91. ICH Harmonized Tripartite Guideline, *"Quality Risk Management, Q9"*, January 2023.

92. ICH Harmonized Tripartite Guideline, *"Pharmaceutical Quality Systems, Q10"*, June 2008.

93. ICH Harmonized Tripartite Guideline, *"Guideline to Good Clinical Practice"* E6(R3) May 2023 (Draft).

94. IDA Programme of the European Commission, *"Model Requirements for the Management of Electronic Records"*, www.cornwell.co.uk/moreq.html, October 2002.

95. IEEE, *"Guide to the Software Engineering Body of Knowledge,"* Rev 3.0, 2014.

96. IPEC, *"Data integrity for pharmaceutical grade excipients,"* April 2020.

97. ISO 9001:2015, *"Quality Management Systems – Requirements."*

98. ISO 11799: 2003(E), *"Information and documentation — Document storage requirements for archive and library materials."*

99. ISO 12207:1995[10]*"Information technology – Software life cycle processes."*

100. ISO 13485:2012, *"Medical devices -- Quality management systems -- Requirements for regulatory purposes."*

101. ISO 8601:2004, *"Data elements and interchange formats - Information interchange - Representation of dates and times."*

102. ISO/IEC 17025, *"General requirements for the competence of testing and calibration laboratories,"* November 2017.

103. ISO/IEC 1799:2005, *"Information technology — Security techniques — Code of practice for information security management."*

104. ISO/IEC 27001: 2022, *"Information technology— Security techniques — Information security management systems — Requirements."*

105. ISPE GAMP Forum, *"Risk Assessment for Automated Systems Supporting Manufacturing Processes – Part 2 – Risk to Records,"* Pharmaceutical Engineering, Vol. 23, No. 6, November/December 2003.

106. ISPE, "Regulatory Framework – EMEA," Dr. Kate McCormick, 2009.

---

[10] *Note*: The 1995 revision is not the most recent version.

107. ISPE, *"Regulatory Framework – PIC/S and ICH,"* Dr. Kate McCormick, 2009.

108. ISPE GAMP®: *"A Risk Approach to Compliant GxP Computerized Systems,"* International Society for Pharmaceutical Engineering (ISPE), Fifth Edition, February 2008.

109. ISPE/PDA, *"Good Practice and Compliance for Electronic Records and Signatures. Part 1 Good Electronic Records Management (GERM)".* July 2002.

110. Information Security Committee, American Bar Association (ABA), "Digital Signature Guidelines," August 1996.

111. IT Infrastructure Library (ITIL), *"The Official Introduction to the ITIL Service Lifecycle,"* 2007.

112. ITIL Service Design, Section 5.2 - Management of Data and Information, 2011 Edition.

113. Journal for GMP and Regulatory Affairs, *"Q&As on Annex 11"*, Issue 8, April/May 2012.

114. Kane, A., the sidebar to *"Designing Optimized Formulations,"* Pharmaceutical Technology (4) 2017.

115. López, O., *"21 CFR Part 11: Complete Guide to International Computer Validation Compliance for the Pharmaceutical Industry,"* CRC, Boca Raton, Florida, 1st ed., 2004.

116. López, O., *"A Computer Data Integrity Compliance Model,"* Pharmaceutical Engineering, Vol. 35, No. 2, March/April 2015.

117.   López, O., *"A Historical View of 21 CFR 211.68,"* Journal of GxP Compliance, Vol. 15 No. 2, May 2013.

118.   López, O., *"Annex 11: Progress in EU Computer Systems Guidelines,"* Pharmaceutical Technology Europe, Vol. 23, No. 6 (June), 2011. http://www.pharmtech.com/pharmtech/article/articleDetail.jsp?id=725378.

119.   López, O., *"Annex 11 and 21 CFR Part 11: Comparisons for International Compliance,"* MasterCotrol, January 2012.

120.   López, O., *"An Easy to Understand Guide to Annex 11,"* Premier Validation, Cork, Ireland, 2011, http://www.askaboutvalidation.com/1938-an-easy-to-understand-guide-to-annex-11.

121.   López, O., *"APIC," in Data Integrity in Pharmaceutical and Medical Devices Regulation Operations,* (CRC Press Boca Raton, FL, 1st ed., 2017), pp. 55-56.

122.   López, O., *"Are Data Quality and ALCOA attributes equivalent?"* GMP Journal, Issue #38, November 2023.

123.   López, O., *"CGMP E-Records Risk Assessments,"* Journal of GxP Compliance, Vol. 22, Issue 5, September 2018.

124.   López, O., *"CGMP E-records Risk Management,"* in E-records Integrity Requirements, Eds. (Nova Science Publisher, Inc., NY, 1st ed., 2022), pp. 61-68.

125.   López, O., *"Comparison of Health Authorities Data Integrity Expectations,"* paper presented at the 4th

Annual Data Integrity Validation, Cambridge, MA, 15-16 August 2018.

126. López, O., *"Computer Infrastructure Qualification for FDA Regulated Industries,"* PDA and DHI Publishing, LLC. 2006.

127. López, O., *"Computer Technologies Security Part I - Key Points in the Contained Domain,"* Sue Horwood Publishing Limited, West Sussex, United Kingdom, ISBN 1-904282-17-2, 2002.

128. López, O., *"Computer Systems Validation,"* in *Encyclopedia of Pharmaceutical Science and Technology,* Fourth Edition, Taylor and Francis: New York, Published online: 23 Aug 2013; 615-619.

129. López, O., "Control of Records," in Pharmaceutical and Medical Devices Manufacturing Computer Systems Validation (Routledge/Productivity Press, New York, NY, 1st ed., 2018), pp. 138-140.

130. López, O., *"Data Integrity and your E-recs During Processing,"* LinkedIn, July 2017.

131. López, O., *"Data Integrity Expectations of EU GMP Inspectors,"* Pharmaceutical Engineering Data Integrity, Expectations of EU GMP Inspectors. *"Data Lifecycle and its Integrity,* (Book Publishing Pros, Los Angeles, CA, 1st ed, 2024), September 2024.

132. López, O., *"Data Integrity in Pharmaceutical and Medical Devices Regulation Operations: Best Practices Guide to Electronic Records Compliance,"* CRC Press, Boca Ratón, FL, 2017.

133. López, O., *"Data Integrity in Manufacturing Environments,"* in Manufacturing Systems: Progress and Future Directions, M. Arezki Mellal, Eds. (Nova Science Publishers, Hauppauge, NY, 1st ed., 2021).

134. López, O., *"Defining and Managing Raw Manufacturing Data,"* Pharmaceutical Technology Europe, Volume 31 Number 6, June 2019, p19-25.

135. López, O., *"Digital Date and Time Stamps,"* LinkedIn, June 2017.

136. López, O., *"Electronic Records Controls: Records Retained by Computer Storage,"* in Data Integrity in Pharmaceutical and Medical Devices Regulation Operations, (CRC Press Boca Raton, FL, 1st ed., 2017), pp. 169-177.

137. López, O., *"Electronic Records Governance,"* in Data Integrity in Pharmaceutical and Medical Devices Regulation Operations, Eds. (Taylor & Francis Group, Boca Ratón, FL, 1st ed., 2017), pp. 133-141.López, O., "Electronic Records Integrity in the Data Warehouse Environments," Journal of Validation Technology, Vol. 22, No. 2, April 2006.

138. López, O., *"Electronic Records Lifecycle,"* Journal of GxP Compliance, Vol. 9, No. 4, December 2015.

139. López, O., *"Electronic Records Life Cycle,"* in Data Integrity in Pharmaceutical and Medical Devices Regulation Operations (CRC Press, Boca Raton, FL, 1st ed., 2017), pp. 39-45.

140. López, O., "*Ensuring the Integrity of Electronic Health Records*," Taylor & Francis Group, Boca Ratón, FL, 2021.

141. López, O., "*E-records Integrity Requirements*," Nova Science Publisher, Inc., NY, 1st ed., 2022.

142. López, O., "*E-records Lifecycle Revisited*," in Ensuring the Integrity of Electronic Health Records, López, O, Eds. (Routledge, Boca Ratón, FL, 1st ed., 2021), pp 7-15.

143. López, O., "*E-records Vulnerabilities*," in E-records Integrity Requirements, López, O., Eds. (Nova Science Publisher, Inc., New York, NY, 1st ed., 2022), pp. 147-158.

144. López, O., "*EU Annex 11 and Data Integrity: Designing Data Integrity into your Practices*," paper presented at the 2014 ISPE Annual Meeting, Las Vegas, Nevada, 12-15 October 2014.

145. López, O., "*EU Annex 11 and the Integrity of Erecs*", Journal of GxP Compliance, Volume 18 Number 2, May 2014.

146. López, O., "*EU Annex 11 – Changes to Computer Systems Guidelines in the EU*", LinkedIn, August 2017.

147. López, O., "*EU Annex 11 Guide to Computer Validation Compliance for the Worldwide Health Agency GMP*," CRC, Boca Raton, Florida, 1st ed., March 2015.

148. López, O., "*Generation, Capture, and Recording of Raw Data*," in E-records Integrity Requirements, Eds.

346

(Nova Science Publisher, Inc., NY, 1st ed., 2022), pp. 79-90.

149. López, O., *"Introduction to Data Quality,"* Journal of Validation Technology, April 2020.

150. López, O., *"Maintaining the Validated State in Computer Systems."* Journal of GxP Compliance, Vol. 17 No. 2, August 2013.

151. López, O., *"Maxims Electronic Records Integrity,"* Pharmaceutical Technology, Vol. 43, No. 6, June 2019.

152. López, O., "*Metadata,*" in E-records Integrity Requirements, Eds. (Nova Science Publisher, Inc., NY, 1st ed., 2022), pp. 129-137.

153. López, O., *"Operational Checks,"* in 21 CFR Part 11: Complete Guide to International Computer Validation Compliance for the Pharmaceutical Industry, Eds. (Interpharm/CRC, Boca Raton, Florida, 1st ed., 2004).

154. López, O., "Overview of Technologies Supporting Security Requirements in 21 CFR Part 11 – Part I," Pharmaceutical Technology, February 2002.

155. López, O., *"Overview of Technologies Supporting Security Requirements in 21 CFR Part 11 – Part II,"* Pharmaceutical Technology, March 2002.

156. López, O., "Pharmaceutical and Medical Devices Manufacturing Computer Systems Validation," CRC Press, September 2018.

157. López, O., *"Points to consider when validating Big Data Environments,"* Journal of Validation Technology, October 2019.

347

158. López, O., *"Records Retention on Raw Data,"* in Data Integrity in Pharmaceutical and Medical Devices Regulation Operations, (CRC Press Boca Raton, FL, 1st ed., 2017), pp. 55-56.

159. López, O., *"Regulations and Regulatory Guidelines of Computer Systems in Drug Manufacturing 25 Years Later,"* Pharmaceutical Engineering, Vol. 33, No. 4, July/August 2013.

160. López, O., *"Requirements Management,"* Journal of Validation Technology, May 2013.

161. López, O., *"Requirements for Electronic Records Contained in 21 CFR 211,"* Pharmaceutical Technology, Vol. 36, No. 7, July 208.

162. López, O., *"Reporting,"* in E-records Integrity Requirements, D. Amorosa, Eds. (Nova Science Publisher, Inc., New York, NY, 1st ed., 2022), pp. 139-146.

163. López, O., *"Technologies Supporting Electronic Records Integrity – Part I,"* GXP Journal Articles, Vol. 21, No. 5, May 2017.

164. López, O., *"Technologies Supporting Electronic Records Integrity Part II,"* GXP Journal Articles, Vol. 21, No. 5, September 2017.

165. López, O., *"The Importance of Computer Systems I/Os Accuracy Checks,"* GxP Lifeline, June 2012.

166. López, O., *"Trustworthy Computer Systems,"* Journal of GxP Compliance, Vol. 19, No. 2, July 2015.

167. López, O., *"Vulnerabilities of E-records,"* Ensuring the Integrity of Electronic Health Records, Eds. (Routledge, Boca Ratón, FL, 1st ed., 2021), pp. 63-74.

168. McDowall, R.D., *"Comparison of FDA and EU Regulations for Audit Trails,"* Scientific Computing, January 2014.

169. McDowall, R.D., *"Computer Validation: Do All Roads Lead to Annex 11?",* Spectroscopy 29(12), December 2014.

170. McDowall, R.D., *"Data Quality and Data Integrity Are the Same. Wrong!,"* Spectroscopy, Vol 34 Issue 11, November 2019, pages 22-29.

171. McDowall, R.D., *"Ensuring Data Integrity in a Regulated Environment,"* Scientific Computing, March/April 2011.

172. McDowall, R.D., *"Maintaining Laboratory Computer Validation - How to Conduct Periodic Reviews?",* European Compliance Academy (ECA), GMP News, April 2012, http://www.gmp-compliance.org/pa4.cgi?src=eca_new_news_print_data.htm&nr=3085.

173. McDowall, R.D., *"The New GMP Annex 11 and Chapter 4 is Europe's Answer to Part 11",* European Compliance Academy (ECA), GMP News, January 2011, http://www.gmp-compliance.org/eca_news_2381_6886,6885,6738,6739,6934.html.

174. McGuire, M., *"Defining Your Data Strategy: Balancing Offense and Defense,"* December 2023.

https://www.dataedification.com/p/defining-your-data-strategy-balancing

175.   Mell, P., and Grance, T., "*The NIST Definition of Cloud Computing*", NIST Special Publication 800-145 National Institute of Standards and Technology, Gaithersburg, Maryland, September 2011.

176.   MHRA and FDA Join paper, "*Data Integrity in Global Clinical Trials*," December 2020.

177.   MHRA, "*GMP/GDP Consultative Committee Note of Meeting*," October 2015, (https://www.gov.uk/government/uploads/system/uploads/attachment_data/file/483846/GMP-GDP_CC_minutes_Oct_2015_FINAL.pdf).

178.   MHRA, "*Good Manufacturing Practice (GMP) data integrity: a new look at an old topic, part 1*," June 2015, https://mhrainspectorate.blog.gov.uk/2015/06/25/good-manufacturing-practice-gmp-data-integrity-a-new-look-at-an-old-topic-part-1/.

179.   MHRA, "*GxP Data Integrity Guidance and Definitions*," March 2018.

180.   MHRA, "*Good Laboratory Practice: Guidance on Archiving,*" March 2006.

181.   MHRA, "*MHRA expectation regarding self-inspection and data integrity*," December 2013, (https://webarchive.nationalarchives.gov.uk/ukgwa/20140507015402/http://www.mhra.gov.uk/Howweregulate/Medicines/Inspectionandstandards/GoodManufacturingPractice/News/CON355490).

350

182. United Kingdom Medicines and Healthcare Products Regulatory Agency (MHRA), *"GxP Data Integrity Guidance and Definitions,"* March 2018.

183. Murphy, L., *"How to make the business case for data quality & data governance Initiative,"* February 2020, https://www.linkedin.com/pulse/how-make-business-case-data-quality-governance-leo-murphy/?trackingId=78vWhB34RJyL8KnY4zA29w%3D%3D.

184. NARA, *"Records Management Guidance for Agencies Implementing Electronic Signature Technologies,"* October 2000.

185. NARA, *"Universal Electronic Records Management (ERM) Requirements,"* Version 3.0, June 2023.

186. National Medical Products Association (NMPA (former CFDA)), *"Drug Data Management Practices Guidance,"* December 2020.

187. National Health Surveillance Agency – ANVISA, *"Guide for Computer Systems Validation,"* April 2020.

188. National Information Standards Organization, https://www.niso.org/.

189. NIST, *"An Introduction to Computer Security: The NIST Handbook"*, Chapter 6, Computer Security Risk Management (Special Publication 800-12), June 2017.

190. NIST, *"Guidelines for Media Sanitization"* (Special Publication 800- 88r1), December 2014.

191. NIST, *"Managing Information Security Risk"* (Special Publication 800-39), March 2011.

192. NIST, *"Recommendation for Key Management, Part 1: General"*, (Special Publication 800-57 Part 1 Rev 5), May 2020.

193. NIST, *"Recommendation for Key Management: Part 2 – Best Practices for Key Management Organizations,"* (Special Publication 800-57 Part 2 Rev 1), May 2019.

194. NIST, *"Systems Security Engineering: Considerations for a Multidisciplinary Approach in the Engineering of Trustworthy Secure Systems,"* (Special Publication 800-160 Vol 1), March 2018.

195. NIST, *"Underlying Technical Models for Information Technology Security,"* December 2001, (Special Publication 800-33, withdrawn: August 2018).

196. NIST, *"Validating the Integrity of Computing Devices,"* SP 1800-34, December 2022.

197. OECD (2021), GLP Data Integrity, OECD Series on Principles of Good Laboratory Practice and Compliance Monitoring, No. 22, OECD Publishing, Paris, https://doi.org/10.1787/45779212-en..

198. OECD, *"Application of GLP of the Working Group on GLP,'* April 2021.

199. OECD, *"The Application of GLP Principles to Computerized Systems,"* OECD Guidance Document, November 2022.

200. Offutt, J., *"Quality Attributes of Web Software Applications,"* IEEE Software, March/April 2002, pp. 25-32.

201.   PDA, Technical Report No. 31, *"Validation and Qualification of Computerized Laboratory Data Acquisition Systems,"* PDA Journal of Pharmaceutical Science and Technology, September 1999, Vol. 53, No. 4, Section 4.5.

202.   PDA, Technical Report No. 32, *"Auditing of Supplier Providing Computer Products and Services for Regulated Pharmaceutical Operations,"* PDA Journal of Pharmaceutical Science and Technology, Sep/Oct 2004, Release 2.0, Vol. 58 No. 5.

203.   PE 009-16, *"Guide to Good Manufacturing Practice for Medicinal Products Annexes,"* Pharmaceutical Inspection Co-operation Scheme (PIC/S), February 2022

204.   PI 011-3. *"Good Practices for Computerised Systems in Regulated "GXP" Environments,"* Pharmaceutical Inspection Co-operation Scheme (PIC/S), September 2007.

205.   PI 041-1, *"Good Practice for Data Management and Integrity in Regulated GMP/GDP Environments,"* Pharmaceutical Inspection Co-operation Scheme (PIC/S), July 2021.

206.   Pressman, Roger S., *"Software Engineering – A Practitioner's Approach"*, McGraw-Hill, 2010.

207.   Roemer, M., *"New Annex 11: Enabling Innovation,"* Pharmaceutical Technology, June 2011.

208.   Russian Federal State Institute of Drugs and Good Practices (FSI SID&GP), *"Data Integrity and Validation of Computerized Systems (Rev 1), July 2022.*

209.   Safe Harbor US –*EU Agreement on Meeting Directive*   *95/46/EC*
http://www.export.gov/safeharbor/index.asp.

210.   Sampson, K., "*Data Integrity,*" Update, Issue 6, pp. 6-10   (2014). http://www.nxtbook.com/ygsreprints/FDLI/g46125_fdli _novdec2014/index.php#/0.

211.   Scientific Archivists Group (SAG), "*A Guide to Archiving of Electronic Records,*" February 2014.

212.   Schmitt, S., "*Data Integrity*", Pharmaceutical Technology, Volume 38 Number 7, July 2014.

213.   Schmitt, S., "*Data Integrity - FDA and Global Regulatory Guidance,*" IVT, October 2014.

214.   Stenbraten, A., "*Cost-effective Compliance: Practical Solutions for Computerised Systems,*" paper presented at the ISPE Brussels Conference, GAMP – Cost Effective Compliance, 2011-09-19/20.

215.   Stokes, D., "*Compliant Cloud Computing – Managing the Risks,*" Pharmaceutical Engineering, 33 (4) 1 - 11, 2013.

216.   Stokes, T., "*Management's View to Controlling Computer Systems,*" GMP REVIEW, Vol 10 No 2, JULY 2011.

217.   Syncsort Editors, "*Data Integrity vs. Data Quality: How   Are   They   Different?*" https://blog.syncsort.com/2019/01/data-quality/data-integrity-vs-data-quality-different/, January 2019.

218. Australia TGA, *Australian Code of Good Manufacturing Practice Human Blood and Blood Components, Human Tissues and Human Cellular Therapy Products*, April 2013.

219. Australia TGA, "*Data Management and Data Integrity (DMDI),*" April 2017, https://www.tga.gov.au/data-management-and-data-integrity-dmdi.

220. Techopedia.com, "*What is Data Loading?*", https://www.techopedia.com/definition/25329/data-loading#:~:text=Explains%20Data%20Loading-,What%20Does%20Data%20Loading%20Mean%3F,da ta%20storage%20or%20processing%20utility.

221. UK Government, "*The Data Lifecycle,*" in the Government Data Quality Framework, https://www.gov.uk/government/publications/the-government-data-quality-framework/the-government-data-quality-framework#The-Data-Lifecycle.

222. US FDA, 21 CFR Part 11, "*Electronic Records; Electronic Signatures; Final Rule.*" Federal Register Vol. 62, No. 54, 13429, March 1997.

223. US FDA 21 CFR Part 58, *Good Laboratory Practice for Non-Clinical Laboratory Studies*.

224. US FDA 21 CFR Part 110, Current Good Manufacturing Practice in Manufacturing, Packing, or Holding Human Food.

225. US FDA 21 CFR Part 211, *Current Good Manufacturing Practice for Finished Pharmaceuticals*, December 2007.

226. US FDA 21 CFR Part 312, *Investigational New Drug Application.*

227. US FDA 21 CFR Part 606, *Current Good Manufacturing Practice for Blood and Blood Components.*

228. US FDA 21 CFR Part 803, *Medical Device Reporting.*

229. US FDA 21 CFR 1271, *Human Cells, Tissues, and Cellular and Tissue-Based Products.*

230. US FDA, "*CPG Section 425.100 - Computerized Drug Processing; CGMP Applicability to Hardware and Software (CPG 7132a.11),*" September 1987.

231. US FDA, "CPG Section 425.200 - Computerized Drug Processing; Vendor Responsibility (CPG 7132a.12)," September 1987.

232. US FDA, "*CPG Section 425.300 - Computerized Drug Processing; Source Code for Process Control Application Programs (CPG 7132a.15),*" April 1987.

233. US FDA, "*CPG Section 425.400 - Computerized Drug Processing; Input/Output Checking (CPG 7132a.07),*" September 1987.

234. US FDA, "CPG Section 425.500 Computerized Drug Processing; Identification of 'Persons' on Batch Production and Control Records (CPG 7132a.08)," September 1987

235. US FDA CDER, "*Artificial Intelligence in Drug Manufacturing,*" March 2023.

236. US FDA, *"Data Integrity and Compliance with Drug CGMP - Questions & Answers - Guidance for Industry,"* December 2018.

237. US FDA, *"Electronic Systems, Electronic Records, and Electronic Signatures in Clinical Investigations Questions and Answers Guidance for Industry,"* March 2023 (Draft).

238. US FDA, *"FDA PAI Compliance Program Guidance, CPG 7346.832, Compliance Program Manual",* May 2010, http://www.ipqpubs.com/wp-content/uploads/2010/05/FDA_CPGM_7346.832.pdf.

239. US FDA, *"General Principles of Software Validation; Final Guidance for Industry and FDA Staff,"* CDRH and CBER, January 2002.

240. US FDA, *"Guidance for Industry: Blood Establishment Computer System Validation in the User's Facility",* April 2013.

241. US FDA, *"Guidance for Industry Computerized Systems Used in Clinical Investigations,"* May 2010.

242. US FDA, *"Guidance for Industry: Contract Manufacturing Arrangements for Drugs: Quality Agreements,"* November 2016.

243. US FDA, *"Guidance for Industry: Electronic Records; Electronic Signatures — Scope and Application,"* August 2003.

244. US FDA, *"Guidance for Industry: Electronic Source Data in Clinical Investigations,"* September 2013.

245. US FDA, *"Guidance for Industry - Process Validation: General Principles and Practices,"* January 2011.

246. US FDA, *"Guidance for Industry - Use of Electronic Health Record Data in Clinical Investigation,"* July 2018.

247. US FDA, *"Guide to Inspection of Computerized Systems in the Food Processing Industry,"* April 2003.

248. Veregin, H., *"Data Quality Parameters,"* Geographical Information Systems, 1999.

249. Vibbert, J.M., *"The Internet of Things: Data Protection and Data Security,"* Global Environment Information Law Journal, Volume 7 Issue 3, Spring 2016.

250. Wechsler, J., *"Data Integrity Key to GMP Compliance,"* Pharmaceutical Technology, Volume 38, Issue 9, September 2014.

251. *WHO Guideline on data integrity.* In: WHO Expert Committee on Specifications for Pharmaceutical Preparations: fifty-fifth report. WHO Technical Report Series No. 1033, Annex 4. Geneva: World Health Organization; 2021 data(https://www.who.int/publications/m/item/annex-4-trs-1033).

252. WHO, Technical Report Series No. 981, Annex 2, *"WHO Guidelines on Quality Risk Management"*, 2013.

253. WHO (TRS 996 Annex 5), *"Designing and validating systems to assure data quality and*

reliability," Guidance on sound data and record management practices, 2016, pp. 183-186. Note: This guidance document was replaced by the WHO Guideline on Data Integrity (TRS No.1033, Annex 4) in March 2021.

254. WHO Expert Committee on Specifications for Pharmaceutical Preparations, fortieth report. *Appendix 5: Validation of computerized systems. Geneva: World Health Organization; 2006: Annex 4 (WHO Technical Report Series, No. 937*; http://apps.who.int/medicinedocs/documents/s20108en/ s20108en.pdf).

255. Wingate, G., "*Validating Automated Manufacturing and Laboratory Applications: Putting Principles into Practice*," Taylor & Francis, 1997.

256. Yves, S., "*New Annex 11, Evolution and Consequences*", www.pharma-mag.com, January/February, 2012.

Appendix IV
Data reliability through various standards and frameworks

Introduction.

Data is considered reliable if it provides a complete and accurate representation of subsequent transactions or activities and can be relied upon during these transactions or activities. This reliability is crucial for informed decision-making.

These attributes ensure that data is trustworthy for decision-making, analysis, or the development of machine learning models. Reliable data, which is free from errors, inconsistencies, and biases, and consistently reflects the actual state of the phenomena or systems being measured, is crucial for these processes.

Ensuring data reliability is not just a technical requirement; it is foundational for building trust in data-driven processes and systems.

Data Reliability Standards and Frameworks.

This section discusses the reliability of data regarding various standards and frameworks.

ISO/IEC 25012:2008.

ISO/IEC 25012, titled "Data Quality Model," is a data quality standard that provides a comprehensive framework for defining and evaluating data quality characteristics, including reliability.

This standard, an element of the Systems and Software Engineering -- Systems and Software Quality Requirements and Evaluation (SQuaRE), https://www.linkedin.com/pulse/software-product-quality-requirements-evaluation-orlando-lopez-a9zte/?trackingId=SXLR8xfsTdqspu836X1HdQ%3D%3D, provides a framework for evaluating data quality.

This standard defines data reliability as the extent to which data is available and accessible when required, along with the confidence level in its accuracy and correctness.

Data reliability ensures that the data we work with is trustworthy and dependable. It is about ensuring that the data is there when we need it and that we can have confidence in its accuracy and correctness. This definition emphasizes the importance of data not only being present and accessible but also reliable and accurate for its intended use, which is crucial for our daily work.

ISO/IEC 27001:2022.

ISO/IEC 27001, titled "Information Security Management", is an information security management system (ISMS) standard. While it does not explicitly define "data reliability," data reliability is implied as part of ensuring the overall security and trustworthiness of data within an organization.

Within the context of ISO/IEC 27001, data reliability refers to the assurance that data is accurate, consistent, and readily available when needed. It also involves implementing controls and procedures to ensure the integrity and availability of data, as well as mechanisms for monitoring and managing data throughout its lifecycle to maintain its reliability. This definition underscores the practical application of data reliability in ensuring the overall security and trustworthiness of data within an organization.

ISO 9001:2015.

ISO 9001, titled "Quality Management Systems," emphasizes ensuring data reliability in quality management systems (QMS). While it does not explicitly define "data reliability," it emphasizes the quality and reliability of processes and outputs, including data.

Data reliability within ISO 9001 is not just a technical term but a key driver for maintaining high-quality products and services. It ensures data is collected, stored, processed, and communicated effectively and accurately to support organizational objectives. This alignment underscores the importance of implementing controls, procedures, and documentation to ensure that data is reliable and can be trusted for making informed decisions and improving organizational processes.

COBIT

Control Objectives for Information and Related Technologies (COBIT) is a framework for governing and managing enterprise IT. While it doesn't explicitly define "data reliability," it includes principles and guidelines for ensuring data reliability, such as data governance, management, and control contributing to reliability.

Within COBIT, data reliability can be understood as the extent to which data can be trusted to be accurate, consistent, and available when needed to support business processes and decision-making. This includes ensuring data integrity, completeness, and timeliness throughout its lifecycle.

Specifically, COBIT emphasizes the following aspects related to data reliability:

- Data Governance involves establishing policies, procedures, and responsibilities for managing and controlling data to ensure reliability and quality.

- Data Quality Management involves implementing processes and controls to monitor and improve data quality, including measures to address data accuracy, completeness, consistency, and timeliness.

- Data Security: Protecting data from unauthorized access, alteration, or loss to maintain reliability and confidentiality.

- Data Management Processes: Defining and implementing data management processes to ensure the proper collection, storage, processing, and dissemination of data according to organizational requirements and objectives.

- Monitoring and Assurance: Monitoring data reliability through regular assessments, audits, and reviews to identify and address any issues or discrepancies.

In summary, within the COBIT framework, data reliability is closely tied to data governance, quality management, security, and effective data management processes to ensure that data can be trusted and relied upon to support business operations and decision-making.

NIST SP 800-53:2020.

NIST SP 800-53, titled "Security and Privacy Controls for Federal Information Systems and Organizations," provides a comprehensive set of security controls and guidelines for federal information systems in the United States. While it doesn't explicitly define "data reliability," it addresses aspects of data integrity, availability, and protection contributing to reliability.

Within NIST SP 800-53, data reliability can be understood as the assurance that data is accurate, consistent, and available when needed to support organizational missions and functions. Here are some critical aspects related to data reliability as outlined in NIST SP 800-53:

- Data Integrity ensures that data remains accurate and unaltered during storage, processing, and transmission. Keeping data accurate and unaltered includes implementing data validation, cryptographic controls, and access controls to prevent unauthorized changes.

- Data Availability involves ensuring that data is accessible and available to authorized users when needed. It also includes implementing redundancy, backup, and disaster recovery measures to minimize downtime and ensure continuous access to critical data.

- Data Protection involves implementing controls to protect data from unauthorized access, disclosure, or destruction, including encryption, access controls, authentication mechanisms, and monitoring to safeguard sensitive data from threats and vulnerabilities.

- Data Management involves establishing policies, procedures, and responsibilities for managing data throughout its lifecycle. It includes data classification, retention, disposal, and archival processes to ensure the reliability and integrity of data over time.

- Monitoring and Incident Response: Implementing monitoring mechanisms and incident response procedures to detect and respond to data breaches, unauthorized access, or other security incidents that may affect data reliability.

In summary, NIST SP 800-53 closely relates data reliability to data integrity, availability, protection, management, and monitoring, all of which aim to ensure the trustworthiness and dependability of data within federal information systems and organizations.

COSCO.

The Committee of Sponsoring Organizations of the Treadway Commission (COSO) is known for its framework on internal control, particularly the COSO Internal Control Integrated Framework. While COSO primarily focuses on internal control and risk management, it does not provide a specific definition for "data reliability." However, within the context of COSO's principles and objectives, data reliability can be understood as follows:

Data reliability refers to the accuracy, completeness, and consistency of data used within an organization's processes and decision-making. It involves ensuring that data is reliable and trustworthy to support effective internal control and risk management practices. This encompasses measures to verify the accuracy of data inputs, maintain data integrity throughout processing and reporting, and ensure that data is available and accessible to support decision-making and accountability.

In the COSO framework, data reliability is integral to achieving the objectives of reliable financial reporting, effective operations, and compliance with laws and regulations. It involves implementing controls and procedures to mitigate data accuracy, integrity, and availability risks and ensuring data is used appropriately to support organizational goals and objectives. Data reliability within the COSO framework aligns with the broader goals of internal control and risk management in safeguarding assets, ensuring compliance, and achieving organizational objectives.

ITIL.

The Information Technology Infrastructure Library (ITIL) provides a framework of best practices for IT service management. While ITIL doesn't explicitly define "data reliability," it emphasizes the importance of ensuring that data supports the delivery of IT services effectively and efficiently. Within the context of ITIL, data reliability can be understood as follows:

Data reliability refers to the trustworthiness and dependability of data used to support IT service management processes. It ensures that data is accurate, up-to-date, and accessible, enabling informed decision-making, efficient problem resolution, and effective service delivery. Data reliability within ITIL encompasses measures to validate the accuracy and completeness of data, maintain data integrity throughout its lifecycle, and ensure that data is available when needed to support IT service management activities.

Data reliability is critical for achieving service excellence and meeting customer expectations in the ITIL framework. It involves implementing processes and controls to manage data effectively, including data collection, storage, analysis, and reporting. By ensuring data reliability, organizations can improve the quality of IT services, optimize resource utilization, and enhance overall performance and customer satisfaction.

Key Points.

The following are the key points about how different frameworks and standards define or relate to the "data reliability" concept.

ISO/IEC 25012:2008 (Data Quality Model).

- Explicitly defines data reliability as "the extent to which data is available and accessible when required and the level of confidence in its correctness."
- Emphasizes availability, accessibility, and accuracy/correctness of data.

ISO/IEC 27001:2022 (Information Security Management).

- Implies data reliability by ensuring security, integrity, and data availability.

ISO 9001:2015 (Quality Management Systems).

- Emphasizes accuracy, consistency, and integrity of data to support quality products/services.

COBIT (Control Objectives for Information and Related Technologies IT Governance Framework).

- Relates it to data governance, quality, security, and management processes for ensuring trustworthy data.

NIST SP 800-53:2020 (Security and Privacy Controls for Federal Information Systems and Organizations).

- Relates it to data integrity, availability, protection, and management to ensure trustworthy data.

COSO (Committee of Sponsoring Organizations of the Treadway Commission Internal Control Framework).

- Relates it to accuracy, completeness, and data consistency for reliable reporting/compliance.

ITIL (Information Technology Infrastructure Library).

- Emphasizes trustworthiness and dependability of data for effective service delivery

While some standards define data reliability, others imply or relate it to ensuring organizational data's accuracy, integrity, availability, security, and trustworthiness through various management practices and controls.

The accuracy and consistency of data are common factors in many of these standards.

Appendix V
Data Reliability in Medicinal Products Manufacturing

Introduction.

Data reliability [1] is critical for human medicinal products and has a significant global impact. It involves the accuracy, consistency, and trustworthiness of the data generated at various stages, including research, development, clinical trials, submissions, manufacturing, post-market surveillance, and distribution.

The worldwide human medicinal products regulatory authorities require that medicinal products be safe, efficacious, and high-quality.

This appendix covers the manufacturing of human medicinal products.

In this context, data reliability is vital. The documentation collected during the manufacturing of these products must demonstrate that the products were manufactured according to the specifications and applicable regulatory requirements.

Data Reliability in Medicinal Products Manufacturing.

The following are some key points to remember when manufacturing medicinal products.

Regulatory Compliance.

Regulatory health authorities in each country play a pivotal role in ensuring the reliability of medicinal product manufacturing data. Compliance with regulations such as Good Manufacturing Practice (GMP) and Good Documentation Practice (GDP) is heavily reliant on accurate and reliable data. Regulatory submissions and audits are also dependent on this data, making its reliability a critical factor in the regulatory process.

Quality Control and Assurance.

Maintaining medicinal product quality depends on reliable data. This includes data related to raw materials, manufacturing processes, testing procedures, and final product specifications. Accurate data is crucial for quality control measures to identify and address any deviations from established standards.

Batch Traceability.

Ensuring traceability of medicinal products is vital in the pharmaceutical industry. Reliable data facilitates identifying and recalling specific batches in case of quality or safety issues.

Supply Chain Integrity.

The production of medicines is a global effort that involves intricate supply chains. Reliable data is crucial to managing the movement of raw materials, intermediates, and finished products across different regions. This helps ensure that the entire supply chain is maintained with integrity.

Data Integrity Systems.

Pharmaceutical companies implement robust systems to prevent and detect data inaccuracies or tampering. These systems involve secure data storage, access controls, audit trails, and regular monitoring to maintain the data's reliability and integrity.

Real-time Monitoring and Reporting.

Real-time monitoring of manufacturing processes and immediate data reporting are key elements in maintaining data reliability. This approach allows for the timely identification of any deviations from established quality standards, enabling swift corrective actions to be taken, thereby ensuring the continuous maintenance of product quality.

Global Collaboration.

Effective collaboration among pharmaceutical companies and their stakeholders globally requires reliable data exchange and communication to ensure accurate and consistent information is accessible to all parties.

Summary.

Data reliability is an essential aspect of the global pharmaceutical manufacturing industry. It ensures regulatory compliance, product quality, supply chain integrity, and global cooperation. Pharmaceutical companies invest in advanced technologies and robust systems to maintain the highest data reliability standards throughout the product lifecycle.

References.

1. Data reliability relationship with complete, consistent, accurate, and trustworthy data - https://www.linkedin.com/pulse/data-reliability-relationship-complete-consistent-accurate-lopez-rgqec%3FtrackingId=6sUtKpauuemcvvUXVGg6AQ%253D%253D/?trackingId=6sUtKpauuemcvvUXVGg6AQ%3D%3D

Appendix VI
Are Data Quality and ALCOA attributes equivalent?

Introduction.

The ALCOA attributes play a pivotal role in evaluating the integrity of data and records in the life sciences sector. Their relevance is particularly pronounced in pharmaceutical research, clinical testing, and the supply chain. These attributes, which ensure data quality in activities covered by the medicines' manufacturing practices applicable regulation, are not just a set of principles but a cornerstone of our work in the regulated industries.

Stan Woollen introduced ALCOA [2] as a criterion for United States (US) Food and Drug Administration (FDA) Good Laboratory Practices (GLP) inspectors to assess data quality.

The ALCOA attributes are not just a local standard. They are recognized and endorsed by regulatory agencies and competent authorities worldwide. Their universal association with the quality of data collected to demonstrate the safety and efficacy of medicinal products is a testament to their global acceptance.

This article compares the attributes of ALCOA in the context of medicinal products authorities and data quality in the context of data engineering to find if the ALCOA attributes can be used to assess data quality.

The following are brief explanations of each component of ALCOA, ALCOA+, reliability, and Data Quality [3] used in this article. As ALCOA, these contain criteria to assess data collected during the execution of activities covered by practices regulation.

ALCOA.

ALCOA is an acronym for Attributable, Legible, Contemporaneous, Original, and Accurate. Each of the criteria is used to assess data quality.

Here's a brief explanation of each component of the ALCOA acronym:

Attributable.

All data should be linked to a specific source or individual related to activities, including data generation, modification, or deletion. This link ensures accountability and transparency in the documentation process.

Legible.

All records should be clear and easy to read to minimize the risk of misinterpretation or errors (e.g., safeguarding electronic records to ensure data recovery in an emergency).

Contemporaneous.

Documentation should be recorded in real-time or as close to the time of the activity as possible.

Original.

Original data includes the data and information initially collected and all subsequent data required to fully reconstruct the activity's implementation, including electronic data in automated manufacturing systems (e.g., SCADA, Historian, DCS, and so on).

Accurate.

Data accuracy is the degree to which data reflects the valid values or facts it represents [4]. One example is the records generated during the validation of computer systems that generate, administer, distribute, or archive e-records.

Data architecture is critical for organizations because it helps ensure data accuracy.

Adhering to the ALCOA principles helps to prevent errors or misconduct in the documentation process, ultimately contributing to the safety and efficacy of products and services.

The original ALCOA principles have not remained static. They have evolved into ALCOA+ and ALCOA++, incorporating additional components to ensure data integrity in regulated industries. These updates are a reflection of the principles' adaptability and their continued relevance in the ever-changing landscape of data management.

ALCOA+.

ALCOA+ expands upon the original ALCOA acronym by adding three additional components to ensure data integrity in regulated industries. The original principles remain, but the three additions are complete, Consistent, and Lasting.

ALCOA+ includes:

Complete.

Complete data refers to data that contains all the necessary information required to make accurate and reliable conclusions. It means that all the relevant variables, observations, and measurements have been recorded, and there are all values and data points, including all relevant information necessary to understand the context of the activity.

Consistent.

Documentation practices should be standardized across all records, systems, and personnel to ensure uniformity and consistency in data collection.

Enduring.

Data should be preserved, maintained, or disposed of safely and securely during and after the computer system's decommissioning throughout its entire life cycle, including all raw data, metadata, and associated documentation. Enduring is achieved by implementing processes to ensure the data is stored, archived, or disposed of safely and securely during and after the computer system's decommissioning.

Adhering to ALCOA+ principles ensures that data is accurate, reliable, complete, consistent, and well-preserved, which is critical for ensuring regulatory compliance and maintaining data reliability throughout the data life cycle.

ALCOA++.

ALCOA++ is an extension of the ALCOA and ALCOA+ components, including additional requirements to ensure data integrity in highly regulated industries.

ALCOA++ includes:

Traceable.

All data should be traceable to its raw form, demonstrating its history and the history of data form, and have a clear audit trail demonstrating its creation to its current state.

Available.

Data should be readily available and accessible to authorized personnel as needed while ensuring appropriate security controls prevent unauthorized access or modification. Data architecture is critical for organizations because it helps ensure data is available when needed.

Secure.

Data should be protected against unauthorized access, modification, or destruction, and security controls should be in place to ensure data confidentiality, integrity, and availability.

Adhering to ALCOA++ principles ensures that data is accurate, complete, consistent, well-preserved, traceable, available, and secure. This is crucial for ensuring regulatory compliance, maintaining data quality, and protecting sensitive information.

By implementing these principles, organizations can maintain the highest data reliability and trustworthiness standards, critical in highly regulated industries such as healthcare, pharmaceuticals, and finance.

Data Quality attributes [5].

Data quality is not just a technical aspect of our work but the foundation for deriving valuable insights and driving better decision-making processes. It is the key that unlocks the potential of our data and the value of our work at any stage in its lifecycle.

Data quality consists of several attributes, including consistent accuracy, suitability, conformity, completeness, consistency, integrity, validity, reliability, timeline, and consistency with the intended use of data quality. These attributes ensure that the data is both correct and valuable.

Accurate.

All data should be precise, complete, and truthful, reflecting what occurred. Data architecture is critical for organizations because it helps ensure data accuracy.

Data accuracy is the degree to which data reflects the valid values or facts it represents [6].

Auditability.

Data audit-ability refers to the ability to trace and verify the raw data, integrity, and lineage of data [7].

Conformity.

Conformity measures how well data adheres to specific formatting, coding, and content guidelines.

Completeness.

The degree to which data captures all relevant information about a particular phenomenon or activity.

Consistency.

Data architecture is the degree to which data is accessible from contradictions or discrepancies with other data sources. It is critical for organizations because it helps ensure data consistency.

Integrity.

Data integrity is the property that data has not been retrieved or altered without authorization since creation and until disposal [8].

E-records integrity service maintains information as entered/captured and is auditable (e.g., audit trails) to affirm its traceability.

Validity.

Validity is the extent to which data elements comply with internal or external standards, guidelines, or standard data definitions, including data type, size, format, and other features.

Reliability.

A record is reliable if its content can be trusted as a complete and accurate representation of the transaction, activities, or facts it attests to. It can be dependent upon the course of subsequent transactions and activities. (NARA)

Reliability refers to the quality and accuracy of the data being collected. Data collected can include incomplete, inaccurate, or unreliable information, so it is essential to ensure its trustworthiness before using it for analysis. Data validation [9] is relevant to ensuring the reliability of the collected data.

Timely.

Timely is the degree to which data is up-to-date and reflects the current state of the activity.

Consistent

Consistent data ensures that the same information is represented in the same way, regardless of where it is used or accessed.

High-quality data is trustworthy [10], relevant [11], and fit for its intended purpose. Data quality can lead to correct insights, flawless decision-making, and decreased costs, risks, and efficiencies.

High-quality data requires proper management processes, including regular quality checks, cleaning, validation, and governance. Regulated companies should also invest in high-quality data management systems and training programs to ensure employees have the skills to manage data effectively.

Organizations can implement data quality frameworks, tools, and best practices to ensure that data is accurate, auditable, conform, complete, consistent, with integrity, valid, reliable, timely, and consistent. It meets the business and analytical needs of the organization.

Data integrity, data reliability, and data quality.

Data with integrity, reliability, and quality are essential for data management, but they are also referred to as different data characteristics.

Worldwide regulatory agencies or competent authorities define data integrity as the "degree to which data are complete, consistent, accurate, trustworthy, and reliable and that these characteristics of the data are maintained throughout the data life cycle."

The key word in this definition is "trustworthy." Trustworthy data is considered reliable, authentic, with integrity, and usable.

It is implied that reliable data is part of many attributes, with integrity being one of many attributes. However, integrity alone does not define reliable data. The definition of data integrity designated by worldwide regulatory agencies or competent authorities must be corrected and consistent with worldwide standards [12].

Based on United States and worldwide standards such as the NIST SP 800-57P1, IEEE, ISO-17025, INFOSEC, 44 USC 3542, 36 CFR Part 1236, and others, data/e-records integrity is the property that data/e-records have not been retrieved or altered without authorization since created and until disposal. 21 CFR Part 211 requires that all raw data be recorded and maintained, even if the data is manipulated. The data integrity characteristic is accomplished by properly managing the raw data. Changes to the raw data must be traceable throughout the data life cycle, and security controls must be established for the computer system to ensure data protection. Any changes to the data should be documented as part of the metadata (e.g., audit trail).

To consider that *data has integrity*, the data must be protected from unauthorized changes, tampering, or corruption. Controls should be in place to ensure that data remains reliable, even when it is stored, moved, or integrated with other data sources.

Data security protects data from unauthorized access, use, or disclosure. It involves safeguarding data against unauthorized access or theft, ensuring data is available when needed, and protecting data from damage or loss.

Data is reliable if its content can be trusted as a complete and accurate representation of the transaction, activities, or facts it attests to. It can be depended upon during subsequent transactions and activities [13].

Data reliability refers to the consistency and repeatability of data over time, regardless of the methods or tools used to collect it. A dataset is considered reliable if it consistently produces the same results, regardless of whether it is measured multiple times or obtained by different researchers or methods. For instance, if an experiment yields the same results every time it is performed, it is considered reliable.

Trusted is a term pertinent to reliability. Reliable data is accurate, authentic [14], with integrity, usable, and can be confidently used for decision-making, analysis, and other purposes.

Trusted data is critical for making informed decisions and achieving positive outcomes. It requires a combination of data quality, integrity, and security to ensure that data is reliable, accurate, and trustworthy. Decisions based on reliable or accurate data can lead to good outcomes and negative consequences.

Several factors, including data quality, integrity, and security, must be considered to ensure the trustworthiness of data.

Data quality is their intended purpose.

Several attributes, including accuracy, suitability, conformance, completeness, consistency, integrity, validity, reliability, timeliness, and consistency with the intended use, determine data quality. These attributes ensure that the data is trustworthy.

The data must be accurate and error-free, including duplicates or missing values. It must also be complete, with all required fields populated, consistent across all sources, and relevant to the problem being addressed.

High-quality data is free from errors, bias, and inconsistencies and relevant to the questions or decisions made. For instance, if a company's customer data is accurate, complete, and current, it can be used to make informed business decisions.

In summary, data reliability is focused on. In contrast, data quality concerns the accuracy, completeness, and relevance of data consistency and repeatability. In contrast, data quality concerns accuracy, completeness, and relevance to its intended use.

A data set containing quality data is also reliable and has integrity. However, only some data in a data set containing integrity is reliable, and only some of the data in a data set containing reliable data has quality.

Comparison of Data Quality, ALCOA, and others.

The following table depicts the dimensions of ALCOA and ALCOA+. ALCOA++, reliability, and Data Quality. Data Quality dimensions based on the EU medicinal regulations [17] are listed for reference only.

The table also associates ALCOA with the attributes to assess the quality of the collected data and demonstrate medicinal products' safety and efficacy.

Dimension (15)	Frameworks [16]					
	ALCOA	ALCOA+	ALCOA++	Data Reliability	Data Quality	Data Quality EMA (17)
Accurate	x	x	x	x	x	
Attributable	x	x	x			
Auditable / Traceable			x		x	
Available			x			
Completeness		x	x	x	x	x
Conformity					x	
Consistent		x	x	+	x	x
Contemporaneous	x	x	x			
Coverage						x
Enduring		x	x			

384

Dimensio n (15)	Frameworks [16]					
	AL CO A	ALC OA+	ALC OA++	Data Relia bility	Dat a Qu alit y	Dat a Qu alit y EM A (17)
Integrity	+			x	x	
Legible	x	x	x			
Original	x	x	x			
Relevance						x
Reliabilit y				x	x	x
Secure			x	x		
Timely					x	x
Validity					x	

From the above table, it can be established that data requires at least four pillars to work.

1. Complete refers to data containing all the information required to make accurate and reliable conclusions.

2. Validity refers to whether the data accurately reflects what it claims to represent.

3. Timeliness refers to when the data was collected and when it is being used or analyzed.

4. Accurate refers to whether the data values stored for an object are correct. The accuracy characteristics are precise, truthful, and reflect what occurred.

It can be established the following relationships.

1. Data completeness results from the data accuracy, precision, and reflection of what occurred contemporaneously. By adding "complete" to ALCOA, ALCOA+ is directly establishing this relationship.

2. If the data reflects what occurred during the data lifecycle, the data can be considered with integrity. The data has been protected from unauthorized changes, tampering, or corruption, even when stored, moved, or integrated with other data sources.

3. The only two frameworks containing the dimension of traceability are ALCOA++ and Quality Data. It is relevant to the raw data [18] changes that must be traceable throughout the data life cycle.

The controls related to data integrity can be summarized as follows:

- Security-related controls.

- Traceability of the modification to the raw data.

The controls related to data reliability can be summarized as follows:

- Data integrity controls.

- Accurate.

- Complete.

- Consistent.

Implementing workflows meeting 21 CFR Part 11.10(f) and data flows meeting the Annex 11-5 (Rev 1) to the EU GMP guideline verifying the data accuracy, completeness, and consistency determine if data is missing or unusable.

The controls related to data quality can be summarized as follows:

- Data reliability-related controls.

- Consistency-related controls determine whether data values do not conflict with other data values and whether they adhere to a standard format (e.g., conformity).

- Duplication-related controls which determine the repeated records.

Based on the above, it is easy to determine that "the controls required for integrity do not necessarily guarantee the quality of the data generated" [19].

The dimensions [15] of ALCOA and ALCOA+ can be correlated to the data's reliability dimensions, and the dimensions related to ALCOA++ can be correlated to the data quality dimensions.

References.

[1] López, O., *"Are Data Quality and ALCOA attributes equivalent?"* GMP Journal, Issue #38, November 2023.

[2]https://www.linkedin.com/feed/update/urn:li:activity:7046255838855856128?commentUrn=urn%3Ali%3Acomment%3A%28activity%3A7046255838855856128%2C7047292986165968896%29

[3] Data quality is defined as fitness for purpose for users' needs about health research, policy-making, and regulation and that the data reflect the reality they aim to represent. (European Health Data Space Data Quality Framework, Deliverable 6.1 of TEHDAS EU 3rd Health 567 Program (GA: 101035467). May 18th, 2022)

[4] EMA, *"EMA Questions and answers: Good manufacturing practice Data Integrity,"* Aug 2016.

[5] López, O., *"Introduction to Data Quality,"* Journal of Validation Technology, April 2020.

[6] Moses, B., Gavish, L., Vorwerck, M., *"Data Quality Fundamentals - A Practitioner's Guide to Building Trustworthy Data Pipelines"*, O'Reilly Media, Inc., Sebastopol, CA, September 2022.

[7] Data lineage represents information about everything that has "happened" to the data. Whether it was moved from one system to another, transformed, aggregated, etc., ETL (extraction, transformation, and load) tools can capture this metadata electronically. (DataManagementU)

[8] NIST SP 800-57P1, IEEE, ISO-17025, INFOSEC, 44 USC 3542, 36 CFR Part 1236, and others standards.

[9] Data Validation is the procedural control of verifying collected data/e-records by a second operator or by validated electronic means to ensure that data/e-records are consistent, accurate, and trustworthy. In addition, it is ensured that these data/ e-records are accurately transcribed into machine-readable form.

[10] Trustworthy data - Reliability, authenticity, integrity, and usability are the characteristics used to describe reliable data from a record management perspective. (NARA)

[11] Data relevancy - Data relevance refers to the degree to which data is valuable, meaningful, and aligned with the business or analytical objectives.

[12] Worldwide standards are a set of globally recognized specifications, guidelines, or requirements that define how products, services, or systems should be designed, manufactured, and operated to meet quality, safety, and performance criteria. International organizations develop these standards.

[13] United States National Archives and Records Administration (https://www.archives.gov/)

[14] Authenticity - The property of being genuine and being able to be verified and trusted; confidence in the validity of a transmission, a message, or message originator. See authentication. (NIST Special Publication 800-18)

[15] A dimension represents one or more related aspects or features of reality.

[16] A framework is a natural or conceptual structure intended to serve as a support or guide for the building of something that expands the structure into something useful

[17] EMA, *"Data quality framework EU medicines regulation,"* September 2022 (draft).

[18] Raw data - The original records (data) and certified true copies of original records, including source data and metadata and all subsequent transformations and reports of this data, which are recorded at the time of the GxP activity and allow complete reconstruction and evaluation of the GxP activity. (WHO)

[19] MHRA, *"GxP Data Integrity Guidance and Definitions,"* March 2018.

About the Author

Highly skilled and detail-oriented data reliability subject matter expert with 30 years of experience ensuring data accuracy, reliability, and security.

His recent publications can be found at https://www.routledge.com/authors/i8734-orlando-lopez, https://novapublishers.com/shop/e-records-integrity-requirements/ and https://tinyurl.com/LifecycleIntegrity.

You can read more about the author at https://www.linkedin.com/in/orlandolopezrodriguez/

www.ingramcontent.com/pod-product-compliance
Lightning Source LLC
Chambersburg PA
CBHW070052030426
42335CB00016B/1856